First and Second Kings

INTERPRETATION
A Bible Commentary for Teaching and Preaching

INTERPRETATION
A BIBLE COMMENTARY FOR TEACHING AND PREACHING

James Luther Mays, *Editor*
Patrick D. Miller, Jr., *Old Testament Editor*
Paul J. Acthemeier, *New Testament Editor*

RICHARD D. NELSON

First and Second Kings

A Bible Commentary for Teaching and Preaching

John Knox Press
ATLANTA

Library of Congress Cataloging-in-Publication Data

Nelson, Richard D. (Richard Donald), 1945–
  First and Second Kings.

  (Interpretation, a Bible commentary for teaching and preaching)
  1. Bible. O.T. Kings—Commentaries. I. Title.
II. Title: 1st and 2nd Kings. III. Series.
BS1335.3.N45 1987   222'.507   87–9883
ISBN 0–8042–3109–5

© copyright John Knox Press 1987
10 9 8 7 6 5 4 3 2 1
Printed in the United States of America
John Knox Press
Atlanta, Georgia 30365

SERIES PREFACE

This series of commentaries offers an interpretation of the books of the Bible. It is designed to meet the need of students, teachers, ministers, and priests for a contemporary expository commentary. These volumes will not replace the historical critical commentary or homiletical aids to preaching. The purpose of this series is rather to provide a third kind of resource, a commentary which presents the integrated result of historical and theological work with the biblical text.

An interpretation in the full sense of the term involves a text, an interpreter, and someone for whom the interpretation is made. Here, the text is what stands written in the Bible in its full identity as literature from the time of "the prophets and apostles," the literature which is read to inform, inspire, and guide the life of faith. The interpreters are scholars who seek to create an interpretation which is both faithful to the text and useful to the church. The series is written for those who teach, preach, and study the Bible in the community of faith.

The comment generally takes the form of expository essays. It is planned and written in the light of the needs and questions which arise in the use of the Bible as Holy Scripture. The insights and results of contemporary scholarly research are used for the sake of the exposition. The commentators write as exegetes and theologians. The task which they undertake is both to deal with what the texts say and to discern their meaning for faith and life. The exposition is the unified work of one interpreter.

The text on which the comment is based is the Revised Standard Version of the Bible. The general availability of this translation makes the printing of a translation unnecessary and saves the space for comment. The text is divided into sections appropriate to the particular book; comment deals with passages as a whole, rather than proceeding word by word, or verse by verse.

Writers have planned their volumes in light of the requirements set by the exposition of the book assigned to them. Biblical books differ in character, content, and arrangement. They also differ in the way they have been and are used in the liturgy, thought, and devotion of the church. The distinctiveness and use of particular books have been taken into account in decisions about the approach, emphasis, and use of space in the commentaries. The goal has been to allow writers to develop the format which provides for the best presentation of their interpretation.

The result, writers and editors hope, is a commentary which both explains and applies, an interpretation which deals with both the meaning and the significance of biblical texts. Each commentary reflects, of course, the writer's own approach and perception of the church and world. It could and should not be otherwise. Every interpretation of any kind is individual in that sense; it is one reading of the text. But all who work at the interpretation of Scripture in the church need the help and stimulation of a colleague's reading and understanding of the text. If these volumes serve and encourage interpretation in that way, their preparation and publication will realize their purpose.

The Editors

Contents

Abbreviations used in citations

ANET	Ancient Near Eastern Texts
Ant	Flavius Josephus, Antiquities of the Jews
AV	Authorized Version
CBQ	Catholic Biblical Quarterly
HUCA	Hebrew Union College Annual
Interp	Interpretation
JB	Jerusalem Bible
JBL	Journal of Biblical Literature
JSOT	Journal for the Study of the Old Testament
LXX	Septuagint, Greek version of the Old Testament
MT	Masoretic text, the Hebrew Old Testament
NEB	New English Bible
NIV	New International Version
RSV	Revised Standard Version
TEV	Today's English Version of the Holy Bible
VT	Vetus Testamentum

Introduction

Reading the Book of Kings Today

The Book of Kings is about the past. It is history, a word which to us is almost synonymous with "irrelevant." "History is a bucket of ashes," wrote Carl Sandburg, and many modern readers of First and Second Kings might be tempted to agree. At first glance Kings seems to be nothing but history, the record of rulers long dead and battles long forgotten. Read with the critical eye of the sober historian, Kings provides useful information about Israel and Judah in the monarchical period. Yet the relevance of such matters for the contemporary Christian is hardly obvious.

This problem has become even more acute since the passing of the "history of salvation" school of Old Testament theology. There was once something of a consensus that the historical books testify to a series of "mighty acts of God" to which the preacher or theologian might point as earlier examples of God's actions that culminated in the Christ event. This consensus has dissolved under the pressure of increasing historical skepticism, coupled with a tendency to read the historical books more and more as theological literature rather than as sources for history.

The history recorded in Kings no longer has any direct impact on us. This observation goes deeper than the obvious fact that we are not Jews of the sixth century B.C.E. A more fundamental problem is that Kings no longer meets our modern standards for history writing. The narrative of Kings is "history like" in that it has a chronological framework, the individual stories are structured into a unitary whole, and it is a fairly reliable source for historical evidence. Yet there is no critical evaluation of the sources from which the narratives are drawn, something even Herodotus offered. Large portions of the narrative can no longer be considered "actual history" by any modern definition. There are legends, miracle stories, folktales, and fictional constructions. Kings draws moral lessons from events,

1

a concern far removed from that of modern history writing. Most fundamentally, causation for events in Kings shifts from human to divine and back again without any embarrassment. Some awareness of psychological (I Kings 1:6), social (12:4), or geo-political (II Kings 17:4) causation in history is present; but the primary causative agent in Kings is God and God's offended sense of what is right. We have not written serious history from that perspective since the Renaissance.

Instead, it may prove more fruitful for us to read Kings as a piece of theological literature which happens to be in the form of history writing. Kings is not just history; it is "preached history." It has a kerygmatic intent. It was written to transform the beliefs of its first readers, to get them to re-evaluate their identity before God. To do so, Kings takes the form of history writing, providing information about past events and a framework for their interpretation. However, Kings is not really focused on the past but upon the situation of its original audience. It was designed to change their inner orientation to God, who (it claims) had turned against the people and undone the exodus by sending them back into exile.

Whether or not Kings makes sense to us or seems relevant to us as history, it remains a powerful theological narrative. As *theological* narrative it finds its relevance in the person of God. The Christian church confesses that the God of Kings is the very God the church worships, the God who raised Jesus from the dead. Read from a theocentric perspective, Kings offers us insight and perspective on the nature of God, as Jesus himself recognized (Luke 4:24–27). When read from an anthropocentric perspective, as theological *narrative,* its very nature as story fills Kings with human interest. Readers find themselves moved and touched by the art of fine story-telling. Once again, the relationship between humanity and its God is explored and exposed.

What to Expect from This Commentary

The reader will find this commentary different from other commentaries on Kings in being less concerned with it as a historical document and more concerned with it as theological literature. The focus is on the Book of Kings itself, not the history behind it. Reported events are treated more as "plot" than as "history." This commentary treats Kings as a piece of theological literature which happens to be historiography (his-

2

tory writing). The goal of the commentary is to open up Kings for the preaching and teaching of the Christian church. This commentary concentrates on the literary impact, the "meaning effect," that the text of Kings has on its modern readers and tries to trace the theological trajectories which result from this impact. It focuses on Kings as a canonical whole rather than as a collection of earlier materials or as the last portion of the Deuteronomistic History. The final exilic shape of Kings and its exilic audience is the focus, rather than any earlier stage in the book's literary history. For practical reasons, the Hebrew text of Kings used by the Revised Standard Version is the object of study (with occasional exceptions). References are made to the verse and chapter divisions of the English Bible.

This commentary does not provide pat answers or attempt to dictate what the text "means." Instead it intends to draw the reader into an intimate engagement with the text itself. Meaning will grow out of the effect the text has on the reader after such an encounter has taken place. This commentary intends to facilitate this process, not short-circuit it or replace it. It is designed to be a lens through which the text can be read more closely, highlighting and magnifying certain aspects, but remaining essentially transparent. It provides readers with a map or guidebook for their own journey through Kings, hoping to open up a more aware and informed experience with the text. This commentary will start the process of engagement. The rest is up to the reader!

For this reason, the bulk of this commentary is devoted to an explanation of how the Book of Kings functions as literature. How does the book have the effect it has on us? How do plot and character interact with the book's theological concern? What factors in the narrative structure are not obvious at first reading but show themselves when the text is read more closely and deliberately? Near the end of each section, the commentary explores some of the difficulties and problems which may arise when that portion of Kings is used as Scripture within the church today. It also suggests some directions for the use of that text in preaching and teaching, drawing out connections between its original purpose and the characteristic situations in which members of the Christian community find themselves. These remain, however, only suggestions and hints. They are not a substitute for the reader's own close encounter with the text.

The Book of Kings once constituted the final segment of the Deuteronomistic History, a long historiographic work which included Deuteronomy, Joshua, Judges, and Samuel as well. For an introduction to this literary complex, the reader is directed to the books by Fretheim, Mayes, and Noth in the Bibliography.

Kings was considered to be a single book in the Hebrew canon. It was not divided into two books until the advent of printed Hebrew Bibles. In this commentary we shall follow this canonical tradition and read Kings as a single, self-contained whole. There are several excellent commentaries in English that deal with Kings from the traditional perspectives of historical criticism. The reader is directed to those listed in the Bibliography for more extensive discussions of such matters than can be provided here. Reading the excellent introduction to the commentary by G. Jones is probably the best preparation for exegetical work in Kings. For form-critical matters, the reader should consult B. Long's contribution to the FORMS OF THE OLD TESTAMENT LITERATURE series (Vols. 9 and 10).

The Original Audience

Kings took its final shape in the early years of the Babylonian exile. The last event within the horizon of Kings is the death of Jehoiachin, the last king of Judah. This probably took place during the reign of the Babylonian king Nabonidus (555–539 B.C.E.) or one of his immediate predecessors. Although Kings is often thought to have been composed in Palestine, the ease of communication among the Jewish communities of this period (Jer. 44:1; Ezek. 33:21) should lead us to consider all exilic Jews as the intended audience, whether they lived in Judah, Babylonia, or Egypt.

Those who remained in Palestine faced difficult times. Archaeology testifies to extensive destruction and serious depopulation in Judah. Territory in south Judah was being absorbed by encroaching Edomites. The temple was a ruin (Lam. 1:10; 2:7), although Yahweh worship of a sort continued on the site (Jer. 41:5). There was serious hunger, at least in the early years (Lam. 1:11, 19; 2:19b, 20; 4:4, 10). Those with control of stored provisions gained important influence (Jer. 41:8). The established social classes were upset (Lam. 4:5; 5:8, 12). The peasants apparently were employed as labor gangs on Babylonian-sponsored agricultural projects, and there was at least some foreign control of the land and its resources (II Kings 25:12; Lam. 5:2, 4).

4

At least in the early period, political unrest continued, as witnessed by the assassination of Gedaliah and the third deportation of 582 B.C.E. (Jer. 40:7—41:18; 52:30).

Those exiled to Babylon were first put into agricultural internment settlements (Ezek. 3:15) where they could build houses and farm (Jer. 29:5–6). In the scramble for limited resources, leaders tended to protect their own interests at the expense of the common folk (Ezek. 34:1–10). Nevertheless, the Babylonian exiles seem to have had a reasonable amount of freedom and to have enjoyed relative prosperity. At a later period, the Jews of Babylonia would begin to enter the world of commerce and a few of them would grow rich. To protect their national identity, the exiles began to emphasize practices such as Sabbath-keeping and circumcision, which set them off from their pagan neighbors.

Babylon was not a stable empire. A period of rapid turnover on the throne was followed by the accession of the religious visionary Nabonidus, devotee of the moon god Sin. Resented by loyal worshipers of the national god Marduk, Nabonidus was to become a prototype of the dangerous, mad, heretical king in Mesopotamian literature (ANET pp. 312–16). He provides an intriguing parallel to the villains of the Book of Kings, such as Jeroboam and Manasseh. This was a period marked by antiquarian interests and religious unrest. Cyrus was already casting his shadow on Babylon's future as early as 550 B.C.E.

A third important community lived in Egypt. Under Amasis (568–526 B.C.E.), Egypt was a cosmopolitan melange of native Egyptians and Greek mercenaries and merchants. Herodotus, in his gossipy presentation of this period (II, 172–82), speaks of great material prosperity. Jews had already come to Egypt as mercenaries even before the exile. We know of exiles settled in Migdol, Tahpanhes, Memphis, and upper Egypt (Jer. 44:1). The Elephantine Jewish mercenary colony was probably founded under Amasis or perhaps earlier.

The books of Jeremiah, Lamentations, and Ezekiel give us insight into the theological opinions of the original audience of Kings. There was a general feeling of depression and disorientation. Many railed at God as unfair: "The way of the Lord is not just . . ." (Ezek. 18:25), they complained. Our ancestors sinned, but we are unfairly bearing their punishment (Ezek. 18:2; Lam. 5:7). Others seem to have laid the blame for their punishment

5

on betrayal by lying prophets (Lam. 2:14). Psalm 79 reflects the spirit of the times: Why pick on us, God? We know you and call on you, unlike those foreign nations whom you should be punishing. Do not blame us for our ancestors' sins, but forgive us our own. Avenge us seven times on our taunting enemies.

Many who did understand God's judgment as just and necessary (Lam. 1:5, 18; 2:17) had lost all hope under the weight of their guilt; "how then can we live" (Ezek. 33:10)? The institutions in which they had hoped had been blasted away: priest, king, prophet, holy city (Lam. 2:6, 9b; 4:12, 20). "Our hope is lost," they said; "we are clean cut off" (Ezek. 37:11). Psalm 137 is a typical vignette of exilic life. The homesick exiles remember Jerusalem and vow never to forget. Tormented by their captors, they react with pathos seasoned by the desire for bloody vengeance. On the other hand, those who remained in the land were sometimes smug, imagining that in contrast to the exiles God's special favor had fallen on them (Ezek. 11:15; 33:24).

Loyalty to Yahweh had hit rock bottom. To some the lesson of history was clear. When our ancestors burned incense to the Queen of Heaven, things went well. When we abandoned her in favor of Yahweh, trouble came. So let us go back to our old syncretistic ways (Jer. 44:15–19). Egyptian exiles burned incense to other gods, forgetting the wickedness of their ancestors and former kings, still disobeying God's law (Jer. 44:8–10). They built a syncretistic temple at Elephantine. Babylonian exiles are quoted as thinking, "Let us be like the nations . . . and worship wood and stone" (Ezek. 20:32). The people violated dietary laws, lifted their eyes to idols, committed murder and fornication. They inquired of prophets but did not obey their words and treated them like artistic performers (Ezek. 33:25–26, 31–32).

It is possible to learn a great deal about the intended audience of Kings by reading the book itself. Kings expects its audience to have read Deuteronomy, Joshua, Judges, and Samuel and makes reference to events, people, and laws in those books. Readers are expected to know Israel's saving traditions: the patriarchs (I Kings 18:36), the exodus (I Kings 6:1), Moses (II Kings 18:4), Horeb and the traditions of theophany (I Kings 19), the conquest (I Kings 21:26), and the judges (II Kings 23:22). They remember something about the ancient tribal system (I Kings 7:14; 8:4; 12:21, 23, 31; 15:27). They are expected to know well the geography of Jerusalem (I Kings 1:9; II Kings 20:11;

22:8, 13) as well as the exterior of the temple (II Kings 12:10; 22:11), although they may be curious about its interior (much of I Kings 6). The readership is conversant with Palestinian geography but needs to have the archaic Canaanite month names explained by the contemporary system of numbering months (I Kings 6:37; 8:2). Readers are supposed to be used to dating events by the exile year of Jehoiachin in coordination with the Babylonian calendar (II Kings 25:27).

Kings expects a measure of literate sophistication from its audience. Readers are expected to have access to literature such as the Book of the Acts of Solomon and the Books of the the Chronicles of the Kings of Judah/Israel. They are expected to appreciate antiquarian and exotic references to almuggin wood, baboons (?), Cerethites and Pelethites, and the names of ancient sages. They are presumed to be interested in lists of Solomonic officials (I Kings 4:2–6, 8–19) and the bizarre names given to foreign gods (II Kings 17:31). They can appreciate world geography and have some idea where far off places like Ophir, Sheba, and Kue might be found. Kings feels comfortable dropping names like Tiglath-pileser, Shalmaneser, and Tirhakah and expects readers to know, without being told, what a Rabshakeh was.

Kings implies an audience that cares deeply about the law of Deuteronomy (I Kings 3:2) and will relish details of Israel's exalted past, such as Solomon's ivory throne (I Kings 10:19–20). Further, these readers are expected to have a sense of humor in order to enjoy the droll parts of the Mount Carmel contest story, the little jokes of Micaiah and Jehu, and Gehazi's clowning. Kings implies an audience that may have doubts about Yahweh's fighting prowess (I Kings 20:25, 28; 3:9–27; 6:17) and about God's power beyond the borders of Palestine (II Kings 5:15, 17–18). As might be expected of exiles, the implied readers are touchy about the idea of slave labor (I Kings 9:22). They are not expected to balk at literal, detailed prophetic prediction (I Kings 13:2) or extraordinary miracles. They were expected to be concerned about the possibility of forgiveness and return to the land of promise (I Kings 8:34) as well as what to expect from captivity (8:50). Were they still God's heritage (8:53)?

The theological questions posed by the fall of the nation were critical ones. Was Marduk stronger than Yahweh? What did defeat and exile mean for a people who had once considered themselves Yahweh's own choice? What was the relationship between the individual and the nation in matters of sin and punishment? What had happened to God's promises about the Davidic dynasty and the city of Jerusalem? Is there any hope at all? The Book of Kings was presented to an audience which had to respond to this crisis of faith or lose its identity.

The Structure of Kings

Kings presents to its readership a number of concerns and themes, held together in loose connection. A great variety of sources were used to construct the book; and yet Kings gives an overall impression of unity. This unity is not created by a single structure or scheme. Rather Kings offers a complicated network of overlapping patterns.

The most obvious structure, and the one most congenial to the modern Western reader, is that provided by *chronology*. For example, I Kings 6:1 links the narrative to all that has gone before in Israel's story. Near the end of Kings, the chronology shifts from an internal national one to that of the Babylonian empire, thus linking the story to the wider stage of world events (II Kings 24:12; 25:8).

Although chronological matters are relatively straight-forward for Solomon and after the fall of the Kingdom of Israel, this temporal structure is more complex than it appears on the surface. Kings synchronizes the chronologies of the separate states of Judah and Israel by reporting on the entire reign of one king and then "backtracking" to report on the reigns of the king or kings of the other kingdom who had come to the throne during the first king's rule. Kings "closes a file" on Solomon in I Kings 11:43 and implicitly opens one for Jeroboam, although without the usual formula. Jeroboam's file is closed by I Kings 14:20. Then with verse 21 Kings backtracks twenty-two years to open a file on Rehoboam. Some events of his reign are reported, then the file is closed by verse 31. Kings then treats Abijam of Judah, whose reign fell within that of Jeroboam of Israel. Next Asa's file is opened in the twentieth year of Jeroboam and continues down for forty-one years. Events of his reign are reported in this file, including some involving Baasha, before it is closed by I Kings 15:24. The chronology then backtracks about forty years to open and close files on Nadab, Baasha, Zimri, and Omri of Israel, all of whom came to the throne during the rule of Asa of Judah. Ahab's file is opened by I Kings 16:29 and remains open to include stories about him and Elijah until I Kings 22:40.

8

The long narrative sections of Kings rest within the open files of the kings: Elijah within Ahab and then Ahaziah, Elisha within Jehoram of Israel, Isaiah within Hezekiah. Usually the files are opened and closed by accession and death formulas, but sometimes narratives perform this function, as in the case of Jehu's revolt. The narrator's sermon in II Kings 17 closes Hoshea's file.

The rhythm of openings and closings provides the reader with instructions for reading Kings. Thus we are instructed to read all the Ahab material from I Kings 16:29 to 22:40 together and to consider everything up to Solomon's death (I Kings 11:43) as something of a whole. The chronology provides backbone and sequence for the narrative and underscores the cumulative nature of the people's history.

This chronological structure has the effect of intimately linking the stories of the sister kingdoms, uniting North and South into a synoptic problem. It provides a sort of "carrier wave" to bear the stories told within the open files so that narrative time and chronological time drive each other. The carrier wave of chronology holds within it points of rest for narrative. An interesting texture is created by the interplay of narrative time and chronological time. A musical analogy may be helpful. The chronological structure serves as a driving bass line to move the piece along through time. At points this line is interrupted by shorter or longer melodic passages as the composition lingers over important themes: Elijah and Ahab, Elisha and Jehoram, Jehu, Athaliah, the sermon of II Kings 17, Isaiah and Hezekiah, Manasseh, Josiah and the end. Chronological time is especially strong in I Kings 14:19—16:34 and II Kings 13:1—16:20. Narrative time takes over in places like I Kings 17:1—22:40 or II Kings 3:4—8:15.

The system is not rigidly enforced, however. There are two major gaps. Elijah's translation and Queen Athaliah lie completely outside the structure, affecting the way we read each of these narratives. At one point two files are open at once. Jehoram and Ahaziah of Judah are both dealt with before Jehoram of Israel has been murdered. Jehoash of Israel's file is closed twice. The first closing (II Kings 13:13) eliminates the Elisha and Benhadad episode from the structure; the second (14:16) interferes with Amaziah's open file. These disturbances create dislocating effects on the reader.

A similar disorientation is created by the numbers offered

9

by the chronology. Heroic efforts have been made by historians and text critics to make some sort of sense out of the chronology of Kings. As it stands, however, it makes no sense at several points, even to the casual reader. Rather than attempt harmonizations or historical explanations for these irregularities, this commentary will attempt to analyze their impact on the reader.

A second major structural principle is that of *parataxis*. Found also in Herodotus, parataxis means the placing of short items side by side to build up larger wholes. In paratactic structure there is no subordination of some items to others. There is no hierarchy of position. The items are simply laid out without the first or last items being more important than the middle ones. There is no climax. The story is finished when the last item has been related, without any need for summary or conclusion. This is why Kings ends on what seems to us to be such a lame note. Parataxis explains why chapters 20 and 21 of First Kings can be reversed in the Greek recension without causing any major shift in meaning. Parataxis is especially visible in the material about Solomon and the stories about Elijah and Elisha.

Various techniques are used to build up larger wholes from the paratactic units in Kings, one of which is the practice of opening and closing reigns described above. Two larger wholes are visible in the narratives about Solomon. First we are presented with a paratactic chain of items positive to Solomon (I Kings 3—10), followed by a chapter of negatives (chap. 11) in which the adversaries of Solomon are offered to us, not in chronological order but in dramatic order. Other examples of larger wholes are created by the drought theme (I Kings 17:1; 18:2, 41–46) and Elijah's threefold program (I Kings 19:15–17).

A third literary technique used to create unity in Kings is *analogy*. The individual narratives in Kings are interrelated by a rich network of analogy. Thus the reign of every king with its similar introductory and concluding formulas is analogous to every other reign, each an opportunity to obey or disobey God's law. A few examples of narratives which fall into analogous pairs are:

two mothers and their sons	I Kings 3:16–28 and II Kings 6:26–31
queenly death	II Kings 9:30–37 and 11:13–16

theophanies to Solomon	I Kings 3:4–15 and 9:1–9
wisdom and folly with visitors	I Kings 10:1–13 and II Kings 20:12–19
the death of a son	I Kings 14:1–18 and 17:17–24
resurrection	I Kings 17:17–24 and II Kings 4:18–37

Kings draws analogies between Jeroboam and Baasha, Elijah and Elisha, the purges of Solomon and Jehu, the enthronement of Solomon and Joash, Jeroboam and Manasseh. There is a threefold analogy involving the reformers Joash, Hezekiah, and Josiah. In a larger sense, the contrast between the peace and prosperity of Solomon in the early chapters and the apostasies, famines, defeats, and follies of the rest of the story, including the final undoing of all of Solomon's works, provides the overarching structure for the plot of the entire book. Analogy provides inner unity to the otherwise loose paratactic structure of Kings. It bridges the divisions caused by the chronological structure of the reigns. It provides rich harmonies and overtones to the individual narratives when they are read with a sense of the whole.

Another sort of structure is provided by the words of the *prophets*. The prophets prove to be the reader's guides through the plot, pointing out what to expect and interpreting events. Ahijah prepares us for Jeroboam's rise and fall along with that of Israel as a whole. The man of God from Judah in I Kings 13 forecasts Josiah's reform thirty-two chapters later. Elijah's threat (I Kings 21:21–24) gives shape to events through the death of Jezebel, and the divine commission laid on him (I Kings 19:15–17) structures events through the revolt of Jehu. Isaiah and Huldah point forward to the climactic disaster.

There is also an *evaluative structure* by which the various kings are judged by the narrator. In the story of Israel, the pattern is that of hope offered by new kings, (Jeroboam, Jehu) followed by their almost immediate failure. The story of Judah oscillates between bad and good kings. Near the end, the evaluative swing becomes wider between the nearly perfect Hezekiah, the ultimate villain Manasseh, and the saintly Josiah. Jeroboam's grim shadow clouds the story of the Northern Kingdom. David provides the touchstone for evaluating the kings of

11

Judah. The evaluations are most obvious in the judgment formulas (such as I Kings 22:43) by which the various kings are linked to their predecessors. This evaluative structure is also present in the prophetic oracles to the kings, the central thematic episodes and speeches, the affectionate description of the temple, and especially in the patterns of apostasy and reform.

Finally, there is the structure of *apostasy and reform.* The theme of reform interweaves a considerable number of passages in Kings. Even political moves, such as foreign princesses, revolutions, and submission to foreign powers, are presented as matters of religious apostasy or reform. To create this structure, the author was even willing to compose fictional reform accounts without reference to sources. For example, it seems likely that the reform of Josiah is heavily dependent on that of Jehoiada (II Kings 12:4–16; 22:3–7). Details may be added for verisimilitude, but the reports are basically artistic creations by the author. The vocabulary of reform and apostasy is typical and timeless rather than specific and historical. Reform and apostasy are basic principles of the plot which determine its course. Seen this way, Kings is a religious history periodized by apostasy and reform. Solomon's infidelity lays the groundwork for apostasy in both North (Jeroboam) and South (Rehoboam). Ahab establishes a negative model for his successors, while Asa provides a good examplar for his. Then follow the twin reforms of Jehu and Jehoiada. One leads to the fall of Israel and the other points to the policies of Ahaz. Kings concludes with the violent contrast between Manasseh on the one hand and Hezekiah and Josiah on the other. At this point, the apostasy and reform structure shocks the reader with its dissonance. The rules of the game seem to change at the last minute, for Josiah's reform makes no impression whatsoever on God's iron will to punish.

Kings as Theological Literature

Kings is an example of the literary genre of historiography (history writing). J. Van Seters has written an excellent comparative study of ancient historiography (Bibliography 1.). One philosopher of history (J. Huizinga) has defined historiography as "the intellectual form in which a civilization renders account to itself of its past." Historiography, like all literature, is a cultural artifact, a societal tool with a definite purpose, function, and intention. It provides answers for the vital questions of a people. Who are we? How did we get to be who we are and where we

12

are? What effect should our understanding of the past have on how we act and feel now?

Kings is the account which the Jews of the sixth century B.C.E. rendered to themselves of their past. Some of these Jews were alien minorities of displaced persons in Egypt and Mesopotamia. Others were an economically devastated and demoralized people living in Palestine. Important core institutions, religion, government, and the economic system, which once gave identity, pattern, and meaning to life had been destroyed or maimed. Kings was one response to this crisis, the last part of a longer story (the Deuteronomistic History) that began with Moses on the plains of Moab. It was a literary tool intended to replace what had been lost by defeat and exile: identity, pattern, and meaning for life. The fact that Kings still exists shows that it worked. The community it was designed to save read it, eventually canonized it, and bequeathed it to us.

Kings performs its historiographic task from an unabashedly theological perspective. God is the central actor in the plot of Israel's history. God demands the total loyalty of the people and is intolerant of other loyalties and commitments. God rewards virtue and punishes sin, but does not do so mechanically. Repentance leads to restoration, but the outcome of repentance still remains in God's hands. God is sovereign over the events of history and nature. God keeps promises, but is not bound by human expectations.

The Book of Deuteronomy always hovers in the background. Deuteronomy is the key to obedience, especially its requirement that all sacrificial worship be centralized (chap. 12). For Kings, the Jerusalem temple is the central sanctuary promised in Deuteronomy, the place God has chosen. Deuteronomy promised the continuation of a prophetic office like that of Moses (chap. 18). In Kings the prophetic word is trustworthy and powerful, but the problem of false prophecy (Deut. 13:1–5; 18:21–22) is not ignored. Deuteronomy has its own jaundiced view of the king (Deut. 17:14–20). In Kings, David was the ideal king who met this Deuteronomic standard. As a result he was given the promise of an eternal dynasty. Yet later kings did not measure up to Deuteronomy's demands, and deadly punishment resulted.

The central task of Kings is to respond to a theological crisis that may be stated this way: How does the Book of Deuteronomy apply to our situation in exile? How can a book about

13

temple, land, and community function in a time when these things have been destroyed? How can scripture that promises life for obedience (Deut. 28:1–14) work when disobedience has brought its curse of death (Deut. 28:15–24)?

PART ONE

A Kingdom of Shalom

I KINGS 1—10

I Kings 1
Solomon Sits on the Throne

The Book of Kings opens with a dramatic power struggle for the throne of the impotent King David. Chapter 1 raises the key question of who will sit upon the throne of David (vv. 20, 27) and then answers it decisively: "Long live King Solomon" (vv. 34, 39)!

At an earlier stage in its literary history, chapters 1—2 formed the conclusion of the throne succession story (II Sam. 9—20; see Jones, pp. 49–57). In the context of the Book of Kings, however, these chapters constitute a beginning rather than an ending. The former epoch of David has run its course. The enthronement of Solomon marks a new, auspicious start, the inauguration of an era of peace and prosperity. Chapter 1 has a dramatic plot that moves from exposition (vv. 1–10) to complication (vv. 11–27) through climax (vv. 28–40) to denouement (vv. 41–53). Its intention is clear—to explain how Solomon came to the throne and to do so in an entertaining way. It stands on its own as dramatic story, but it also makes important theological points.

In the exposition to follow, some explanatory details will be offered in order to make the story more understandable for the modern reader. Then will come an examination of the literary techniques used by the narrative to shift the story focus from David to Solomon. After this, we shall return to the narrative itself for a detailed look at how the plot works. Then will follow

15

the implications of this story for the Book of Kings and present-day readers.

Bridging Gaps with the Reader

Although the modern reader has no difficulty appreciating this story, some explanations are needed to bridge the gap between text and reader. For example, Abishag was sought out to resolve a constitutional crisis, not just to comfort the shivering old king. The physical and sexual vigor of a king was a matter of national concern. It was believed that there was a definite link between his natural powers and the power and effectiveness of his rule. David's personal servants sought to renew his waning vigor by contact with the contagious vitality of a younger person, who moreover was a desirable virgin (NEB, NIV). Abishag became both a nurse for David's failing health and the prescribed medicine for his impotence. David remains impotent, however, and this failure precipitates a political crisis to which first Adonijah and then Nathan respond. The ensuing conflict indicates that the succession of the oldest son was not yet an assured constitutional principle at the time of this narrative.

Adonijah's public relations ploy (v. 5) is clear enough to modern readers, who recognize the importance of an entourage of limousines and security personnel for a political celebrity. Good looks (v. 6) were as important then as now (I Sam. 9:2; 16:12; II Sam. 14:25). Adonijah's sacrifice meal was not necessarily the occasion for an unauthorized coronation, although the wily Nathan makes it out to be just that. It may have been only a way of building good will among his potential supporters. Although the narrator leaves our suspicions unconfirmed either way, most commentators have for some reason bought Nathan's story at face value.

Nathan's proposal (through Bathsheba, v. 20) was not for Solomon to replace David as king but for a co-regency. This political mechanism of an older and younger king reigning jointly helped assure dynastic stability. David would remain king with Solomon (vv. 43, 44, 47, 48).

Bathsheba's exclamation in verse 31 is not really out of place, in spite of David's advanced age, but is a generalized wish that the royal vitality be carried on by the present king and in his descendants. The picture of Solomon riding the royal mule (v. 33) fails to convey to us the intended impression of

16

glory and dignity. The original readers would have recognized this as a potent symbol of ancient royal office (Zech. 9:9). Similarly, David's use of the word *nagid* (v. 35; RSV "ruler") harks back to leadership traditions from Israel's pioneer past (I Sam. 9:16; 10:1).

Focusing in on Solomon

The story delivers its point powerfully: Solomon was God's choice as king, and he inaugurated a new era of peace and prosperity. The narrative makes its point through a skillful use of several literary techniques, one of which is spatial perspective. Spatially the reader is moved from David as center to Solomon as center. David is the passive spatial center at first. The reader begins at his bedside (vv. 1–4), then moves away to the outside (vv. 5–10), both spatially and in regard to narrative time (vv. 5–8). Next the reader is moved back through the palace (vv. 11–14) to the king's chamber once more (vv. 15–27). David's passivity is underlined by his inability to get warm, have sex, or control his son. He does not know what is going on outside the palace. Nathan and Bathsheba are the active ones. As Bathsheba begins her part of their plan, the reader is reminded once more of David's helpless passivity by a parenthetical reminder about Abishag (v. 15).

Verse 27 marks a turning point. The passive center becomes the active center. Nathan's speech and his penetrating questions rouse David to action. For the moment at least (vv. 28–37), David takes control. He summons his forces and issues orders. David's orders take us back outside (vv. 38–40). As Solomon is made king, however, David fades into the background again, into the speech of Jonathan. David's words and actions now take place off stage (vv. 43–44, 47–48). He is bedfast once more (v. 47). As the story moves from bedchamber to Gihon (vv. 38–40) to En-rogel (vv. 41–49) to the altar (v. 50), a change in center takes place. When we return to the palace (vv. 51–53), it is to discover a new center. Solomon has become the active center, into whose presence Adonijah comes and from whom he is ordered to go.

The narrative also uses other techniques to shift the reader from David to Solomon. Bathsheba and Nathan bow to David at the start (vv. 16, 23, 31). David himself bows to a blessing of Solomon in the middle (v. 47). At the narrative's end, Adonijah does obeisance to Solomon, the new center (v. 53). This same movement is underscored by the way Solomon is named. He begins as brother to Adonijah and son to Bathsheba (vv. 10, 12, 13, 17, 21, 30), but the conspirators move to speak of him as David's "servant" (vv. 19, 26). At the climax, David refers to Solomon as "my son" (v. 33). Then David (v. 34), all the people (v. 49), the messenger and Adonijah (v. 51), and finally the narrator (v. 53) call him "King Solomon." By contrast, his rival is identified only as "Adonijah" or "Adonijah son of Haggith," except in Nathan's questionable assertion in verse 25. In a similar way, the stylized address of elevated courtly language is directed first to David (vv. 2, 17–21, 24–27, 31, 36–37) but at the end to Solomon by the subservient Adonijah (v. 51).

The narrative also focuses on Solomon by providing the reader with the viewpoints of several characters. We get an insight into Bathsheba's inner perspective from her fearful words in verse 21. She and her son would be "offenders" (that is, "traitors," II Kings 18:14) under Adonijah's regime. Jonathan son of Abiathar reveals the point of view of public opinion. He is as omniscient as the narrator himself, reporting events at Gihon, in the throne room and even in David's bed chamber. Through a subtle temporal distortion (he arrives at the moment of the trumpet blast, but reports the subsequent enthronement and blessing, vv. 46–48), Jonathan brings news to Adonijah's potential supporters and to the readers as well. This causes Adonijah's public support to evaporate, but Jonathan has already made the common citizen's decision: "our lord King David has made Solomon king" (v. 43).

Things are especially interesting when the story is told from Adonijah's point of view (vv. 5–10, 42, 50–51). Of all the characters, only his inner psychology is revealed. He begins as a spoiled royal brat (vv. 5–6). Most of the critical events happen in his absence, while he is celebrating unaware. We leave him at En-rogel in verse 9 and come back to him there in verse 41 after the climax. His statement in verse 42 now shows him as being uncertain and anxious, grasping at straws (cf. II Sam. 18:27). In the end he is fearful (v. 50). Again the narrative has gotten its point across effectively. Solomon is king.

Other effective literary techniques strike the careful reader. Repetition delays the action (vv. 34–35, 38–39, 44–45), emphasizes the division between the parties (vv. 7–8, 9–10, 19, 25–26), and hammers home important points (vv. 11 and 18; 13, 17, and 30; 20 and 27). Circumstantial details of local geogra-

18

phy, court etiquette, and the exotic Cherethites and Pelethites add color and verisimilitude. Characters reveal themselves through their speech: Bathsheba as the frantic mother, Nathan as the wily manipulator, Benaiah as the loyal and obedient officer. Both David (v. 35*a*) and Benaiah (vv. 36–37) foreshadow future events in their speeches. There are effective contrasts between the old, cold David and his hot, aggressive son; between Nathan the crafty instigator and Bathsheba the fearful co-conspirator; between the impotent David and the David roused to decisive executive action. Irony pervades the narrative, but much of it depends on the assumption that the reader has already read Second Samuel. David who seduced Bathsheba now cannot "know" Abishag. Adonijah is skillfully tarred with Absalom's brush (v. 5 and II Sam. 15:1; v. 6 and II Sam. 14:25). Nathan's counter deception reminds us of Hushai's (II Sam. 17:5–13).

How the Story Works

In a well-crafted story, the exposition (vv. 1–10) sets the stage and tells us what is amiss. In this case what is amiss is David's advanced age (vv. 1–4). The old order is on the way out. What will replace it? The robust, handsome Adonijah? Abishag's introduction hints at certain romantic expectations (cf. Esther), but she soon turns out to be only a signal of David's impotence and Bathsheba's uncertain position. She will also provide a way to get rid of Adonijah in chapter 2. Adonijah provides an emphatic contrast to David's powerlessness and proves to be a character of central importance. The general circumstances pertaining to Adonijah are given in verses 5–8. "I (rather than someone else [the emphatic pronoun is used]) will be king," he has been thinking.

The action really begins with his feast in verse 9, the first event in the narrative present. The narrator drops comments into the exposition (vv. 6, 8, 10) hinting that Adonijah's plan will not go smoothly. The last name on the list of those not invited is especially problematic for his hopes, "Solomon his brother." The subtle invocation of Absalom's ghost constrains us to see Adonijah's moves in the worst possible light. We are led to view him as treasonous rather than simply prudent.

Verse 11 begins the complication (vv. 11–27) to Adonijah's hopes. Conspiracy is met by counter-conspiracy, deception by deception. The Hebrew moves from circumstantial sentences

19

into straight narrative tense. The plot moves from plan (vv. 11–14) to execution (vv. 15–27) to the desired result (vv. 28–37). Nathan insinuates by his question to Bathsheba that Adonijah already reigns, drops the name of her rival Haggith (v. 11), points out her mortal danger (v. 12), and outlines what Bathsheba should say. Repetition and some delaying business involving obeisance and entrances wrap the passive king into a web of half truths and motivations to take action.

Having read no such vow (v. 13) in Second Samuel, we suspect that Nathan is pulling a deception on the senile king, although the narrator cannily keeps us in the dark about this, as well as about Adonijah's actual intentions at En-rogel. Bathsheba repeats Nathan's unsubstantiated allegation about this gathering (v. 18). She motivates the king by invoking the expectations of his subjects, who look to him for leadership (v. 20), and the danger she and Solomon would face (v. 21).

Next it is Nathan's turn. He mixes insinuating questions (vv. 24, 27) with what seems to be an outright lie (v. 25, "Long live King Adonijah"). He carefully implicates the supposed traitors, but makes it clear that both he and Solomon are David's loyal servants (v. 26). Bathsheba's focus had been Solomon. Nathan shifts the focus to the treachery of Adonijah by reversing (in feigned innocence) David's alleged vow (v. 24) and concluding with an incredulous question (v. 27) that echoes Bathsheba's statement (v. 20). Both conspirators emphasize David's ignorance (vv. 11, 18), intent on rousing him to angry action. We are not quite taken in by Nathan, his memory of a vow called out of thin air, his half truths and unsubstantiated allegations, his deferential speech, or his contrived confirmation of Bathsheba's words. But David is, and the throne passes to Solomon by a trick. Solomon, however, is kept carefully out of the conspiracy, unsullied by unsavory court politics.

The narrative reaches its climax in verses 28–40. The old king is roused to one last burst of decisive action. He believes that he has made the vow (vs. 30), recognizes the danger, and knows who is loyal and disloyal. He calls in his staff, snaps out crisp orders. He sets in motion the steps for a formal coronation (vv. 33–35): a procession to Gihon, anointing, acclamation by the populace, and enthronement. Three of these steps are described in verses 38–40; the enthronement will be reported by Jonathan. Solomon continues to be the passive object of all of this (vv. 38–40, 43–44). His throne rests solidly on David's solemn oath (v. 30) and command (v. 35) and the support and acclamation of others (vv. 36–37, 39–40), which hyperbolically splits open the earth.

This noise provides a bridge back to En-rogel, where, in verse 9, we left Adonijah. The effects of the climax unfold in the denouement (vv. 41–53). The rising curve of Solomon reaches its apex on the throne; Adonijah's falling curve hits bottom as he grasps the altar in terror, then bows before his rival. Jonathan's report retells and then completes Solomon's triumph. The piled up "moreovers" (vv. 46a, 47a, 48a; the same Hebrew word is translated by three different expressions in the NEB) strike repeated blows at Adonijah's hopes. The guests scatter, in vivid contrast to Solomon's solid support from the city, the king, and Yahweh (v. 48).

Adonijah's panic and submission contrast effectively with his earlier self-assurance. Solomon appears for the first time as an active character in verses 51–53. Now he is king; his word is life and death. There is a reconciliation of sorts between the estranged brothers, but the future lies entirely in Solomon's hands. Solomon responds to Adonijah's simple plea with an ambiguous "maybe." The condition imposed on Adonijah is deceptively simple, because Solomon alone will be the judge of worthiness. Adonijah goes home, but the story is clearly not over.

God Did It!

So "Solomon sits upon the royal throne" (v. 46). This is the narrative's central message, recounted three times (vv. 32–35, 38–40, 41–48) for unmistakable emphasis. But Solomon himself had nothing to do with the tawdry deceptions that brought him there, or so the narrative wishes us to believe anyway. Perhaps the choice of Solomon seems arbitrary, almost immoral in the light of Adonijah's priority. By whose will then was he enthroned? On one level it was by the will of David, who recognized his limits and voluntarily relinquished his throne to Solomon (vv. 47–48). David himself made the vow (v. 30) and the appointment (v. 35). Notice the repetition of "my" in verses 30, 35, 48 (cf. 13, 17, 24). Of course, on another level, David was only a pawn of Nathan and Bathsheba, and Solomon the unwitting beneficiary of their intrigue. Yet even this is not the whole story.

Benaiah wishes that Yahweh would second David's initiative (v. 36), but David sees more deeply into what the story intends to reveal (v. 48). Yahweh has brought this about. Solomon was Yahweh's choice for king. As is so often true in biblical literature, God's transcendent will has operated behind unworthy human motives and plots (Gen. 50:20; Ruth 4:14; II Sam. 12:24–25; 17:14). Yahweh is an unindicted co-conspirator in this palace intrigue. As the Book of Kings unfolds, the reader will recognize Yahweh as a master of deception, with other tricks up the sleeve (Micaiah, Jehu, Huldah). Perhaps it is offensive that no moral judgments are made on these shady characters, or worse, that the God of universal history should be involved in a sleazy harem intrigue. So be it! This Yahweh will offend pious sensibilities more than once in the pages to follow. Yahweh's plan and will must be effected, and for God, at least, the ends justify the means. The God of the Book of Kings seems willing to go to any extreme to bring about the divine will, even to the point of undercutting divine promises, destroying the temple, dismissing the beloved Davidic dynasty, and nearly liquidating the chosen people.

God's involvement in the seamy world of politics seems problematic to the modern reader. Devious political machinations, the sudden coup, the establishment of absolutist power have all too often been justified on religious grounds. We may wish to pause and ponder the dark realities of power in our world. The good news is, however, that God is in charge even of the dark side, even of political intrigue. The political structures of this world are not running wild, outside of God's control. They too are part of God's rulership for the good of humanity (Rom. 13:1–7; I Peter 2:13–14). When governments fail to do justice and provide security, God will overthrow them (chap. 12; II Kings 9).

The good news is precisely that our God is singleminded, perhaps, if necessary, even devious, in bringing the divine will into being for us. In a sense, the cross shows us God at God's most determined, most in control of the crooked plots of the politically powerful (Acts 4:27–28), working through human evil to save God's people in the end (Gen. 50:20). The good news is that after the coup of Easter, God's candidate now sits on the throne of the universe (Hebrews 1:3, 8–9, 13).

22

The accession of Solomon sets in motion a complex succession of events to follow in the Book of Kings. The theme of God's promise to David receives its first fulfillment (v. 48). Adonijah's is the first of many conspiracies to follow (Baasha, Zimri, Jehu, Athaliah and others). Solomon's reign will be a glorious one (vv. 37, 47). He reigns explicitly over Israel and Judah (v. 35), but that unity will not last. Kings ends in tragic contrast to this hopeful beginning as a powerless descendant of David sits on a purely symbolic throne, the lackey and sycophant of a foreign monarch (II Kings 25:27–30). For the original readers, thus, the question of this first chapter remained an open one. Who shall now sit on David's throne, if anyone? But we have been given fair warning. In all that follows, Yahweh will be in complete control of events. The will of God powers the dramatic action of the Book of Kings, and the plan of God shapes the course of its plot.

In the more immediate context, however, the focus will be on Solomon's reign—its consolidation (v. 52 and chap. 2) and its unsurpassed peace and prosperity (v. 37 and chaps. 3–10). Solomon's throne will be even greater than David's (v. 47).

I Kings 2
Politics and the Promise of God

This narrative about the consolidation of Solomon's power has a familiar ring to it. We know all too well the concept of the enemies list, the brutal violence of the one-party state, and the utility of moral justifications for politically advantageous crimes. The "bloodless coup" is a rarity in human history. Solomon's was no exception. "All modern revolutions have ended in a reinforcement of the power of the State" (Albert Camus). Again, Solomon's was no exception. After introducing some cultural concepts that may be unfamiliar to the modern reader, we shall examine in some detail how the narrative of chapter 2 moves. Then will follow a look at the chapter's thematic relationship to the rest of Kings and its implications as Scripture.

Some Unfamiliar Concepts

Certain aspects of this story may require some explanation. For example, the narrative assumes that the reader appreciates the high status awarded the queen mother in Judah, reflected by Solomon's courtesy to Bathsheba (vv. 19–20), and that eating

23

at the king's table (v. 7) was the ancient equivalent to a pension. In addition, the reader is expected to know the stories of Joab (II Sam. 3:22–29; 20:8–22), Barzillai (II Sam. 17:27–29), and Shimei (II Sam. 16:5–13).

The scene of an ancient hero summoning his successor(s) to offer last words is common in the Bible (Gen. 49:1; Josh. 23:1; 24:1). David's charge to Solomon also shows similarities to the Egyptian literary format of "instruction," in which a king is represented as passing on political wisdom to his successor. The themes of executing rebels, punishing criminals, and rewarding loyal followers are present in these Egyptian examples (ANET, pp. 414–19).

The issue of blood guilt is raised by verse 5, which emends the Masoretic text to indicate that Joab's bloody deed led to a persistent, objective guilt borne by David, who as king was responsible for his subordinate's actions. Emendations aside, this is also what Solomon claims as justification for executing Joab (v. 31). Blood guilt, viewed as something objectively real, had to be neutralized lest the Davidic house be put in mortal danger. It is this same danger of blood guilt that Solomon seeks to avoid by making it clear that the death of Joab was really Yahweh's revenge and that any guilt must fall on Joab's family and not on the descendants of David (vv. 32–33). A violent death for Joab (vv. 6, 31) would balance out the accounts for David and his family.

The problem of Shimei (vv. 8–9) involves the concepts of the irrevocable curse and the inconvenient oath. In the Old Testament a word is a powerful, objective thing. Even though David had pardoned Shimei for his crime (II Sam. 16:5–11; 19:21–23), his "grievous curse" (literally the "sickening curse") still hung suspended over David's house. Since David's own oath to Shimei was also irrevocable, he was unable to do anything about the problem. Solomon, however, was free to take action and arrange a violent death in order to disarm the curse.

Adonijah's request for the hand of Abishag may seem touching, even romantic to us. The narrator chooses to leave us uninformed about Adonijah's real motivation, but Solomon seizes on a darker possibility, one that in part depends on the expectation that we have read II Samuel 16:21–22. According to this line of thinking, Adonijah's request was intended as an indirect claim to the throne. Taking over the harem of a former king implied just such a claim (II Sam. 3:6–7; 12:8).

Joab seeks asylum at the altar of Yahweh. The idea behind this ancient conception seems to have been that he would be under divine protection as God's guest. According to the law of asylum found in Exodus 21:12–14, at least, Joab would not have been entitled to protection. The narrator fails to tell us whether Solomon was legally justified in violating sanctuary, but Benaiah seems to have had serious qualms (vv. 29–30).

Not every aspect of this story can be easily explained, however. Probably because of a complex literary history, the chapter reveals certain irreducible inner tensions. Did Joab die because of his past crimes (vv. 5, 31–33; the official line of David and Solomon) or because of his support of Adonijah (v. 28; the suspicion of Joab)? Does Solomon take these actions from a high moral purpose (vv. 31–32, 43–44) or out of fear for his throne (v. 22*b*)? On a structural level, Solomon does not take up the problem of the sons of Barzillai bequeathed to him by David's final speech, whereas David for his part never mentions either Adonijah or Abiathar.

The Narrative Movement

Chapter 2 falls naturally into two parts: David's farewell and death (vv. 1–12) and the establishment of Solomon's power (vv. 13–46). The basic movement in chapter 2 is from David's commission through Solomon's obedient action. This movement is effected by the subject change between "David charged Solomon his son" (v. 1) and "Solomon sat upon the throne of David his father" (v. 12). The commission section is enclosed by the subject of David's death (vv. 1 and 10), the action section by the repeated formula of verses 12*b* and 46*b*.

David's last words start with generalities (vv. 2–4) and move to specifics (vv. 5–9). Each of his three specific directives is backed up by a brief justification. The order is justification/negative directive (vv. 5–6), positive directive/justification (v. 7), justification/negative directive (vv. 8–9). The first and third in the series are yoked together by parallel expressions about wisdom and violent death. David's words lead on to Solomon's actions, both directly in the instructions concerning Joab and Shimei and indirectly in that the admonition to "be strong" (v. 2) points to Solomon's decisiveness. David's references to wisdom (vv. 6, 9) anticipate Solomon's clever opportunism.

Yet David's farewell speech has a wider frame of reference as well. The themes of prosperity, wisdom, and keeping the law give us a guide for evaluating the glories of Solomon's reign in chapters 3–10 (cf. 3:3; 4:25; 10:8). The conditional promise of the throne of Israel (v. 4) foreshadows the loss of that throne in chapters 11 and 12. Therefore, David's speech provides a transition from the age of David to the new age of the kings and guidance for interpreting Solomon's coming reign. Verses 10–12 reinforce this transition with a summary of David's ideal forty-year reign and his peaceful death.

Between the brackets of verses 12b and 46b, Solomon takes four actions on the basis of David's last words (vv. 25, 27, 34, 46). These result in the firm establishment of his reign. In two of these actions the other party takes the initiative (Adonijah, Joab); in two Solomon makes the first move (Abiathar, Shimei). All four are linked to events in the career of David. The Adonijah incident implicitly provides the motive for the deposition of Abiathar and explicitly triggers the Joab episode. The fates of Joab and Shimei result from David's specific commission (vv. 6,9). Three of these episodes provide Solomon with a chance to make self-justifying speeches. These bloody deeds are done, he claims, for the safety of the regime (vv. 22–24), for the future of the Davidic house (vv. 31–33), and to protect the sanctity of oaths (vv. 42–45). Sole responsibility for each death supposedly rests with the victim. The greater good of the state and dynasty (vv. 33, 45) provides Solomon with an allegedly noble motive.

In contrast to the deceptions of Nathan or the soft-headed leniency of David (1:6; 2:7–8), Solomon here takes his father's advice to "show yourself a man" (cf. I Sam. 4:9) with bold, decisive action. He demonstrates his "wisdom" (vv. 6, 9) by his clever seizure of the opportunities provided by Adonijah, Joab, and Shimei. Doubtless the original audience was thoroughly appreciative of Solomon's stratagems, although we may have moral hesitations.

Let us look more closely at each of these four "liquidations." The *Adonijah episode* (vv. 13–25) is crafted in two dialogues. The first scene consists of four exchanges between Adonijah and Bathsheba (vv. 13, 14, 15–16, 17–18) by which Adonijah circumspectly approaches his sensitive request. In addition to providing a tension-building delay into the story, this dialogue firmly establishes Adonijah as the petitioner, reduced to employing wheedling tactics: "Feel sorry for me (v. 15). It is only one thing. He will not turn you down." Adonijah

26

ostensibly agrees with the narrator that Yahweh was behind the recent turn of events and unambiguously refers to his rival as "King Solomon." At the same time, his words plant a seed of suspicion in the reader's mind. Coming from this man (again v. 15), this is a dangerous request. Yet this remains no more than a suspicion, for the narrator tells us nothing of Adonijah's motives.

The second scene, between Bathsheba and Solomon (vv. 19–24), also delays matters with the king's courtly expressions of respect. Bathsheba repeats some of Adonijah's motivational language in verse 20. The narrative gently leads the reader to anticipate a positive response. It is only a small thing. Solomon will not refuse the mother he has bowed to and set at his right hand. Indeed, he has promised to grant her request. But then our expectations are shattered by Solomon's outburst with its bitter sarcasm, its rough syntax (v. 22; NIV is close to the difficult Hebrew), its deadly oath. Adonijah's request is a prima-facie case of treason, and with this justification Benaiah receives his first assignment (v. 25).

The *Abiathar episode* is a paragraph subordinate to the previous episode, simply a brief report followed by a notice of the fulfillment of an oracle. The reference to the oracle against the house of Eli (I Sam. 2:27–36) reminds the reader for a moment of the greater story, of which Solomon's kingdom is just a part, the saga of Yahweh's dealings with Israel from exodus to exile.

The tension in the *Joab episode* (vv. 28–35) is provided by the concept of sanctuary. Solomon's order is blunt and decisive (v. 29), but how will Benaiah carry it out? His attempt to lure Joab out of sanctuary with a purported royal command is frustrated by Joab's intransigence. Benaiah reports back with his dilemma, but Solomon overrides his lieutenant's scruples. Joab has predicted his own death. Give him what he has called for! Then follows Solomon's second speech of self-justification. Joab is only getting what he deserves. Solomon is doing God's work (v. 32). The family of David must be protected from bloodguilt so that eternal shalom might rest on the dynasty. The replacements reported in verse 35 are a further indication that the kingdom is solidly established in Solomon's hand. Benaiah is suitably rewarded.

27

The plot of the *Shimei episode* moves from the imposed agreement (vv. 36–38) through its violation (vv. 39–40) to the consequences (vv. 41–46*a*). The narrator may intend the reader to realize that Solomon had a political motive for keeping Shimei on the Jerusalem side of the Kidron (v. 37), away from his pro-Saul kinfolk in nearby Bahurim (v. 8). Yet Shimei's violation occurs in the opposite direction and for an innocent reason. There is no political danger in his action. He transgresses only the letter (v. 37), not the spirit, of the prohibition. Solomon is a "wise man" (v. 9), however, and takes this as an opportunity to eliminate Shimei's "grievous curse" (v. 8). In his third justification speech (vv. 42–45), Solomon throws the blame on Shimei and declares himself guiltless. Not only has Shimei violated his own solemn oath, but his long-standing hostility against David has now rebounded upon him. Once more Solomon is really doing Yahweh's judging work (v. 44; cf. v. 32).

Themes and Implications

Chapter 2 launches themes on trajectories that will arch through the rest of Kings. For example, the *word of Yahweh* (v. 27) will continue to provide an interpretive structure for events.

The *Deuteronomistic voice* also makes its first appearance. In verses 2–4 this special voice speaks through David, using the vocabulary and style of the Book of Deuteronomy. It will continue to have its say at intervals throughout the Book of Kings. This Deuteronomistic voice is an evaluative voice, using the law of Deuteronomy to judge kings and the people. In some chapters it is absent (4; 7; 12; 17—20; II Kings 1—7; 11; 19—20). In others it is obtrusively audible (8; 11; 14—16; II Kings 17; 21—24). Usually it speaks as the narrator (as in II Kings 17), but the narrator does not always evaluate in this voice. Sometimes in First Kings it speaks through characters such as Solomon (8:15–53), Ahijah (14:15–16), or even the Queen of Sheba (10:9). Very often this voice is identical with the voice of God as in verse 4 of this chapter (cf. 9:3–9; 11:31–38; and elsewhere).

This Deuteronomistic voice represents the editorial comments of the author of Kings, the Deuteronomistic Historian. It introduces the evaluative key for the rest of the Book of Kings. David's farewell speech establishes the theological ideal by which each king to follow will be judged. David foreshadows the high potential reached by Hezekiah and Josiah, the ideal pious king from Deuteronomy 17:14–20. His speech emphasizes the importance of keeping the law of Moses as written in the Book of Deuteronomy for national prosperity and success.

The *eternal dynasty* of David is another important theme (vv. 33, 45). Solomon looks forward to an eternal establishment of the Davidic throne and the peace that shall be upon it forever. On one level this can be read as little more than conventional blessing language intended to offset the dangerous potential of bloodguilt, which is fixed firmly on Joab and Shimei. In the broader context of Kings, however, these words must be taken literally. Yahweh has promised an eternal dynasty to David unconditionally (11:36; 15:4; II Kings 8:19). This unconditional covenant sets up one of the critical ideological stress points in the book, for only a parody of this eternal throne is left in the last chapter (II Kings 25:27–30).

The conditional promise of verse 4 seems at first to undercut this unconditional covenant. This same conditional promise is repeated in 8:25 and 9:4–6. Most interpreters have taken the expression "throne of Israel" as a reference to the throne of the United Kingdom. They see this as a conditionalization of the unconditional dynastic promise to David's house expressed in 11:36; 15:4; II Kings 8:19. The presence of both unconditional and conditional promises to the house of David would create intense theological dissonance in Kings.

A closer look, however, indicates that the conditional promises are only offered within the material on Solomon and refer only to the "throne of Israel." The unconditional promises, on the other hand, are distributed more widely and speak of an unending reign in Jerusalem. It is most natural, therefore, to understand "throne of Israel" in 2:4; 8:25, and 9:4–6 as a reference to reign over the Northern Kingdom. Verse 4 means that God promised David rule over the northern half of the United Kingdom forever if David's sons were to keep the law with Deuteronomistic rigor (cf. Deut. 17:18–20). Solomon, of course, ultimately failed in this (chap. 11) and the "throne of Israel" was lost to David's house and offered on similar terms to Jeroboam (11:38).

The *priesthood* is a theme of some importance as well. Here Abiathar's line is excluded from Jerusalem and Zadok's is established by the will of Yahweh. Later the book will report about the pseudo-priests set up by Jeroboam (12:31; 13:33), the coup of Jehoiada (II Kings 11), the priests sent by the Assyrians (II Kings 17:27–28), and Josiah's exclusion of the non-Jerusalem priesthood (II Kings 23:9), which returns again to the issue of the sole legitimacy of the Zadokites.

This section intends to convince the reader that the royal power was firmly established for Solomon by his own decisive, wise action. He was justified in every move he made. Moreover, he was doing Yahweh's righteous work (vv. 32, 44) and fulfilling Yahweh's word (v. 27). In that sense Yahweh was behind the establishment of the kingdom in Solomon's hand. Indeed Solomon and Adonijah both assert this explicitly, and the narrative intends the reader to agree. This section points beyond itself to the shifting fortunes of the Davidic dynasty. More narrowly it prepares the reader for the peace and prosperity (vv. 33, 45) of the Solomonic kingdom (chapts. 3–10) and raises the issue of the throne of Israel (v. 4) to be decided in chapter 11.

The modern reader may be unwilling to buy what sounds like crude political propaganda. We are highly suspicious of Solomon's self-justifying rhetoric. Verse 22 sounds more loudly in our ears than all his high-sounding moral rectitude. We have heard too often the claim that government does God's work by its violent deeds. Marxist, capitalist, and Third World states all have their variations on this theme. How else could the Benaiahs of our world be convinced to violate the modern equivalents of sanctuary? For the preacher and teacher, this chapter may open up new perspectives on the shoddy foundations of political ideology. It might alert the church to the danger of being co-opted by established governments or revolutionary movements for their own purposes.

In tension with this observation, however, it is also true that this chapter insists that Solomon's reign was actually a different matter altogether from what we suspect. As canonical text, this chapter has the goal of overcoming our suspicions and persuading us, perhaps against our better judgment, that God was indeed behind the consolidation of Solomon's power and that Solomon was indeed justified in what he did. The text suggests that when the welfare of God's people is at stake God is willing to employ the most ruthless of political processes. The death of Egypt's first born and the death of God's own Son are the classic examples. Why God should care so much to establish and protect the throne of David's son may only become clear when one reads Matthew 1:6–16 and Revelation 22:16.

I Kings 3:1–15
The Pattern for Kingship

"So the kingdom was established in the hand of Solomon" (2:46*b*), but what sort of kingship would this be? In the ancient world, stories of dreams and divine appearances often answered such questions of political ideology (one example is the Sphinx Stele, ANET, p. 449). Let us look first at the choice that Solomon made concerning the pattern for his kingship, then at the details of the narrative itself, and finally at the wider implications of this passage for the structure of the Book of Kings as a whole and as Christian Scripture.

The Pattern Chosen

In Solomon's dream at Gibeon, the nation's "most important high place" (v. 4, NIV), two competing patterns of kingship are set before the reader: a kingship of glory and a kingship in the spirit of Deuteronomy. Solomon chooses the second pattern.

What Solomon does not ask for are the trappings of glory and worldly success that made up much of the royal ideology: long life (Ps. 72:15), riches (Ps. 21:3, 5; 72:15–16), and death to the opposition (Ps. 21:8–12). It was just this pattern for kingship that Deuteronomy warned against (Deut. 17:16–17), as had Samuel (I Sam. 8:11–18). These glories would be part of Solomon's kingship (chaps. 3—10), but only as God's gifts, rewards for Solomon's proper focus on an entirely different pattern for kingship. Riches and honor were granted, beyond what any other contemporary king could boast of (v. 13); long life would depend on continued fidelity (v. 14).

Solomon chooses the pattern of kingship under the law. This is the pattern one reads about in Deuteronomy 17:14–20, the sort of kingship later represented by Hezekiah and Josiah (cf. 3:12 with II Kings 18:5–6; 23:25). According to this pattern, the king is God's servant (four times in vv. 6–9), a loyal vassal in a covenant relationship (vv. 6, 14). The goal of this sort of kingship is the welfare of God's people (vv. 8–9), not the glory

31

of the king. In order to govern (literally "judge") this people, the servant king needs the talent for which Solomon asks. This talent is expressed four different ways (the first and fourth expressions and the second and third are linked in a chiastic pattern, *ABBA*):

> A an understanding mind
> >   (literally a "hearing heart"; v. 9)
> > B to discern between good and evil (v. 9)
> > B' understanding to discern what is right
> >   (literally "to hear judgment"; v. 11)
> A a wise and discerning mind (literally "heart"; v. 12)

The description of this pattern of kingship is packed with ideologically loaded vocabulary. The first readers would have recognized echoes of royal ideology in words like "faithfulness," "righteousness" (v. 6), "discern" (v. 9), and "wise" (v. 12). These are some of the characteristics of the ideal king reflected in Isaiah 11:2–5. The word translated as "steadfast love" (v. 6) is *hesed,* covenant loyalty, implying the royal theology that God and David's family were joined by an unconditional covenant relationship (Ps. 89:19–37). The most intriguing expression is Solomon's request for a "hearing heart" (v. 9; RSV, "an understanding mind"; NEB, "a heart with a skill to listen"). The heart is the organ of thought and will in the Old Testament. This expression implies a reason that understands, an instinct for the truth. Solomon's request is for the specific purpose of ruling the people, especially in the judicial arena. The following story of the disputed baby (vv. 16–28) is a perfect illustration of what is meant by verse 9.

The Narrative Structure

In examining how this narrative makes the point that Solomon made the correct and godly choice, we shall begin first with the outer framework (vv. 1–4, 15*b*). There is a clear change in situation from verses 1–4 by the time we reach verse 15*b*. Solomon began by sacrificing at Gibeon, but finishes with sacrifices in Jerusalem. Verse 1 functions to set the story in the time before the temple was begun. This notice concerning Pharaoh's daughter is in the right place chronologically. Kings is now at least three years into Solomon's reign (2:39) and temple construction began in his fourth year (6:1). Verse 3 explains that Solomon still sacrificed outside Jerusalem, and verse 2 provides

32

a justification for his apparent violation of the law of Deuteronomy. To understand the following narrative, it is important for the reader to know that Solomon loved Yahweh and yet still sacrificed at high places (local sanctuaries, raised outdoor platforms). Even though the temple has not yet been built (as vv. 1–2 remind the reader), Solomon's choice of a pattern for kingship means that the locus of sacrifice has already shifted in verse 15.

Within this framework, the narrative itself is fashioned according to the form of a dream epiphany (cf. Gen. 28:12–16), putting into Solomon's mouth a classic petitionary prayer (cf. 8:23–26). Whether the writer used an earlier tradition about a dream appearance at Gibeon or simply created this story is a disputed point. The original audience may have understood Solomon's action in the light of the practice of "incubation," intentionally sleeping in a sanctuary in hopes of receiving a divine revelation. A dream frame is provided by verses 5*a* and 15*a:* Solomon dreams and wakes. The core of the story is a dialogue, and the narrative frames (vv. 1–4, 15*b* and inside this vv. 5*a* and 15*a*) have been kept to a minimum in order to focus on this dialogue.

The basic movement in this dialogue is that the king asks (used eight times) and God gives (five times). This movement is laid out by God's first words, "Ask what I shall give you" (v. 5), followed by "you have asked . . . I give you" (vv. 11–12), and then, "what you have not asked I give you" (v. 13; modified RSV). The motif of asking from God and receiving seems to have been part of the royal ideology (Ps. 2:8; 21:2, 4).

The foundation for Solomon's request is laid by verses 6–8. Verse 6*a* looks back to the past, David's righteousness and God's steadfast love. Solomon's succession is the subject of verses 6*b*–7*a*. There are multiple links back to chapter 1 (to 1:13, 20, 35 and so on). Verses 7*b*–8 bring the problem into focus and lead on to Solomon's request. Solomon's "little child" is a rhetorical way of expressing the humility natural to prayer (Jer. 1:6; cf. David in II Sam. 7:18). "To go out or come in" is a general expression for the duties of leadership, with military leadership especially in mind. The whole section on the request and its justification is unified by interlocking vocabulary: "great and steadfast love" (v. 6*a*, *b*), "thy servant" (vv. 6*a*, 7*a*, 8*a*, 9*a*), and "thy people" (vv. 8*a*, 9*a*, *b*).

Deuteronomistic language is also strongly present: "in righ-

33

teousness and uprightness of heart" (v. 6; Deut. 9:5); "thy people whom thou hast chosen (v. 8; Deut. 7:6). A close thematic parallel to the whole dialogue is provided by Deuteronomy 1:9–18. In fact, both Solomon (vv. 6–8) and God (vv. 12–14) unite in using Deuteronomistic language, a further sign of Solomon's harmony with God's purpose.

God's answer provides the dramatic climax. The reader is given a glimpse into God's mind for a moment (v. 10). Verse 11 gives the background for the response with three negatives (you have not asked) framed by two positives (you have asked). The English versions obscure this patterned repetition, which puts as much emphasis on what is not asked as on what is. "You have asked" is picked up by verse 12a and granted; "you have not asked" is taken up by verse 13a and also granted.

Wider Structural and Theological Horizons

The narrative in 3:1–15 is not isolated. It introduces the positive side of Solomon's reign (chaps. 3—10 as opposed to chap. 11). Verses 1–3 of chapter 3 join with 9:24–25 to provide a bracket around 3:4—9:23, material dealing with Solomon's kingdom from an internal perspective (as opposed to 9:26—10:29 which deals with international affairs). The building projects introduced by verse 1 are described in chapter 6, 7:1–2, and 9:15. The theme of wise judgment (v. 9) is critical to what follows (v. 28; 4:29; 5:7, 12; 10:8–9). Solomon's dream at Gibeon is paralleled by a second appearance of God in 9:1–9.

This narrative also prepares for chapter 11, the negative side of Solomon's reign. Verse 1a leads to 9:24 and on to the negative implications of this woman in 11:1. Verse 1b leads to 9:25b and on to Solomon's apostate building activities in 11:7. His "love" for Yahweh in 3:3 finds its darker side in 11:1, "Solomon loved many foreign women." The mention of high places (v. 2) connects to the threat of 9:6–9 and the judgment of 11:10–13, the consequences of which will reverberate down to the end of the book.

In some ways 3:1–15 is parallel in function to chapters 1—2 and as such is an example of parataxis. Both narratives legitimate Solomon as king. Chapters 1—2 do so from a dynastic, political perspective. The dream narrative speaks of legitimacy from God more directly. The sort of wisdom given here is a dislocating contrast to that sort evidenced by Solomon so far (2:6, 9).

Theologically the reader is offered a way of holding together apparently contradictory ideologies about God's relationship to kingship. The writer is attempting a theological balancing act, a harmonization of unconditional royal covenant theology with a conditional Deuteronomistic insistence on obedience. The reader has already had a preview of this in 2:2–5. There a conditional promise of the throne of Israel (the Northern Kingdom) contingent on obedience to the law of Moses was introduced. Now Solomon is offered a second conditional promise. Long life will be contingent on Solomon's obedience (v. 14).

On the other hand, God's unconditional dynastic promise has already been established on the basis of David's fidelity (v. 6). The unconditional nature of God's promise to the Davidic dynasty goes back to II Samuel 7:14–16 and will be stated explicitly again in 11:36. The dialogue in chapter 3 supports this by emphasizing David's perfect obedience and God's "great covenant loyalty."

In the Book of Kings, this eternal and unconditional dynastic covenant and various conditional promises are coordinated. The unconditional dynastic promise for David's family is solidly based on David's past fidelity. In contrast, lesser promises (the throne of Israel, long life) are conditional, dependent on each king's individual obedience to the law.

The Christian church has had its own struggles with conditional and unconditional language in describing how God relates to us. The extreme poles of this tension are marked by Augustine and Pelagius, and in a less extreme way by Calvin and Arminius. This narrative offers one possible way of balancing these two opposing theological grammars. God's critically important promise rests on unconditional grace, founded on a past act of obedience (David's in the O.T., that of Jesus in the N.T.; cf. Rom. 5:19; Phil. 2:8; Heb. 5:8–9). Conditional promises are of a subsidiary nature. The Christian is comforted by the unconditional and challenged by the conditional.

As far as the Book of Kings is concerned, however, this is a temporary equilibrium only. The reader of Kings will be confronted by this tension again and again. By the time the book has run its course, God's unconditional, eternal covenant with David will have been cast into critical doubt (II Kings 21:10–15; 24:3–4). At the same time, confidence in the conditional Deuteronomistic idea that obedience leads to God's favor will also have been shaken to its roots by God's refusal to take Jo-

35

siah's perfect obedience into consideration. Where this leaves the reader will be considered in the last section of this commentary, II Kings 25:27–30, "Can the Promise Live?"

Thus the picture of "Solomon in all his glory" is set in perspective by an insistence that the king must be God's faithful servant. His central concerns must always be the people chosen by God and obedience to the law. David here is the model for this pattern of kingship, as he will continue to be through the rest of the book (9:4; 11:4, 6, 33; 14:8; 15:11; II Kings 14:3; 16:2; 18:3; 22:2). Solomon's prosperity and glory were his reward for choosing the pattern for kingship that corresponded to the Deuteronomistic ideal.

The question of the proper pattern for kingship faces this century as it has every other. That pattern rejected by Solomon is well represented by governments around the world today, just as it was among the geopolitical structures known to the first readers (the Egyptian and Babylonian states). Yet New Testament Scripture insists that these governments operate under God's mandate (John 19:11; Rom. 13:1–7; I Peter 2:13) and ought to rule in accordance with the servanthood pattern chosen by Solomon. Persons who stand in the biblical tradition may sometimes find themselves in positions of governmental authority and can thus take Solomon's choice directly to heart. Others will find their role with the prophets, calling governments back to their proper place as vassals and servants of God and to their proper service of ruling with a "listening heart." Both groups are reminded by this text that God is vitally concerned about proper and wise government.

In the lectionary shared by many denominations, this story is used on the Tenth Sunday after Pentecost, Year A, in conjunction with Matthew 13:44–52. This Gospel reading includes two parables about the importance of recognizing the priorities of God's kingdom and acting on them. In this text we see Solomon doing this very thing. He becomes a prime example of faithful choice in harmony with God's will and of Jesus' admonition to "seek first [God's] kingdom and [God's] righteousness, and all these things shall be yours as well" (Matt. 6:33).

Finally, the Christian reader cannot fail to recognize that the wise pattern for kingship chosen by Solomon finds its complete realization in the ministry of Jesus, the messianic king, who prescribed this same pattern for his disciples (Matt. 20:25–28).

I Kings 3:16—5:18
Wisdom and Prosperity I

The promise given to Solomon in 3:12–13 unfolds from verse 16 through chapter 5. The same themes and topics will be taken up again in 9:10—10:29 (see "Wisdom and Prosperity II," below). Between these two sections, the story of Solomon's kingdom of shalom rises to its high point in the building and dedication of the temple (chaps. 6—8). This is then followed by a second, more ominous appearance of God (9:1–9).

This section is a characteristic example of paratactic structure. Units are laid out side by side until the whole story is told (see Introduction). First there is a folktale extolling Solomon's judicial wisdom (3:16–28). Then come two lists of royal officials, enriched with additional comments, revealing Solomon's administrative wisdom (4:1–6, 7–28). Next follows a section bracketed by 4:29 and 5:12, developing the theme of Solomon's wisdom and the kings of the earth, particularly Hiram of Tyre (4:29—5:12). Finally the theme of preparations for the temple is completed by the miscellany of 5:13–18.

Solomon's Judicial Wisdom (3:16–28)

A traditional folktale (3:16–28) provides an illustration of Solomon's "listening heart" (v. 9) and his "understanding to discern what is right" (v. 11). The first word ("then," v. 16) ties it closely to Solomon's dream at Gibeon, as does the concluding popular reaction: The wisdom of God is in (literally "inside") Solomon (v. 28). This story confirms that God's promised gift has indeed been given. It also provides an example of what even the commonest citizen could expect from Solomon's wise rule.

The story is told with artistry and wit. It moves by means of dialogue rather than through a direct portrayal of events. Three speeches are made by the women (vv. 17–22*a*), followed by Solomon's speech (vv. 23–25), two more by the women (v. 26), and then the king's judgment (v. 27). The plot moves from the normal situation of the two housemates (vv. 17–18), complicated by death, deception, and the ensuing controversy (vv.

37

19–22), to resolution (vv. 23–27) and the popular reaction (v. 28).

The central dilemma for Solomon is repeated three times in verse 18. The women were completely alone, without even so much as a customer present (a meaning implied by the Hebrew), so the normal juridical practice of hearing witnesses is precluded. The usual procedure in such a difficulty would be to rely on God's judgment through the casting of sacred lots, an oath of purgation (Exod. 22:9–10), or an ordeal (Num. 5:11–15). In this case, however, the "wisdom of God" is available directly from the king.

The repetitious dialogue has the effect of tiring and bemusing the reader. For example, the chiasm of verse 22 is repeated by Solomon in verse 23, as if to say that the argument was going around in circles. The Hebrew shows a repetitive word play in verses 18, 20, 25, obscured in the English. Solomon's final directive is an exact reproduction of the mother's urgent plea: "Give her the living child and by no means slay it" (vv. 26, 27; RSV modified).

The reader's sympathy is naturally directed at the woman who speaks first. She is polite and a bit chatty ("in the house ... in the house;" "in the morning ... behold ... in the morning, behold"). In contrast, her opponent snaps back a brusque reply, and the argument is on (v. 22)! Even though the narrative does not say so, the reader assumes that this first speaker is telling the truth and thus is the compassionate woman, the real mother. The compassionate woman's "maternal feelings were stirred" (v. 26, literally "her wombs") out of compassion for her son. She uses an especially maternal word (*yalud,* "born one") for the infant in place of the more objective "son" or "child" employed earlier. Her opponent, on the other hand, is inhumanly cold. Even when she has won the baby by the compassionate woman's capitulation, she still insists on the fifty-fifty split which would be objectively "fair" (Exod. 21:35) but morally monstrous. The reader is glad things turn out the way they do and admires Solomon for pulling off this psychological *tour de force* in the best traditions of Hercule Poirot or Inspector Maigret.

But wait! Is the reader being fooled in the process? Think again. For one thing, we cannot be sure our favorite first speaker really is the woman of compassion. More seriously, Solomon has not really proved that the compassionate woman is the biological mother, only that she is more fit to be a parent. His demonstration is psychologically reasonable but not logically watertight. Does her heart yearn (v. 26) for a son presently under the threat of a sword or for a son already dead? Moreover, the woman who loses the judgment is such a monster that she strains her credibility with the reader to the breaking point. She is inexplicable either as true mother or liar. Finally, perhaps a truly perverse reader might even wonder how wise Solomon would have looked if both women had urged him to preserve the child's life, which seems the most likely scenario! If the reader is being fooled, however, the story does such a good job of it that no one really minds. The reader is perfectly willing to agree with the populace that the wisdom of God and its resulting justice are present in Solomon.

One hallmark of God's justice is that it is fair to all, even to a pair of disreputable prostitutes. Human justice has always been available to the well heeled or the well connected. In contrast, God's justice "raises up the poor from the dust" (I Sam. 2:8; cf. Luke 1:52–53). It is justice for the outcast which transcends what may be objectively fair. It is justice for a woman in a man's world. One who has read the Bible's whole story, including John 8:3–11, recognizes that this tale about Solomon displays the genuine character of God's justice in a wisdom that goes beyond mere cleverness. Where such justice is done today, the wisdom of God may be perceived to be at work.

Solomon's Administrative Wisdom (4:1-28)

The structure of 4:1-28 is based on two registers of officials (vv. 1–6 and 7–28), the second of which has attracted various comments and extra details. The concept of "all Israel" (vv. 1, 7) focuses the beginning of each list. The second section (vv. 7–28) is held together by the repetition of the chief duty of these officers (better: "district governors," NIV) in verses 7 and 27–28. The intention is to induce awe and wonder over the prosperity, extent, peacefulness, and stability of Solomon's kingdom. This "kingdom of shalom" was all anyone could ever wish for, a political and economic paradise.

The first list emphasizes Solomon's continuity with David's rule (cf. II Sam. 8:15–18; 20:23–25). Certain names reach back into the past (Zadok, Abiathar, Benaiah, Jehoshaphat son of Ahilud). One name and office, that of Adoniram, also points

39

forward to a darker future (12:18). There are plenty of priests in this utopia. Even the deposed Abiathar is mentioned. This is a kingdom under God. Yet it also is flavored with the sophistication of Egyptian court practice (see the commentaries).

The second register lists Solomon's twelve administrative districts. The first seven (vv. 8–14), with geographic names, make a clockwise inner circle. The next five (vv. 15–19a, reading "Gad" for "Gilead" in v. 19a) trace a counterclockwise outer circle north and south and identify the districts with tribal names. Again a continuity with David appears with the inclusion of Ahimaaz and a son of Hushai (II Sam. 15:27, 37). Israel's tribal past is part of Solomon's new organization (the tribal names). But the Canaanite tradition is present as well in the geographic shape of the first seven districts and the Canaanite-style patronymic names of many of the officials ("Ben-hur" and so forth). The reader is intended to marvel at the complexity of a kingdom requiring such a sophisticated system, to note the stability implied by the presence of Solomon's sons-in-law (vv. 11, 15), and to remember that all this land was really the gift of God (4:13 and 19 reflect Deut. 3). These lists provide the reader with a sense of reality and verisimilitude. This utopia was no never-never land. It involved real people and real geography.

The material inside the brackets of verses 7 and 27–28 is arranged in a chiasm (apart from v. 26). Summary statements of general prosperity and happiness are in verses 20 and 25; verses 21 and 24 describe the extent of the empire; and verses 22–23 itemize the vast provisions needed to support the king's magnificent household. Each sentence adds to the reader's wonder. These verses are parallel in style and function to ancient self-laudatory inscriptions such as that of Azitawadda of Adana (ANET, pp. 653–54). Solomon's kingdom was the fulfillment of God's promises to the patriarchs in regard to both population (v. 20; Gen. 22:17; 32:12) and extent (Gen. 15:18; Deut. 1:7). There was security within the traditional borders from Dan to Beersheba, and each peasant owned the prerequisites for a modestly prosperous lifestyle (v. 25; cf. the vision of eschatological peace in Micah 4:4). This empire actually realized the courtly exaggerations of royal ideology (vv. 21, 24; Ps. 72:8, 10–11, 16). Solomon's household was vast; thousands ate from his bounty. He kept a huge force of horses for the chariots that guarded the "peace on all sides round about him" (v. 24).

40

Solomon and the Nations (4:29—5:18)

"God gave Solomon wisdom" and "the Lord gave Solomon wisdom" (4:29 and 5:12) bracket 4:29—5:12. The topic is first Solomon's wonderful wisdom in general. Then 4:34 provides a transition to a narrowed topic, how Hiram, one of "the kings of the earth," related to David's "wise son" (5:7). This latter topic not only underscores Solomon's administrative wisdom but also prepares for his most important achievement, the temple. This transition to the temple, with a description of Solomon's forced labor, is completed in 5:13–18.

The author has utilized a sophisticated structure to surround the temple construction with Solomon's other glorious achievements. Each part of 4:29–5:18 has its mirror image on the other side of the temple chapters. Verses 29–34 correspond to 10:1–13 and 5:1–12 corresponds to 9:10–14. The next part, 5:13–18, has its twin in 9:15–23.

The reader is intended to marvel at the wisdom of Solomon eulogized in 4:29–34. The sentences are loosely joined to each other, although the English versions supply connectives. Verse 29 takes the reader back to the dream at Gibeon. Solomon's wisdom surpassed all recognized sources and authorities. The numbers are impressive. Verse 33 indicates that he made lists of natural phenomena in the best traditions of ancient wisdom and sought wisdom from his observation of plants and animals (cf. Prov. 30:25–26).

The basic structure of 5:1–12 is provided by the sending of messages (vv. 1, 2, 8). First comes Hiram's initiative to retain his relationship with David, "love" being a verb used in treaty parlance. Then follows Solomon's proposal, and finally Hiram's modified acceptance of it. The result is a commercial agreement, peace, and a treaty between the two kings (vv. 10–12). There is some movement in the negotiation, for Hiram modifies Solomon's original offer (v. 6) with a program of divided responsibility. Hiram's people will deliver the logs to the harbor; Solomon's crews will take it from there (NIV and NEB reflect this more clearly than RSV). Solomon's enormous yearly payment of wheat would have supplied his own house for seven months (cf. v. 11 with 4:22; RSV uses "measure" for *"cor"* in 4:22).

The presence of the Deuteronomistic voice in chapter 5, **41** used here by both Hiram (v. 7) and Solomon (vv. 3–5), alerts the reader that the narrative is returning to theological basics once more. Solomon motivates his petition to Hiram with theological language actually directed at the reader. Negotiations are set in the context of God's promise to David (v. 5 reflects II Sam. 7). God has given "rest" to Solomon (v. 4; II Sam. 7:1, 11). The temple will be for the "name" of Yahweh (v. 3; II Sam. 7:13). With a traditional "blessed be Yahweh," Hiram praises God for setting Solomon over this "great people" (v. 7; cf. 3:8). The story of Solomon is beginning its ascent to the glorious climax of his reign, the building and dedication of the temple. One small sign of this is the repeated mention of "cedar" (vv. 6, 8, 10), a key word in chapters 6–7 (fourteen times).

This transition to temple construction is concluded in 5:13–18. The structure is loose, but simple. Verses 13–14 speak of timber workers, 15–17 describe those who provided stone. The concentration is on numbers, job descriptions, and organization. Verse 18 summarizes these two groups of workers. Sources for the two basic construction materials have been secured. The effort to impress is obvious in the huge numbers. These are not just any stones, but "great stones, costly stones, . . . dressed stones" (v. 17; RSV modified). Skilled workers are imported even from Gebal (Byblos). The numbers of workmen in verses 15–16 seem to have been computed on the basis of 9:23 and added later (see the commentaries), indicating that early readers of this text appreciated the effort to impress them and joined in it. Along with 5:1–12, this material serves to increase the reader's anticipation for the start of actual construction.

Overall, 3:16—5:18 has the upbeat character of a modern public relations effort, but the reader also senses a muted negative subtheme. Was Solomon as wise with those two women as he seemed? Adoniram's presence in 4:6 and Judah's apparent exemption from the district taxation system (4:19; JB, NIV, NEB, TEV; RSV adds "Judah" here) foreshadow a darker future. Solomon's boast that he has no "adversary" (5:4) takes on an ironic twist in the light of the upcoming reports of 11:14, 23.

Finally, the last verses, 5:13–18, raise the explosive issue of forced labor. At this point the institution is treated positively, or at least neutrally. This is not the permanent reduction in status to serfdom imposed on the Canaanites (9:20–22) but a temporary conscription for what the narrator sees as the worthiest possible cause (5:5). We might remind ourselves of the dedication and joy of those who labored on Europe's cathedrals in assessing the way forced labor is presented in Kings up to this point. The dangers for the future, however, are already all too apparent.

God has given rest (5:4). Shalom (4:24; 5:12), wisdom (3:28; 4:29–34; 5:7), and prosperity (4:20, 22–23, 25) envelop the kingdom. The materials are ready for building to begin. The workers are ready. The reader is ready. Yet underneath it all is a realization that this fragile shalom could be broken if Solomon should fail to live in fidelity to God's command (2:3–4; 3:14).

Many European and North American Christians will see their own economic, cultural, and political situations reflected in this utopian vision of Solomon's wisdom and prosperity. They may wish to use the subtle ironic flavors of this text to plumb beneath the glossy surface layer of peace and prosperity which characterizes Western culture. Do prostitutes and other outcasts receive justice (3:28)? Do the poor actually have their own vines and fig trees (4:25)? Are tax systems (4:7–19) and labor policies (5:13–14) really in harmony with the goals of God's wisdom? Do substantial defense systems (4:26) blunt the awareness of hidden adversaries (5:4)? As Kings tells the story, Solomon's prosperity was a gift of God, the result of the king's faithful prayer for wisdom. But it all hung by the slenderest of threads, the continued obedience of the one who held power. Knowing how the story finally turns out, the comfortable and secure dare not read these chapters feeling smug.

I Kings 6—7
Building the Temple

This section should sound familiar to anyone who has ever taken a guided tour of a famous building. This is the voice of the typical tour guide, rattling off statistics (in cubits and baths) and dates (6:1, 37–38), pointing out interesting features, sometimes at random, spinning out anecdotes (6:7; 7:13–14, 46–47). Like a tour guide, the narrator of this section wishes to impress, to awe, to fix in the reader's mind a general impression of this particular attraction.

The purpose of these chapters is not to provide a blueprint from which the original temple of Solomon might be reconstructed but to overawe the reader with the grandeur and glory

43

of the building. Stone is covered with cedar, and cedar with gold. Skilled carving adorns every wall and door. The text recreated an image of the demolished temple for the original readers, some of whom would have remembered it (Ezra 3:12). We shall first look at how this description is structured to produce this desired effect, then reflect on the theological implications for the Book of Kings and for today's reader.

A Guidebook to the Temple

Solomon's building activities are described in chapters 6 and 7. The major emphasis rests on a description of the temple, which precedes (6:1–38) and follows (7:13–51) a more cursory look at the other public buildings of Jerusalem (7:1–12). The emphasis is on the interior of the temple and its furnishings, which the average person would never have seen, although the exterior is not ignored. Perhaps some sort of archival source was used to write this, or a literary reworking of the instructions given to the artisans, but this description could easily have been created from on-the-spot observation or memory. One is reminded of Josephus and the Mishnah describing the later Second Temple after its destruction. A golden aura of memory overlays the concrete reality of stone and cedar.

The presentation lacks the order and structure of a modern guidebook, but it still impacts the reader with a strong sense of wonder and awe, even though the building is not impressive by modern standards. This mental picture is generated dynamically with narrative verbs: "he built, he made, he lined, he carved." Held into this narrative structure are simple descriptions using nominal sentences. There is a considerable degree of textual confusion. Many of the details are hidden from us, for we no longer understand the architectural terms employed. However, the original readers probably did not understand them either! Consider the piling up of glosses to explain "nets" in 7:17.

Chapter 6 describes the building itself, bracketed by the chronological notices of verses 1 and 38. A mental picture of the outside of the temple builds in verses 2–10: the overall dimensions (vv. 2–3, actually the interior measurements), around the outside walls (vv. 4–6, 8), the roof (v. 9, again seen from the inside), and back again to the structure running around the outside (v. 10). The focus is on stone until the summary statement of verse 9a, then on wood (vv. 9b–10).

After a second summary statement (v. 14), verses 15–36 take the reader through the interior. The focus moves around like a panning camera, zooming in on details of carving (vv. 18, 29). Gold glitters from every surface. Verses 16–28 concentrate on the inner sanctuary, the holy of holies, giving the reader a chance to gawk at the cherubim. With a grammatical shift to perfect verbs, verses 29–36 indicate a change in subject. The reader now stands outside the innermost holy of holies, looking at the walls (v. 29), the floor (v. 30), and then back at the doors to the holy of holies (vv. 31–32). The reader is then taken out the main door (vv. 33–35) for a glance at the inner court (v. 36). The section closes (vv. 37–38) with a chronological reflection of verse 1 and a reversal of the refrain "he built the house and completed it" (vv. 9, 14; v. 1 "he built the house") with "the house was completed . . . and he built it" (v. 38; Hebrew literally).

The cursory description of Solomon's secular buildings in chapter 7, verses 1–12, is full of lexical, grammatical, and textual difficulties. It is only on the basis of excavations of the *bit-hilani* architectural style, especially at Megiddo, that we recognize that verses 6–8 probably describe an integrated complex of buildings. The descriptions are brief, with only the most salient features noted. The reader is not intended to become too interested in them. In verse 1 "house" is a general heading encompassing the entire palace complex. First the buildings are described (vv. 2–8), then the materials (vv. 9–12). Most attention is given to an interior view of the house of the forest of Lebanon, which will be mentioned again in 10:17, 21.

There is a chronological distortion in that Kings understands the thirteen years of verse 1 to have come after the seven years of temple construction (9:10). But by moving these buildings forward in time, sandwiching them between material on the temple and integrating them architecturally with the temple (v. 12), the narrator firmly subordinates these secular buildings to the house of the Lord. Both the house of the forest of Lebanon and the complex described in verses 6–8 are substantially larger than the temple, but they have been effectively relegated to the status of interesting footnotes. They highlight Solomon's glory without diminishing the wonder of the temple.

Verses 13–50 first describe the bronze work with Hiram as subject (vv. 13–47), then the gold furnishings with Solomon as subject (vv. 48–50). First Hiram is introduced in a way cal-

45

culated to attract admiration. Each item is introduced by a narrative sentence with Hiram as subject (15*a*, pillars; 23*a*, sea; 27*a*, stands; 38*a*, lavers; 40*a*, miscellaneous items), followed by nominal descriptive sentences, first giving measurements and then (mixed with a few narrative verbs) other details. Verses 40*b*–45 summarize all this with a slightly varied list of the items described. The concern of verses 46–47 remains bronze, but the grammatical subject shifts to Solomon. This provides a transition to the gold accessories of verses 48–50, as does the use of the word "vessels" in verses 45, 47, 48, 51. Verses 46–47 also make it clear that Solomon was the prime mover behind Hiram's contributions.

The goal of impressing the reader continues: the intricate workmanship of the two pillars; the vast size and capacity of the sea, at least by ancient standards; the supposedly portable wheeled stands, each weighing at least a metric ton when full; the artwork; the incalculable weight of bronze. This effort is carried to an extreme in verses 48–50. The repeated words "fine gold . . . gold" at the end of each verse and half verse hammer home an impression of limitless wealth. Finally, verse 51 provides a conclusion for the whole of chapters 6–7.

Theological Concerns

Chapters 6–7 have a theological side as well. This was no ordinary building, but a structure to house the ark (6:19). Nothing could be permitted to violate the integrity of its walls (6:6). No uncouth sound, especially that of an iron tool (Deut. 27:5; Josh. 8:31) marred the construction process (6:7). Hiram's Israelite mother is carefully noted lest it be thought a Gentile had done this holy work (7:14). The twin pillars bear names of security and stability: Jachin, "it is solid," and Boaz, "with strength" (7:21). The sea seems to be a symbol of chaos contained. God's gift of fertility is recalled by the artwork: gourds, flowers, palm trees, hundreds of pomegranates (cf. the erotic flavor to palm trees and pomegranates in the Song of Solomon), even bulls (7:25, 29; NIV, TEV). The guardian cherubim (6:23–29; 7:29, 36) signal God's presence (Ps. 18:10; 99:1; I Sam. 4:4).

The introductory chronology (6:1) makes the event of temple building the culmination of Israel's saga up to this point. It marks the end of a chronology that has been carefully calculated by the Deuteronomistic Historian since Deuteronomy

46

1:3. At the same time it is carefully synchronized with the royal chronology of the Book of Kings which started in 2:11. Thus the construction of the temple is set at the midpoint of Israel's history with God and is coordinated with the primary saving event of the exodus.

Other items in chapter 7 provide positive links to Israel's past as well. Hiram is described as a second Bezalel (cf. v. 14 to Exod. 31:2–3). Some of the bronze work and most of Solomon's gold work are echoes of the furnishings for the tabernacle (cf. v. 40 to Exod. 27:3; vv. 48–50 to Exod. 25:23, 29, 31, 38; 30:3). (In historical-critical terms, Exodus may actually be dependent on Kings; but in canonical terms, the story runs the other way!) Verse 51 of chapter 7 links back to David's dedications in II Samuel 8:10–12 and to Joshua's puzzling dedication of the spoil of Jericho in Joshua 6:24.

Chapters 6—7 also point forward in time, but in a more ominous way. Mention of the exodus from Egypt launches a theological trajectory which is at first positively associated with election, covenant, and the temple (8:9, 16, 21, 51, 53). But the exodus event soon becomes associated with God's threat (9:9; II Kings 17:7; 21:15), and Kings ends with a reversal of this exodus in a traumatic return to Egypt (II Kings 25:26; cf. Deut. 28:68).

Solomon's glorious labor will gradually be undone as the plot of Kings moves down from the high point of temple construction. Shishak will rifle the treasury (14:26). Ahaz will strip the stands and remove the bulls under the sea (II Kings 16:17). Hezekiah will remove the gold from the doors (II Kings 18:16). II Kings 24:13 reports that Nebuchadnezzar cut up the gold vessels that Solomon had made, and in the final disaster Nebuzaradan burns down the temple itself (II Kings 25:9). The gold and silver are melted down and the great items of bronze are broken up (II Kings 25:13–17). This final list is a hollow echo of the confident inventory of chapter 7 (cf. vv. 40, 50 with II Kings 25:14–15; vv. 41, 43–44, 47 with II Kings 25:16; vv. 15–18 with II Kings 25:17.

This odd blend of bright optimism with ominous foreshadowing is focused by God's speech to Solomon in the Deuteronomistic voice (6:11–13). Confidence in Solomon's temple seems to be underscored by God's promise to "dwell among" the people, never forsaking them. The use of the theologically important verb "dwell" *(shakan)* links this promise to the central

47

Deuteronomistic expectation of Deuteronomy 12:5 and hints at the unconditional promises of the theology of Zion (Pss. 68:16; 135:21).

But here God's promise is made the subordinate clause of a conditional sentence. *If* Solomon faithfully keeps the law, *then* God will establish with Solomon the word once spoken to David. What word? This cannot refer to the dynasty promise of II Samuel 7, for this has already been established (II Sam. 7:12–13) and it specifically rejects any possibility of becoming conditionalized (II Sam. 7:14–16). Chapter 6, verse 12 must instead refer to the conditional promise of 2:4, the promise of the "throne of Israel," the Northern Kingdom. Therefore, verse 13 adds a third conditional promise to the two Solomon has already received (2:4 and long life in 3:14). God's continued residence in the midst of the people and a promise never to forsake them rest on the shaky foundation of Solomon's obedience. Things look good so far (3:3), but of course Solomon's fidelity will falter (11:9–10). As it turns out, Israel and Judah actually have no guarantees of God's presence, no certainty that God would not forsake them.

The temple is of central importance to the Book of Kings. This description of its construction, set in the "middle of time," attempts to communicate this importance by emphasizing the glory of the building and its furnishings. From this point on, every king of Israel or Judah will be judged on whether he permitted sacrifice anywhere else but in this temple. Apostasy and reform in temple worship will be a special interest of the narrator.

Important as it is to the Book of Kings, however, Solomon's temple would be no absolute guarantee of God's presence or favor. This will be made clear immediately in 9:6–9. The final chapter of Kings casts a dark shadow over every bright bit of gold and polished brass. Thus the spirit of the Book of Kings as a whole is not too far from that of the prophet Jeremiah: "Do not trust in these deceptive words: 'This is the temple of the Lord'. . . . I will do to the house which is called by my name . . . as I did to Shiloh" (Jer. 7:4, 14).

The New Testament, looking back at the recent destruction of the successor to Solomon's temple (Luke 21:5–6, 20–24) found no permanent value in a temple "made with hands" (cf. the speech of Stephen, Acts 7:44–50). The temple image was instead filled with new meaning—as a metaphor

48

for the death and resurrection of Jesus (Mark 14:58; John 2:19–22), as a symbol of the church (I Cor. 3:16–17; II Cor. 6:16–18), and as the heavenly locus for Christ's saving act (Heb. 9:11–12, 23–26).

The God of the Bible does make guarantees, but they do not involve structures, systems, or human institutions. God's guarantees involve the person and presence of Jesus Christ (Matt. 18:20; 28:20) and the trustworthiness of God's own promises (for example, Matt. 16:18–19). In Revelation's picture of God's coming new world, there is no temple in New Jerusalem. The direct presence of God and the Lamb takes its place.

I Kings 8
Dedicating the Temple

Apparently what one may expect to find on the program of public ceremonies has changed little over three thousand years! A showy procession and impressive religious actions frame a lot of talking: a poem (vv. 12–13), comments on the significance of the occasion (vv. 15–21), an extended prayer directed as much to the audience as to God (vv. 23–53), and a forecast of hopes and expectations (vv. 56–61).

Kings has been building to this high point since 3:1–2 with descriptions of the preparations (chap. 5), the building (chap. 6), and the furnishings (chap. 7). Set carefully into the chronology of salvation (6:1), the dedication of the temple becomes the centerpiece of Solomon's kingdom of shalom, framed by narrative mirror images before and after (3:1–3 and 9:24–25; 3:4–15 and 9:1–9; 4:29–34 and 10:1–13; 15:1–12 and 9:10–14; 5:13–18 and 9:15–23). This chapter lays out the ideological program by which the rest of the Book of Kings must be understood. The reader needs to mark this chapter, at least mentally, and return to it repeatedly at critical points.

We shall trace first the overall literary structure of the chapter. Next we shall take a closer look at each section in turn, focusing especially on the central seven-petition prayer. Following a discussion of the Deuteronomistic theology in Kings, we shall consider the theological importance of this chapter for the book itself and then for present-day readers.

49

Literary Structure

The boundaries of this unit are marked by the movement of the people. Solomon assembles a roster of the leaders, and every Israelite gathers (vv. 1–2). At the close of the dedication, Solomon sends these people away, and they return home rejoicing (v. 66). Although the report insists that the dedication was a group effort (vv. 1, 3–6, 62–63) involving "all the assembly of Israel" (vv. 14 [twice], 22, 55, cf. 65), it is clear that Solomon's actions constitute the real substance of the event and serve to introduce the major sections of the narrative (vv. 1, 12, 14, 22, 54–55, 63, 65).

Scholars agree that chapter 8 is the end product of a complex redactional history. In its final form, however, it displays a high order of theological unity and literary structure. The first and last sections consist of narrative reports about the transfer of the ark and the dedication sacrifices (vv. 1–13 and 62–66). These form a framework for the speeches of Solomon (vv. 14–21 and 56–61), which in turn enclose the theological heart of the Book of Kings, the dedication prayer itself. This structure may be outlined as follows:

> narrative action (transfer of ark) (vv. 1–13)
> theological commentary (vv. 14–21)
> prayer for the dynasty (vv. 22–26)
> transition in (vv. 27–30)
> seven petition prayer (vv. 31–51)
> transition out (vv. 52–53)
> theological commentary (vv. 54–61)
> narrative action (sacrifices) (vv. 62–66)

The narrative action of verses 1–13 sets the stage for the speeches of Solomon. Solomon's first theological commentary gives the theological context for the temple and its dedication (vv. 14–21). This address and its partner (vv. 56–61) bracket the great prayer with commentary, just as they in turn are bracketed by narrative.

Solomon's prayer (vv. 23–53) divides topically into two unequal portions. First there is a petition for the dynasty (vv. 23–26). This is followed by the great litany, describing in seven examples the practical role of temple prayer in the life of Israel. These seven petitions (vv. 32–51) are themselves framed by a transition into the topic of temple prayer (vv. 27–30) and a parallel transition out of the topic (vv. 52–53).

Verses 62–66 conclude on a positive note with a return to the dedication liturgy, a movement secured by the repetition in verse 62 of the sense and grammar of verse 5.

Leading Up to the Prayer (vv. 1–21)

The narrative action (vv. 1–13) begins with a gathering of all the people in the seventh month for the Feast of Booths (vv. 2, 65). To the Deuteronomistic mind this date implies a ceremonial renewal of the covenant (Deut. 31:9–13). The chronology of Kings delays the dedication eleven months after the completion of the temple (6:38), perhaps in order to set it in the four hundred forty-eighth year (divisible by seven) after Moses gave the command to read the law every seven years (Deut. 31: 10–12; cf. 6:1, 38 with Deut. 1:3).

The first verses are crowded with personnel to transport the ark (political leaders, v. 1; elders, v. 3*a;* priests only, vv. 3*b*, 6; priests and Levites, v. 4) due to successive expansions, but the total effect is to suggest the single-minded, unanimous participation of the people: "all the heads . . . all the men of Israel . . . all the elders . . . all the congregation" (vv. 1–5).

A similar impression of concord and unity results from the text's success in bringing together three divergent theological traditions (vv. 4, 7–13). The dominant Deuteronomistic tradition limits the contents of the ark to the tablets of the law and recalls the exodus and the lawgiving at Horeb (v. 9).

A voice in the priestly tradition points to the wilderness tent of meeting and its vessels (v. 4), introducing another element of Israel's past. It describes God's presence in the temple in terms of God's "glory" and the cloud that filled the tabernacle (vv. 10–11; Exod. 40:34–35). An emphasis on the cherubim (v. 7) recalls Exodus 25:20–22 and links back to the descriptions of chapter 6. The poles remain in the ark (Exod. 25:15) to serve as a visible reminder of the hidden ark's presence.

In the poetic dedication (vv. 12–13), a third, creation-oriented, theological tradition makes its contribution. In contrast to the creation of the bright sun (NEB, RSV, TEV following LXX), God has promised to dwell mysteriously in the thick darkness of the temple's inner sanctuary. "Thick darkness" implies the cloud which wraps God in mystery (Deut. 4:11; 5:22;

Ps. 18:10–11; 97:2). Thus one theological tradition emphasizes God's law, one God's transcendent glory, one God's hiddenness. All three agree that the earthly focus of God's presence is the temple, whether the symbol of that presence is the ark, a cloud of glory, or the enigmatic thick darkness of God's dwelling.

Narrative action is followed by Solomon's introductory commentary (vv. 14–21). Solomon faces the assembly (v. 14; cf. vv. 22, 54–55) and speaks in the Deuteronomistic voice. The introductory verse 15 first points to the past with "promised with his mouth" and then indicates the present with the words "with his hand has fulfilled." Verses 16–19 take up the theme of the past with a review of the Nathan oracle of II Samuel 7, emphasizing God's choice of David (vv. 8–9) and the appointment of Solomon to build the temple (v. 13). Verses 20–21 here characterize the present: Solomon sits on the throne of Israel and has carried out his assignment.

The intention of verses 20–21 is almost catechetical. The reader is not to misunderstand the nature of God's presence in the temple but urged to think in orthodox Deuteronomistic terms. The ark is not a throne for God nor a localization of God's presence. It is rather the container for the law tablets (cf. v. 9; Deut. 10:1–5; 31:24–26). God is transcendent and does not actually reside in this building (cf. vv. 12–13), but God's "name," a powerful expression of selfhood, is present there (3:2; 5:3, 5; 8:27). This functions as a theological corrective to the more immanent view of God's presence expressed in verses 10–13. This topic is taken up again in verses 27–30.

Solomon's Dedicatory Prayer (vv. 22–53)

Solomon begins with a prayer for the Davidic dynasty (vv. 23–26). He opens with a hymnic invocation of God as one without equal (Deut. 4:35, 39) who keeps covenant loyalty (3:6; Deut. 7:9, 12), particularly with David. This picks up both the topic and vocabulary of verse 15. God has kept one promise today (v. 24), the promise of a son to build the temple (v. 20). Solomon prays that God will now go on to keep a second promise, to give permanent possession of the "throne of Israel" (the Northern Kingdom) upon which Solomon now sits (v. 20). The granting of this is conditional on Solomon's own behavior (v. 25).

Verses 27–30 and 52–53 provide transitions into and out of the central seven petitions. The first transition sets up in a general way the situation to follow. It introduces the refrain "hear thou in heaven," which holds the petitions together (vv. 32, 34, 36, 43, 45, 49–50). The classic theological tension between the immanence and the transcendence of God is introduced by the parenthetical rhetorical question of verse 27. It is resolved in verses 29–30 in the same way as in the petitions to follow. Prayer is offered in/toward the temple, but the transcendent God hears in heaven. This first transitional section also serves to generalize the specific petitions to follow. "Supplication," "cry," and "prayer" offered "night and day" cover all possible cases.

The transition section (vv. 52–53) that follows the central prayer starts abruptly (Hebrew: infinitive construct) with a repetition of the striking metaphor of verse 29: "that thy eyes may be open . . . to hear" (RSV modified). These verses return the specific examples of the prayer to generalities again, to prayers of both king and people whenever they pray.

The seven petitions themselves (vv. 31–51) describe a catalogue of paradigmatic crises during which an answer to prayer would be critical. Five of the seven relate to the curses threatened by Deuteronomy 28. The intention is to generalize about the act of prayer.

This generalizing paradigmatic effect is created, first, by using a variety of grammatical formats to set up the situations. Second, a variety of expressions are used to describe the place or direction of prayer, ranging from "in this house" (vv. 31, 33) through "towards this place/house" (vv. 35, 38, 42) to "in the direction of land/city/house" (vv. 44, 48; obscured by the RSV). Third, the generalizing effect is advanced by identifying the petitioner variously as the king ("thy servant") and/or Israel. The language is studiously non-specific: "prayer and supplication" (vv. 33, 38, 45, 49), "far off and near" (v. 46). The fourth petition (vv. 37–40) is the most generic of the seven, covering every conceivable agricultural, military, or personal health problem which could be suffered by any individual or by all the people together.

To understand the background of the first petition, judicial oath (vv. 31–32), one needs to read Exodus 22:7–12 and Numbers 5:11–31. The second, defeat (vv. 33–34), reflects the curse of Deuteronomy 28:25 and will be illustrated by Hezekiah's behavior in II Kings 19:14–19. The third, drought (vv. 35–36), reflects Deuteronomy 28:23–24 and will be illustrated

53

by Elijah in chapter 18. The fourth is a general catalogue of crises (vv. 37–40), resting in part on Deuteronomy 28:21–22, 38. Petition number five, the foreigner (vv. 41–43), reminds the reader of Naaman in II Kings 5. The sixth petition concerns war under God's guidance, holy war (vv. 44–45), and will be reflected in the narratives in chapters 20 and 22 and II Kings 3.

The emphasis in this series falls on the seventh petition, exile (vv. 46–51), based on Deuteronomy 28:36–37. This petition is twice as long as any of the others. The topic of exile was naturally of greatest interest to the original readers. Literary artistry reaches a high level with a sevenfold word play on the verbal roots "carry captive" *(shabah)* and "repent/turn" *(shub)* (Levenson, *Hebrew Annual Review* 6:135–38):

> "carried away captive" *(shabah)* (v. 46*b*)
> "if they turn (RSV lay) it to heart" *(shub)* (v. 47*a*)
> "carried captive" *(shabah)* (v. 47*a*)
> "repent" *(shub)* (v. 47*b*)
> "land of their captors" *(shabah)* (v. 47*b*)
> "repent" *(shub)* (v. 48*a*)
> "carried them captive" *(shabah)* (v. 48a)

The situation is described in tension-building detail (vv. 46–48), and the threefold confession is quoted directly to increase its impact (v. 47).

At this point, the original exilic audience of Kings is clearly addressed. They are urged to repent *(shub)*, to pray in the direction of home. But what is it they can hope for? Kings is very reticent at this point. When supplication was possible in the temple itself (v. 33), the prayer indicates that repentant exiles had a good chance of returning home. Perhaps the exiles of Israel and those taken from Judah in 701 B.C.E. are intended. All that is offered to the present exilic audience, however, is the compassion of their captors so that the exiles might achieve a *modus vivendi* with them (v. 50; cf. Ps. 106:46).

Beyond this modest hope nothing more is said directly, but Solomon does remind God, and the reader, that this people was once delivered from the iron furnace of Egypt (v. 51). This is the thinnest possible offer of a chance at return for the exiles, one the narrator dares not even whisper. At the end of Kings, the captive Jehoiachin will experience the good will of the king of Babylon and nothing more (II Kings 25:27–30), a fulfillment of the modest hope of this chapter (v. 50). Yet at that point, too, the future will remain open-ended.

Leading Away from the Prayer (vv. 54–66)

His prayer over, Solomon rises from his knees (v. 54). The reader remembers that the prayer began with him standing (v. 22) and can only conclude that under the weight of his petitions Solomon had sunk to a kneeling position, an act of submission (19:18; II Kings 1:13; Isa. 45:23).

Once more he addresses the congregation, starting as he did in verse 15 by blessing God for an act of grace described in Deuteronomistic theological terms. In the peace and security of Solomon's kingdom of shalom (5:4; cf. II Sam. 7:1, 11), God has given the "rest" promised by Moses in Deuteronomy 12:10.

Solomon begins with two wishes or indirect prayers (vv. 57–58 and 59–60) and concludes with an exhortation (v. 61). First, he hopes for God's continued presence (as conditionally promised in 6:13) so that God can help Israel keep the law. Second, he wishes that the words of his prayer, having an objective life of their own, might be a daily reminder to God to uphold the just cause of king and nation. Then all people would learn the truth of Israel's creed, "Yahweh is God" (repeated from the prayer, v. 23; 18:39; Deut. 4:35, 39). Solomon concludes with an exhortation to keep the law with a true (complete, undivided) heart (v. 61). This section has a paraenetic intention, encouraging readers to keep God's law out of an inner undivided volition (a true heart) and to acknowledge their dependence on God's help in bending their hearts the right way (cf. I Cor. 12:3).

In verses 62–66, the text returns to the narrative mode to report the dedication liturgy. The huge number of sacrificial victims for the communion meals is a way of indicating the total participation of all the people. There were so many that the middle court had to be consecrated to handle the slaughter. The description of the vast extent of Solomon's kingdom makes the same point. The people gathered in verses 1–2 disperse after the seven-day Feast of Booths (Deut. 16:13–15) full of joy and blessing Solomon. The reader is intended to leave the subject of temple dedication with the same attitude. At one point, the narrator addresses the readers directly ("our God," v. 65) as if to remind them that they too have a stake in the God who has shown such goodness.

Deuteronomistic Theology in Kings

This chapter is virtually a primer of Deuteronomistic theology, the dominant ideological perspective in the Book of Kings. (For an introduction to this theology, see Noth, *The Deuteronomistic History*, pp. 89–99 and Rast, *Joshua, Judges, Samuel, Kings*, pp. 42–108.) Israel is the people of God's heritage, chosen by the exodus and separated from other peoples by the gift of the law of Moses (vv. 51, 53; Deut. 4:20; 9:26). God graciously gave to this people the land of inheritance promised to their ancestors (vv. 34, 36, 40, 48; Deut. 4:37–38; 9:4–6).

God's graciousness is summed up in the concept of "goodness/good" (*tob;* vv. 56, 66; see Brueggemann, *Interp*, 22: 387–402). This word describes what one might call the "gospel" of the Book of Kings. "Good" describes the land that is God's gracious gift (14:15) and the prosperity of Solomon's kingdom (10:7; RSV's "prosperity" translates *tob* here). It is significant that God has shown this "good" specifically to David (v. 66; see below).

"Repent/turn" *(shub)* is a second pivotal concept in the Book of Kings (Wolff, "The Kerygma of the Deuteronomic Historical Work," pp. 83–100). In Deuteronomistic theology, when Israel commits sin, calamity naturally follows as punishment (Deut. 4:21; 9:8; the curses of chap. 28). When the people committed apostasy, they "turned" from God (9:6), but the prophets over and over called on them to repent, to "turn" back (II Kings 17:13). The ideal model for such a turning is the piety of Josiah (II Kings 23:25). We shall see in chapter 13 that a word play on the verb *shub* is a basic creator of meaning, and this is also the case with the seventh petition of Solomon's prayer (see above). The causal relationship between sin and its calamitous result is the theme tying together the first, second, third, and seventh petitions of Solomon's prayer. In each case, the people must repent *(shub)*.

A basic theological problem in Deuteronomistic theology involved how one ought to speak of God's presence in the temple (v. 27), the classic tension between the immanence and transcendence of God. Deuteronomistic theologians were unwilling to say simply that God lived there (v. 13; Ps. 46:4–5; 76:2). Their more sophisticated approach was to explain that God's name was present there (v. 29), while God's actual dwelling place was in heaven (v. 30). This idea was based on the social and psychological function of names. The name of someone in authority carries weight even when that person is absent. To call a name over something is to invoke ownership and in some sense the owner. A person's name will always get his or her attention (v. 29). A name in the sense of reputation can travel far and wide.

Impact on the Theology of Kings

Theologically, this chapter seeks to elevate the temple dedication to the status of a saving event and make it clear that the temple and prayers in it or toward it have been vital to the nation's life. The chapter brings together divergent streams in Israel's theological life and centers them on the temple.

Chapter 8 has a powerful effect on the reader because of its central dramatic position and its literary artistry. Its goal is to report Solomon's most important act in a way that evokes admiration for the king, the temple, and God. Solomon's kingdom is the fulfillment of God's promise of promised land "rest" (v. 56) and perfect obedience ("as at this day," v. 61). This marks the high point of Solomon's kingdom of shalom. From here Judah and Israel will begin a long slide to disaster.

The sin of permitting worship outside this temple at the high places and at Jeroboam's sanctuaries will cause their downfall. The penultimate punishments for these offenses would involve the temple itself at times (14:26; 15:18; II Kings 14:14; 16:8; 18:15–16; 24:13). The reform efforts of pious kings would center on it (II Kings 12:4–16; 22:3–7; 23:4–12), as would the acts of the apostate ones (II Kings 16:10–18; 21:4–7). In the end the temple would share the fate of the people themselves (9:8–9; II Kings 23:27; 25:9). The disturbing assertion that the poles of the ark are visible "to this day" (v. 8*b*) may once have strengthened the reader's confidence in the narrative, but in the present context these verses sound a jarring false note, pointing along with the darker topic of Solomon's prayer (v. 46) to this final disaster.

The more immediate crisis of the kingdom's imminent division is introduced by Solomon's words in verses 56–61. While on the surface these verses offer an up-beat paraenesis, they point forward on another level to the vocabulary of Solomon's apostasy. His pagan wives would "incline his heart" (v. 58) after other gods (11:2, 3, 4, cf. 9; RSV obscures the fact that this is the same verb).

While temple sacrifice is important in Kings (vv. 62–64; 9:25), it really has only a negative ideological role: sacrifice is permitted only in the temple (3:2; 13:33–34). What really matters is prayer and faithful obedience. Here, Kings stands in the tradition of the prophets (Amos 5:21–24; Hos. 8:11–13; cf. Ps. 51:16–17). The sacrificial system, although given by God for the sake of the people, could never be a substitute for genuine faith and repentance. For the exilic readers this was good news. Sacrifice was impossible for them, but that was not critical. What mattered was turning back in heartfelt repentance and prayer (vv. 47–48).

The importance of the Davidic dynasty in the Book of Kings is also clarified by this chapter. God chose David (v. 16) and has shown him "good" (v. 66). David obeyed God's law in all things (3:6; 14:8; 15:5) and became the standard by which the behavior of all other kings would be judged (3:3, 14; 11:4, 6, 34, 38; 15:3, 11; II Kings 14:3; 16:2; 18:3; 22:2). Because of his obedience, God favored David with the promise of a son to build the temple (5:5; 8:19) and the promise of continued rule over the Northern Kingdom contingent on similar obedience from Solomon (2:4; 8:25; 9:4–5; cf. 8:20). For David's sake, God would delay the loss of this throne of Israel until Solomon's death (11:12–13, 32, 34). There also is another, far more extraordinary promise to David which has not yet been unfolded in the Book of Kings, the promise of an eternal reign in Jerusalem (11:36; 15:4; II Kings 8:19).

In the end, this complex chapter is less about the character of the temple than it is about the nature of Israel's God. This is a trustworthy God who can be counted on to hold to the covenant and to keep promises (vv. 15, 20, 23–24, 56, 66). This is a gracious God, providing a temple so that Israel could have access to divine favor (vv. 12–13; 17–21; 27–29). This God has chosen Israel as a special people: through the exodus (vv. 16, 51), the covenant law (vv. 9, 21, 53), and the gift of the land (vv. 34, 36, 40, 48). This God is serious about obedience (vv. 58, 61) and punishes disobedience even to the point of exile and national destruction (v. 46). This is a God whose nature is good news to exiles set off from their neighbors by their obedience to the law (v. 53). For this is the God who answers prayer, even prayer from the land of captivity. If the exiles repent wholeheartedly, this God will forgive them and give them some kind of future (vv. 47–50).

Theological Implications

As canonical Scripture, chapter 8 leads readers into at least three areas of consideration: the struggle with God's immanence and transcendence, the role of prayer, and the call for repentance.

Christian faith has always struggled with the dilemma of God's presence. How can we trust that God is reliably present for us (immanent), without forgetting that God cannot be controlled or taken for granted (and thus is transcendent)? How can the God who remains mysterious and awesome, who refuses to be contained by creation, still be closely present to love and save us? Chapter 8 affirms both transcendence and immanence simultaneously and utilizes the "name theology" to hold them together. God is "really present" in the temple in cloud, glory, and ark (vv. 3–13). Yet lest this be misunderstood as suggesting that God is automatically at Israel's beck and call, Solomon insists that even the whole universe cannot contain God. God is only "symbolically present" in the temple through the divine name.

For Christianity this theological tension is approached christologically. Jesus Christ means that the transcendent God who is Wholly Other can be at the same time "God for us" and present with us (Matt. 18:20; 28:20; John 10:29–30). In a sense, all the great trinitarian and christological controversies have focused on this concern. This same problem of immanence and transcendence is at the heart of the ongoing controversy over the nature of the presence of the body of Jesus in the Lord's Supper. The classic formulations of the Council of Trent, Luther, Calvin, and Zwingli form a taxonomy running from divine immanence to transcendence.

The ability to pray is the acid test of faith (Matt. 7:7–11; Luke 18:1–8). In the lectionary shared by most North American Christians, portions of the prayer of Solomon, specifically the prayer of the foreigner (vv. 41–43), are paired with the Gospel text about the healing of the centurion's slave (Luke 7:1–10). Both texts insist that God hears and answers prayer, even the prayers of outsiders.

The call for repentance is basic to Solomon's prayer. "Turning" back to God is the first step in each petition. Solomon confidently assumes that repentance will be followed by God's forgiveness. The text calls for repentance and trust from all who

59

read it, a reorientation of self back to this trustworthy God who hears, forgives, and answers prayer. "Turn" *(shub)* so God may once more shower "good" *(tob)* upon you. So too Jesus: "The kingdom of God is at hand; repent, and believe in the gospel" (Mark 1:15).

I Kings 9:1–9
Promise and Threat

These verses are God's reply to Solomon's prayer. In a second appearance to Solomon, God speaks a promise about the newly-dedicated temple (v. 3) and then follows this with a conditional promise (vv. 4–5) and a threat (vv. 6–9). As is often the case in Kings, the divine speech here uses typical Deuteronomistic language and vocabulary (cf. 2:4; 3:14; 5:5; 6:12–13; 11:11–13).

The Carrot (vv. 1–5)

The text hurries through the narrative setting, referring the reader to 3:4–15 for details, to concentrate on God's response. "I have heard your prayer" (v. 3) is a typical introduction to a divine response (II Kings 19:20; 20:5). God sets up the basis for the temple promise with verse 3a and then delivers it with 3b. In a sense verse 3 is a verbal replay of what has already been described visually by 8:10–11. Also, the promise that God's eyes will be fixed on the temple is a direct reply to 8:29, 52. God's temple promise is "forever, for all time." This sets up a certain tension with verses 7–9, which envision the temple as a "heap of ruins," but this can be explained on the basis of 8:48. The temple will remain a consecrated place of prayer even after its demolition.

There is a sharp contrast between the two conditional statements that follow, although the theme of obedience or disobedience to the law holds the two together. The first is directed at Solomon in the second person singular and ends in a promise for David's dynasty (vv. 4–5). Verse 4 shifts attention from God to Solomon ("as for you") and prescribes what is required of the king in the same terms as 3:6. Solomon is to obey according to the pattern already set by David. The conditional

60

promise of continued rule over the Northern Kingdom comes as no surprise to the reader (cf. 3:14; 8:25). That is the carrot.

The Stick (vv. 6–9)

The stick follows in verses 6–9. The second conditional statement (vv. 6–9) is directed at the Davidic kings in general in the second person plural and concludes with a vivid threat against Israel and the temple. Here the field of vision is widened by the plural address to cover the whole of Kings. Obedience is required especially of the kings (v. 6), although the whole people will suffer the consequences (v. 7). This lays out the tragic plot of the rest of the book. Israel will pay for the sins of Jeroboam, and Judah for the apostasy of Manasseh. Nevertheless, the people themselves also sin and share in the guilt of their kings (v. 9; II Kings 17:17; 21:11–15). This threat against land and temple strikes at the very center of Israel's existence. The threat echoes ironically the good news of verse 3 by reversing its promise ("my eyes will be there") into a threat ("I will cast out of my sight," v. 7; literally, "send away from my face).

The question and answer vignette is chillingly effective (vv. 8–9). Israel, like the exilic readers themselves, has disappeared from the stage. Hissing strangers speak. The very mention of Israel has become a byword (v. 7), like Waterloo, Quisling, or Watergate. The mental picture of a heap of ruins would have been more vivid in the memory of an exilic reader than any of the golden images of chapters 6 and 7.

This second theophany scene is never brought to a narrative ending (contrast 3:15). Thus the looming threat continues to hang suspended over the rest of the book. Continuing the interpretive function of chapter 8, 9:1–9 provides an evaluative key for understanding the ups and downs, apostasies and reforms, rewards and punishments described in the rest of the Book of Kings. For exilic readers, these verses were an explanation of how they got into their present fix. Their kings had not kept the law and neither had they.

One of the most amazing facets of Old Testament faith was the ability to pronounce a "doxology of judgment" in the face of disaster. This was a public confession that God was justified in punishing the sufferer with whatever crisis had struck him or her. When Achan, in Joshua 7, was fingered by the sacred lots for taking and hiding forbidden loot, he was urged to "give glory to the Lord God of Israel . . . and tell me now what you have done" (Josh. 7:19). To confess sin is to glorify the God who punishes sin (Ezra 9:15; Ps. 51:4). In a sense, the entire Book of Kings represents a doxology of judgment, and verses 6–9 provide a focus for this. By producing and using this book, the community of exiles was confessing that it was not God's oversight or weakness or inconstancy that had led to the temple becoming a heap of ruins. It was their own fault entirely, and God was right in doing what had to be done.

Disaster and Sin Today

Modern faith has for the most part lost track of the connection between disaster and sin. Today, at least in their more rational moments, believers no longer directly blame themselves or their sins for the inevitable tragedies of life nor seek to pin the blame on the sins of others. This is all to the good, of course, and it means we have learned the lesson of John 9:3. Yet the generic causal connection between sin in general and suffering in general still is a valid testimony of the biblical witness (Gen. 3:16–19). Jesus taught his followers that suffering and disaster, while not a time for moralistic finger pointing, still provide an occasion for repentance (Luke 13:1–5).

Both the conditionalized promise of verses 4–5 and the frightful threat of verses 6–9 are sobering reminders that fidelity and obedience do not become optional for those who live under God's gracious promise (v. 3). The New Testament too insists that God's grace is not a license to sin (Rom. 6:1–2). Life under promise is instead the context for "faith working through love" (Gal. 5:6). Lest this text become an occasion for proclaiming moralism and legalistic coercion, however, the reader must remember that God's gracious promises always come first (3:11–14; 8:15–16, 20).

I Kings 9:10—10:29
Wisdom and Prosperity II

The rest of chapter 9 and chapter 10 continue and conclude the portrayal of the wisdom of Solomon and the prosperity of his kingdom of shalom. Chronologically, these reports are set by 9:10 into the mature middle life of Solomon's forty-year reign. As is the case with 3:16—5:18, the style is paratactic. Each item of the presentation is laid out side by side with no great concern for historical or logical order. When the last item in the series has been related, the presentation is considered complete and the account breaks off abruptly.

Yet these reports and narratives are bound together by definite literary techniques. For example, these items in chapter 9 are paired with analogous narratives and reports in the corresponding material (Wisdom and Prosperity I) before the temple building and dedication: verses 10–14 with 5:1–12; verses 15–23 with 5:13–18; 10:1–13 with 4:29–34. Moreover, verses 24–25 serve with 3:1–2 to bracket off a section on the internal affairs of Solomon's kingdom, followed by a shorter description of the kingdom from an external perspective in 9:26—10:29.

Internal Affairs (9:10–25)

For the historically-minded reader, Solomon's dealings with Hiram in verses 10–14 seem out of place in a presentation of the positive side of his reign. Once a nation begins to sell off its territory, things may be assumed to be going badly! The Chronicler had the same impression, so he simply reversed the direction of the transfer (II Chron. 8:2). However, the reader who treats this as literature rather than history receives a totally different impression. Here a critical economic crisis has been transformed by the magic of literary artistry into an illustration of Solomon's financial acumen.

The original irritant around which this pearl has formed was an archival note reporting the transfer of territory in verse 11*b*. However, both the grammar and the structure of the story as Kings tells it put emphasis instead on Hiram's visit to his new acquisition and his disappointment with it (vv. 12–13). After twenty years of sending building materials and gold to Solomon and then receiving these towns in return, Hiram's survey does not please him. The reader is left to puzzle out the fragmentary etymological etiology for Cabul (cf. Josh. 19:27). The pun could rest on "as nothing" or perhaps "mortgaged." The really important punch line is saved until last (v. 14). Hiram paid more than four metric tons of gold for these worthless hamlets! The partisan Judean audience must have gleefully appreciated how Sol-

63

omon beat at his own game this king of a merchant nation. The intention is once more to underline the wisdom of Solomon, and the probable historical realities are passed over.

The cycle of forced labor and building from 5:13—7:51 is repeated in brief by verses 15–25. This report again impresses the reader with Solomon's administrative wisdom. Although the section begins with a heading introducing the topic of forced labor, it first lists Solomon's defensive construction projects, arranged from north to south. Inscriptional analogies may be found (in ANET, pp. 320–21 [Mesha] and pp. 655–56 [Zakir]), and archaeology has confirmed Solomon's building activity at Hazor, Megiddo, and Gezer. The list generalizes at the end (9:19), even suggesting building work in Lebanon. This reduces any remaining suspicion the reader might have over the Cabul incident.

The main topic of this section, as the heading suggests, is forced labor. By the standards of the Deuteronomistic narrator, at least, this policy is set in a thoroughly positive light. This is a different institution from the temporary labor which was the civic duty of Israel (5:13–18). The narrator makes this clear by speaking explicitly of "a forced levy of slaves" (v. 21) and by carefully excluding native Israelites from any hint of this (v. 22). The "to this day" of verse 21 means that this demotion in status was permanent, not temporary.

Modern readers may have moral problems with this policy, but the narrative itself presents it as another example of Solomon's wise piety, as obedience to the law (Deut. 20:10–11). These slaves are the remnants of the peoples dispossessed in the conquest (v. 20; Deut. 7:1) who were to be annihilated or kept apart (Deut. 7:2–3; 20:16–18). Israel had been unable to wipe them out completely (v. 21), and to the Deuteronomists they were a potential source of fatal infection (Deut. 7:3–6; Josh. 23:12–13). As Kings tells the story, therefore, Solomon's ancient equivalent of apartheid was a wise and pious policy, an act of obedience to God's law. The parenthetical note of verse 16 (note the bracketing repetition of "Gezer") is also a theological comment on the Canaanites. Even Pharaoh engages in holy war against them, burning Gezer (Josh. 8:28; a detail not confirmed by archaeology) and slaying the inhabitants in unconscious obedience to Deuteronomy 20:16–18.

64

The modern reader ought to judge this sort of political ethic by a higher standard than that of the Deuteronomists

(Matt. 5:9; Luke 7:9). Present day examples demonstrate how natural it is to provide religious justification for acts of barbarism and oppression. Yet it must also be remembered that the God of the Bible has some deadly serious plans for this world and is willing to go to extreme lengths to bring them to fruition. What is good news for one group may inevitably entail bad news for some other group (Exod. 12:29–30; Luke 1:51–53). Even Israel would eventually find itself on the receiving end of God's wrath enforced by fire and sword (II Kings 24—25; Matt. 23:37–38), a solemn warning for modern would-be Solomons.

External Perspectives (9:26—10:29)

The section which treats Solomon's kingdom of shalom from an external perspective is held together by the topic of his wisdom and the riches which resulted from it, as summarized by the programmatic statement of 10:23–25. Wisdom is the particular concern of the Queen of Sheba episode. The topic of riches, summarized in the utopian 10:27, is approached from the perspective of international commerce. The verb "come/bring" echoes through the individuals notices (9:28; 10:10, 11, 22, 25). Solomon's fabulous wealth was without equal (10:10, 12*b*, 21*b*, 27; cf. 3:13). His economic influence reached to the far corners of the world: Ophir (East Africa?), Sheba (Yemen), Arabia, Kue (in present Turkey). Once more the quantity of gold is beyond belief (9:28; 10:10, 14). The income is steady (10:14, 25).

The reader is beguiled with exotic words of uncertain meaning ("almug wood," "apes and peacocks") and the romance of great "ships of Tarshish" on long sea voyages to distant ports. For a people as unused to the sea as the Israelites, this would have had a special impact. The reader is impressed with the luxury of gold drinking vessels and the sophistication of almug wood instruments and exotic pets. The great ivory throne, with its possibly cosmological symbolism of seven levels (six steps and the throne platform) and twelve lions, is a fitting material realization of the "throne of Israel" the reader has heard so much about (2:4; 8:20, 25; 9:5; 10:9). The might of Solomon's chariot force would strike a responsive chord with an audience so recently defeated by the armies of Babylon. The wealth of this kingdom of shalom, the reader is reminded, was a result of the wisdom God had given Solomon (10:24; cf. 3:28).

Wisdom is the particular concern of the Queen of Sheba

episode (10:1–13). Like 3:4–15, this is a legend which seeks to elevate Solomon in the estimation of its readers. Historians have interpreted the Queen's visit as a mundane commercial negotiation; later story-tellers have sought out romantic implications. In the context of Kings, however, this narrative has the same intent as the rest of the section of which it is a part. It underscores Solomon's fame, great wealth, and profound wisdom and provides a concrete example of 10:25.

The boundaries of the narrative are marked by the Queen's arrival and departure (vv. 1, 13). The narrative exposition (vv. 1–3) is hurried through in order to get to the Queen's reaction. Her visit is motivated by the fame of Solomon (and of Yahweh, v. 1). She seeks to match wits with him in a contest of riddles ("hard questions," cf. Judg. 14:12–18), a traditional exercise of ancient wisdom. Solomon solves all her riddles (v. 3). She also witnesses other aspects of his wisdom in his elegant life style and piety. She is left breathless (v. 5; "there was no more spirit in her").

Her concession speech interprets the meaning of her visit for the reader, offering the same positive evaluation of Solomon which permeates the entire context. The text skillfully adopts a feminine point of view for her beatitude in 10:8 (if the emendation of the RSV is correct). In 10:9 she speaks in Deuteronomistic vocabulary to raise up the themes of God's love for Israel (Deut. 7:8, 13), the throne of Israel, justice and righteousness (3:11, 28). She gives Solomon rich gifts, but lest the reader imagine that Solomon was somehow dependent on her generosity, verses 11–12 are inserted from the surrounding material. Solomon, for his part (v. 13, with grammatical emphasis on the subject) loads her with gifts and favors in keeping with his royal generosity (for the same Hebrew expression, cf. Esther 1:7, 2:18).

The presentation of Solomon's kingdom of shalom in 9:10—10:29 gives further evidence that God kept fully the promise to Solomon: "I give you a wise and discerning mind, . . . riches and honor, so that no other king shall compare with you all your days" (3:12–13). The dark undercurrent which has been a counter-theme to this positive evaluation of Solomon is here reduced to the thinnest hints: the careful limitation on Israel's participation in forced labor (9:22; cf. 12:4), the mention of Pharaoh's daughter (9:24; cf. 11:1), perhaps the calf's head on the throne (10:19, following RSV; cf. 12:28).

Yet no one with a Deuteronomistic theological background could ever have missed the broad hint of the last verses about horses from Egypt (10:28–29), which point directly to Deuteronomy 17:16. This provides a transition to the breakdown of shalom in chapter 11 caused by Solomon's violation of Deuteronomy 17:17. The course of events this sets in motion will eventually lead to the fulfillment of the warning about returning to Egypt (Deut. 17:16) by the events of Judah's final disaster (II Kings 25:26). Suddenly, all the glittering gold of Solomon's reign takes on a grimmer aspect, tarnished by the remembered words of Deuteronomy 17:17: "nor shall he (the king) greatly multiply for himself silver and gold."

When read as a whole against the contextual background of Deuteronomy, this text develops into a critique of national pride, high standards of living, and cultural ingenuity. As gifts of God used in faith, such things have the potential for good (3:9; 10:8–9). But human beings more readily follow Solomon in letting wisdom and prosperity grow into forces for injustice, into objects of concern which ultimately prove corrosive to faith (Matt. 6:24–33; Luke 12:13–21).

PART TWO

Shalom Is Broken

I KINGS 11—16

I Kings 11
Solomon's Sin and Its Result

"The rest of the acts of Solomon," reports Kings, as a way of supporting its own credibility, "and his wisdom, are they not written in the Book of the Acts of Solomon?" (11:41). Unlike that earlier lost work, however, Kings goes beyond the architectural, political, and economic externals of Solomon's kingdom of shalom to probe at its theological heart. That probing exposed a fatal sickness, the virulent consequences of which Kings will trace through to the bitter end. Chapter 11 sets this process in motion. Although the material in this chapter is of varied character and origin, the overwhelming presence of Deuteronomistic condemnation, by the narrator and by God, holds it together in a structure that moves from Solomon's sin through God's anger to prophetic announcement. We shall first follow this structure, then trace four theological themes raised by this chapter.

Solomon's Sin and God's Anger (vv. 1–25)

Solomon's sin is described (vv. 1–8) in a vocabulary which reflects ironically on 3:3; 8:58, 61 ("love," "incline/turn away the heart," "true heart"). Solomon fell short of the standard of David set for him in God's two appearances (v. 9; 3:14; 9:4).

What the modern reader may see as the necessary political reality of intermarriage between allied royal families and what the ancient person would have normally interpreted as a witness to Solomon's glorious potency as a ruler (cf. 1:4), the narrator evaluates single-mindedly as a violation of the law of God (Deut.

69

7:3–4). It is not the fantastic number of these wives which is presented as the problem; it is their nationality and religion and Solomon's accommodation to it. Even though Solomon himself did not worship their gods (v. 8*b*, note the plural), it was enough that he had been lured into building places of sacrifice for them. Just as the construction of the temple is presented as the acme of his piety, so these high places are sufficient evidence that "his heart was not wholly true to Yahweh his God" (v. 4).

The narrator uses the organizing principle of "first obedience, then sin." Sin and its punishment are set exclusively in the latter part of Solomon's reign, when he was old (v. 4). Chapters 3—10 have described the wisdom and prosperity of the kingdom of shalom; in chapter 11 shalom is broken. Yet, because verses 21 and 25 make it explicitly clear that the careers of Solomon's two adversaries reach back to the start of Solomon's rule, the reader is aware that the narrator is distorting time in the process. Obedience and sin are more powerful organizers of reality than is mere chronology. Another example of this theological time warp is Solomon's marriage to Pharaoh's daughter (who sticks out roughly in the grammar of v. 1). This was just as much a violation of Deuteronomy 7:3–4 as any of his other marriages, but actually it took place in Solomon's third or fourth year as king (3:1). This is not so much a matter of redactional ineptitude as it is a testimony to the subordination of chronology to ideology. Modern Western readers are apt to rebel against this sort of temporal manipulation; the original audience would have taken it in stride.

The narrator makes us party to God's angry emotions and the reason for them (vv. 9–10). The narrator even seems to share God's anger with an impatient reference to Solomon's obtuseness ("twice"). In what follows, God addresses Solomon with the equivalent of a prophetic judgment speech (accusation, v. 11*a;* announcement of judgment, v. 11*b*). Because Solomon has deliberately (v. 11 TEV; cf. Job 10:13) failed to keep God's covenant, the conditional promise of the throne of Israel (the united kingdom; 2:4; 8:25; 9:4–5) is aborted.

The language of punishment is reminiscent of the tragedy of Saul (I Sam. 15:28), but in this case the damage is limited and the execution of punishment delayed until after the death of Solomon. This mitigation is not due to anything Solomon does, in contrast to the stories told about Ahab (21:27–29) and Jehu

(II Kings 10:30). It is solely the result of God's covenant loyalty to David based on David's unparalleled past obedience (cf. 3:6; 8:16, 23). For this same reason, God's unconditional promise to David concerning Jerusalem, to be explicitly defined in verse 36, will stand firm. As promised in the Nathan oracle, Solomon is to be punished "with the rod of men," but God's "steadfast love" *(hesed)* will not be taken from him, as it was from Saul (II Sam. 7:14–15).

Hadad and Rezon (vv. 14–25) are not explicitly linked to God's threat, which jumps over them to verses 26–40. Yet neither are they figures of mere historical interest, for God raised them up as "adversaries" to Solomon (vv. 14, 23). The reader is left to make the fully justified theological connection between Solomon's sin and their hostility. These two reports expect the reader to be familiar with II Samuel 8:3–8; 13 (LXX). The story of Hadad seems to break off before any mischief (v. 25) is reported; the report on Rezon is even sketchier. Their presence in the narrative has more to do with the interpretive light they throw on Jeroboam. Jeroboam fled from his master, as did Rezon, and found support with Pharaoh until the death of the king, as did Hadad. (The Greek recension carried these parallels even further, marrying Jeroboam into the Egyptian royal family, 12:24e, f.) The implied conclusion is clear: Even though Jeroboam raised his own hand (v. 27) against Solomon, he too was an adversary raised up by God.

Jeroboam and Ahijah (vv. 26–40)

The narrative about Jeroboam's encounter with Ahijah and the fateful word of God (vv. 26–40) begins as though it were going to describe some act of rebellion on Jeroboam's part. The protagonist is provided with several biographical details: name of parents and hometown, social status ("a man of standing" NIV), an industrious character. These have the effect of luring the reader into a positive identification with Jeroboam.

The narrative starts with an exposition (vv. 26–28) which leads the reader to expect a story line concerning some sort of *coup de main* against the king (v. 26b). This is followed by a complication in the shape of an oracle and prophetic act from Ahijah (vv. 29–39). But the expected rebellion never occurs. Instead Jeroboam is put on hold in Egypt to await further developments (v. 40). In respect to plot, then, this is only an episode

71

of a larger story which will reach its climax in chapter 12.

The interest here is concentrated on the verbose, overfull oracle, which provides the reader with guidance on how to interpret what will follow. For now, the "reason" (v. 27) is more important than the events it will cause. Historically-minded scholars quite properly look for the cause of the division of the kingdom in Solomon's inequitable forced labor practices (12:4), but the narrator insists otherwise. Causation is to be sought in God's historical will and the communication of that will through the prophetic word.

The scene between Ahijah and Jeroboam is an example of the genre of "report of symbolic action," divided into the action itself (vv. 29–31) and its interpretation through an oracle (vv. 32–39). Ahijah's act was viewed as something more than just a visual aid or a way of getting attention. The symbolic act of a prophet was thought to have an actual effect on coming events, triggering the future it imitated. That is why the narrative asserts that the cloak was a new one, appropriate for such a quasi-magical act. Readers are intended to remember how Saul's cloak was accidentally torn (I Sam. 15:27–28), presaging the loss of his kingdom to another.

At the time of the composition of Kings, the number twelve had already become a purely ideological number representing the tribes. That the Northern Kingdom of Israel consisted of ten tribes also seems to have been a traditional concept (cf. II Sam. 19:43). David's house could be sure of one tribe. Probably Judah is intended, although perhaps it is Benjamin (12:21). Because these are ideological numbers, the reader should not become overly concerned with the mathematical puzzle of "ten plus one equals twelve," unless it is to realize that there remains something imponderable and hidden about God's purposes in history, even when they are revealed by the prophetic word.

The oracle itself is a tangled interweaving of the fates of Solomon, Rehoboam, and Jeroboam. The complexity is probably the result of the literary history of the passage, but a certain order is still evident. A general oracle against Solomon (vv. 31, 33) is qualified by a limitation of the punishment (vv. 32, 36) and its delay (vv. 34–35). Then a general conditional promise to Jeroboam (vv. 37–38) is qualified by verse 39. The double line of direction qualifying the oracle against Solomon ("limitation" and "delay") leads forward to the events that follow in chapter

72

12. At the same time, the use of the verb "tear" (v. 31; cf. vv. 11, 12) and the names of the foreign gods (v. 33; cf. vv. 5, 7) carry the reader back to God's word to Solomon (vv. 11–13), in which this same double line of direction had already been introduced ("delay," v. 12; "limitation," v. 13).

The key words in the accusation are "they have forsaken me" (v. 33; RSV emends). This concept is programatic for the Book of Kings as a whole. God had promised not to "forsake" the people (6:13; cf. 8:57). What happened instead was that the people and their kings forsook God (9:9; 11:33; 18:18; 19:10, 14; II Kings 17:16; 21:22; 22:17). The final tragedy was not caused by any lapse in fidelity on God's part; the blame rests squarely on the shoulders of the people.

The promise to Jeroboam breaks new ground (vv. 37–38). Basically, Jeroboam is offered the same promise that David received. He will rule over all he desires (cf. Abner's words to David in II Sam. 3:21), over Israel. Solomon's behavior has vitiated the conditional promise of the throne of Israel to David's house. Echoing the Nathan oracle, God promises to be "with" Jeroboam (cf. II Sam. 7:9a) and to build him a "sure house" like David's (cf. II Sam. 7:16a). In short, Jeroboam, with whom the reader has naturally identified (vv. 26, 28), is offered the chance to become a second David if only he will obey as perfectly as David did. Although the narrator will leave this conditional promise suspended in midair to turn to Rehoboam, the reader will not be kept in suspense for long. We learn already from verse 39 that Jeroboam will fail his test. God will afflict the descendants of David "for this" (either as punishment for Solomon's apostasy or for the sake of the promise to Jeroboam), but not forever. The future of Jeroboam's dynasty has already been closed off by prophetic foreknowledge. For David's dynasty, the future remains open.

Four Theological Themes

Chapter 11 launches four theological themes: royal apostasy, the prophetic word, God's control of international affairs, and the eternal promise to David. These thematic trajectories will cut through the rest of Kings, and they will finally deliver their payloads on Jerusalem and Judah in the last chapters of the book. All four of these theological claims have an impact on today's reader as well.

INTERPRETATION

The ebb and flow of royal apostasy and reform provide a structural rhythm to the Book of Kings. The kings are the prime movers in this, but the people as a whole share in both the guilt and the punishment. Apostasy first appears here in chapter 11. The appraisal language of verses 4b, 6, 9–10 links forward to the basic issue of apostasy versus reform as found in the judgment formulas provided for each of the kings. Compare the extensive similarities in vocabulary at 14:22–24; 15:11–15; II Kings 14:3, 5–6; 18:3–6; 21:2–9. This sort of general review of apostasy finds its closest parallel in the direct word to Jehu in II Kings 10:28–31, the sermon against Israel in II Kings 17, and the loose prophetic message evaluating Manasseh in II Kings 21:10–15.

One stream of apostasy was the non-centralized worship of Yahweh at the rural high places of Judah and the shrines of Jeroboam. This will be introduced by 12:26–33. Chapter 11 introduces a different type of apostasy, the worship of foreign gods. Kings will show a continued concern about the worship of foreign gods under the patronage of women from the royal household: Maacah (15:13); Jezebel (16:31); Athaliah (II Kings 8:18, 26–27; 11:1–20). Solomon's apostasy is referred to again in II Kings 23:10, 13, where it is specifically undone by the reform of Josiah. By then, however, Manasseh's worship of other gods has made reform and repentance a dead issue for Judah.

For the community of faith, apostasy has always been a danger. In New Testament times the crisis swirled around Christian participation in cults imbedded in the Hellenistic social and political structure (I Cor. 8:1–13; 10:14–22) and at a somewhat later time the threat of emperor worship (Rev. 13:5–8, 11–18). Today this enticement no longer comes as much from foreign gods as from ideologies and power systems incompatible with faith in a living, loving God. Some of these tempting idolatries may be as close and dear as was Solomon's harem. Each generation must make the difficult decision as to which systems and ideologies are incompatible with Christian commitment. Christians in some nations face this crisis more acutely than others. But chapter 11 makes it clear that the God of the Bible refuses to share the ultimate loyalty of the people of faith with any other god or idol. One consequence of such apostasy may be rips and tears in the fabric of our social and political life.

74

A second theme is the vital power of the prophetic word. In chapter 11 the word of God, spoken both directly and through the prophet Ahijah, provides the driving force for coming events. In verses 11–13 the divine speech is as the prophets will speak, using the genre of a prophetic judgment speech (cf. 13:21–22; 14:7–11; 16:2–4; 20:28; II Kings 1:16). This, coupled with the use of Deuteronomistic language by some of these prophets (especially Ahijah here in vv. 32–34, 36, 38 and later in 14:7–11), leads the reader to trust that the words of the prophets provide true evaluative guidance.

A further confirmation of the trustworthy nature of the prophetic word comes from the persistent and explicit references Kings makes to the fulfillment of individual prophetic threats (12:15; 14:18). When the final disasters crush Israel and Judah, the narrator can confidently assert that everyone had received fair warning from the prophetic word (II Kings 17:13; 21:10–15). The church also lives in dependence upon the word it believes comes from God. It too counts on this word to create faith (John 20:30–31; Rom. 10:14–17), to warn (I Cor. 10:6–11), and to encourage (James 1:22–25).

The third theme is that God controls international affairs, not just the fate of Israel and Judah. This theme will find wider scope in the chapters to follow, but is already present in the reports about Hadad and Rezon. The Hadad narrative especially is interested in the details of the rise and protection of the young national hero, his life among the Egyptians, and the nurture of an heir to the throne of Edom. Hadad's adventures bear a mystifying relationship to the story of Moses. He flees by way of Midian and Paran (part of the traditional geography of exodus); after weaning, his son is raised in Pharaoh's household (cf. Exod. 2:9–10). Rezon exhibits equally intriguing parallels to David: flight from his royal master, being leader of a small private army, elevation to the kingship in another city (Damascus, Hebron). These evocative details testify that the God of Kings is not simply the God of Judah and Israel. This God raises up national liberators for other peoples in ways that echo the stories of Moses and David.

This is the sort of God that Amos knew, a God who granted an exodus to the Philistines and Syrians (Amos 9:7). This God's purposes in history transcend any single-minded, unconditional protection of a chosen people or of only one royal dynasty. In fact, Damascus and Edom are being prepared for future use by this God against the people of promise and the house of David! Here God sets in motion the threat of Damascus that will strike in chapters 20 and 22; II Kings chapters 6 and 16, as well as the threat of Edom, which will lay dormant for the most part until the bitter experiences of the original exilic audience (Ps. 137:7; Isa. 34; Obadiah). Even the fearsome kings of Assyria and Babylon, the reader will discover, do the bidding of this universal God.

It is hard to believe that the God of the Bible is still in control of history in this day of nuclear weapons, hopeless hunger, terrorism, and totalitarian oppression; it must have been just as hard for the victims of Assyrian and Babylonian terror. The New Testament as well affirms God's control of the nations (Rev. 11:15) and God's willingness to coopt political systems to effect divine will (Acts 4:27–28 or 23:6–11 and the events leading up to 28:30–31).

The most ambiguous theme raised by chapter 11 is the promise to the house of David. In verse 36; 15:4, and II Kings 8:19, God promises a "lamp" in Jerusalem for the Davidic house forever. This puzzling word probably ought to be translated "dominion." In contrast to the conditional promise narrowly concentrated on Solomon and the future of the "throne of Israel" (2:4; 8:25; 9:4–5), these promises apply to the descendants of David as a whole and refer unambiguously to an eternal reign over Judah and Jerusalem. Yet the Book of Kings ends with Jerusalem leveled and the last scion of this royal house playing the sycophant's role in captivity.

Thus these unconditional dynastic promises create an intense ideological tension. On the one hand, God has promised David an eternal reign. On the other hand, nothing in Kings does more than hint at a chance for a revival of the Davidic monarchy in Jerusalem. Was this one of God's "lies" (cf. the lie of God in chap. 22) or a theological principle that became "inoperative" (as in the case of Josiah's perfect piety failing to divert God's punishment, II Kings 23:26–27)? Or could the original reader yet dare hope that the affliction of David's house would not be forever? Kings leaves the issue open, but the New Testament holds fast to the promise (Matt. 1:6–16; 21:1–11), while raising the rule of David's house to a higher, transpolitical dimension (Matt. 22:41–46; John 18:33–37).

76

I Kings 12:1–32
Rehoboam's Folly and Jeroboam's Sin

Chapter 12 presents the obverse of the breakdown of Solomon's kingdom of shalom (chap. 11) by tracing the rise of Jeroboam. This chapter intends to answer a double question: Why did Jeroboam succeed and why did Jeroboam ultimately fail? In one sense it is a concentrated parallel to the presentation of Solomon (chaps. 1—11), dealing in turn with Jeroboam's accession, building projects, and eventual condemnation.

The questions of Jeroboam's success and failure are entangled in the mystery of divine and human causation. Human motives are in view where Jeroboam is active (vv. 3, 12). The reason for the split is simply dissatisfaction over forced labor. God is also at work (vv. 15, 24; cf. II Sam. 17:5–14), however, to fulfill Ahijah's threatening word of chapter 11 by an undoing of the future hoped for in 2:4; 8:25. God's motives are highlighted by those places where Jeroboam is passive (vv. 2 MT, 20). On a larger scale, there are analogical parallels to the rejection of Saul and to the prior secret designation of David.

This chapter initiates the pattern of synchronism which will structure the narrative until the fall of Samaria. Because the regnal resumé of 14:19–20 makes it clear that chapter 12 falls into the "file" on Jeroboam (see the Introduction), Jeroboam is intended as the central subject. Rehoboam's turn at stage center will come in 14:21–31. Although the narrative of chapter 12 adopts a Judean point of view (v. 19, cf. vv. 26–27), Jeroboam is nevertheless presented in a thoroughly positive light until verse 26.

Rehoboam's Folly (vv. 1–20)

The story of the nation's division (vv. 1–20), traces a double causation for this tragedy: Rehoboam's folly and God's will (v. 15). Because Jeroboam is the real center of interest, Rehoboam remains basically passive, swayed by his counselors and then reacting lamely to events beyond his control. The story begins as the people come to make him king (v. 1) and ends with them

77

making Jeroboam king (v. 20a). This chain of events starts with Jeroboam as the loser who has fled (11:40), but ends with Rehoboam fleeing instead (v. 18). Two scenes involving Rehoboam and the people enclose Rehoboam's interaction with his advisors (vv. 3b–5 and 12–16). In a structural sense, this folkloristic narrative is a developed story, with exposition (vv. 1–3), complication (vv. 4–15), climax (v. 16), and denouement (vv. 17–20).

The exposition (vv. 1–3) describes a national assembly, probably constitutionally necessary at this early stage of the monarchy (cf. II Sam. 5:1–3). This dramatic device gets all the characters on stage together. In Jeroboam's presence there is a hint of trouble to come. If one accepts the narrative necessity of his presence, then it is not so troublesome that Jeroboam's role in verses 2–3 does not make much sense, especially in light of verse 20. Much of the rationale for text emendation disappears as well. The exposition of this chapter flows from the interrupted exposition of 11:26–28 (see the previous section). Direct links are provided by verses 2, 15. Jeroboam's role in chapter 12 would make no sense without the background provided in chapter 11.

A complication to Rehoboam's hopes comes with verses 4–15. A tension-building delay is provided by verse 5 and the ensuing consultations. Moreover, these verses make Rehoboam a thoroughly unlikable character. He is arrogant, impulsive, and tactless. The repetition of the people's request (vv. 9, 10) also builds tension, while at the same time making it clear that their position was perfectly reasonable. Their deferential politeness contrasts sharply with the arrogance they suffer from the king.

The motif of wise versus foolish advisors can be compared to a parallel incident involving the famous hero Gilgamesh (ANET, pp. 45–46). The contrast is highlighted by the grammatical emphasis on "you" in verses 6, 9. The two groups differ in both experience (age) and loyalty. The old men have already "stood up to" Solomon (implied by the Hebrew of v. 6; cf. Gen. 19:27). The "young" (Rehoboam is 41 according to the chronology of Kings!) men are dependent creations of the new regime, now standing before Rehoboam in government positions.

Rehoboam puts the question in a general way to the old men, not citing the petition of the people: "How" ought I answer. He receives a general opinion in the form of an aphorism. The old men give typically sage advice. Be a servant "today"; they will be your servants for ever ("all the days"). Their point is that the loyalty of a people stems from a king's willingness to act as a public servant. They are suggesting the sort of concessions in taxes and labor obligations that were generally expected upon the accession of any new monarch.

Their choice of words reflects balanced rationality. "Answer them" (contrast "speak" in v. 10) implies being responsive in light of a shared relationship. "Good words" is language specific to covenants and treaties, here implying formal arrangements for release (cf. II Kings 25:28). The grammar of verse 7 (the cognate accusative with the root *dbr*, "speak words") indicates "arrive at a decision through bargaining" (cf. I Sam. 20: 23).

Rehoboam puts the question much more specifically to his young men. He cites the people's request and asks "what" is to be said (contrast "how," v. 7). The "we" of verse 9 shows already where the king's sympathies lie, as does the verb "forsake" of verse 8. The young men seem to mock the people's petition by turning it into rhyming doggerel (v. 10), then offer three aggressive slogans for the new regime, one sadistic ("scorpions"), one possibly obscene ("my little thing" may mean "penis"; RSV "little finger"). Rehoboam chooses slogans over wisdom, machismo over servanthood.

The climax comes in verse 16. Israel has a poetic slogan of its own (II Sam. 20:1). "Tents" seems to have been a politically loaded concept with military and historic implications (cf. "log cabin" in the United States). A paraphrase of their parting shot might be, "mind your own business, David."

The denouement of verses 17–20 unwinds the tension and explores the implications of the climax: the stoning of Adoram (v. 18; a characteristically tactless choice of emissary), the election of Jeroboam (v. 20*a*), and the summary notes of verses 17, 19, 20*b*.

The narrative impetus begun by the national division is continued by the contrasting responses of the two kings. Rehoboam seeks to return (v. 21; root: *shub*) the kingdom by military force, but obeys the word of God and desists. Jeroboam seeks to prevent the kingdom's return to David's house (again *shub;* v. 26) through apostasy.

Rehoboam's Obedience (vv. 21–24)

The response of Rehoboam (vv. 21–24) is an example of the genre "report of prophetic commission," similar to 19:15–18;

21:17–19; II Kings 9:1–3. The report presupposes the role of a prophet in the battles of the tribal militia (cf. 22:5–6). The presentation is highly concentrated with a minimum of description. The focus is on the word and its effect. No attention is paid to the circumstances of its reception; the actual delivery to the king is ignored. Once the reader hears the word and is told of the king's obedient response, the report is over. Although the king had intended to restore (v. 21; root: *shub*) the kingdom, the army instead returns (v. 24; *shub*) home. As far as God is concerned, Rehoboam has become king only of Judah (v. 23). Although verse 24 seems to conflict with 14:30, perhaps the narrator only meant to forbid a full-scale invasion.

The effect of this report is to rehabilitate the obedient Rehoboam in the reader's opinion, especially in light of Jeroboam's coming acts of disobedience. This more positive view of Rehoboam will be supported by the final evaluation of 14:22. Here the sin of Judah is blamed on the people rather than the king, an unusual judgment for the narrator. A second effect is to increase the reader's confidence in the evaluative perspicacity of the narrator, for in verse 24 God supports the narrator's claim of verse 15.

Jeroboam's Sin (vv. 25–32)

The narrative of Jeroboam's religious innovations seeks to undercut the reader's sympathy for Jeroboam, so carefully enhanced in the earlier half of the chapter. The reader gets a glimpse into the king's impious motivation by means of a rare internal monologue (vv. 26–27). The blame is placed directly on his shoulders ("he said in his heart," v. 26, cf. v. 33; "he took counsel" with himself, v. 28; cf. NEB).

By the time the narrator has finished with Jeroboam, the reader has the impression that the king systematically and intentionally violated nearly every principle of Deuteronomic law: non-centralized sacrifice (Deut. 12:5–7), image worship (Deut. 9:8–21 is especially in view); non-Levitical priests (Deut. 18:1–8); the Feast of Booths in the wrong month. The plural of verse 28 adds polytheism to the list of charges, as does the provision of two calves rather than one. The narrator insists that Jeroboam's sacrifices were to these calves (v. 32) rather than to Yahweh, whom they certainly represented in some way. Even the generations-old institution of local high places is blamed on Jeroboam (v. 31).

80

Whether this dark parallel to Solomon's temple building and sacrifices is based on genuine annalistic sources or is pure fiction, in either case it defines the all-important motif of Jeroboam's sin for the rest of the Book of Kings. This sin will be the focus of judgment against all the Northern kings, only to be undone in the end by Josiah (13:2; II Kings 23:15–20). Thus a second type of apostasy takes its place beside that of the worship of strange gods introduced in chapter 11: the improper worship of Yahweh.

Because the narrator is indulging in an anachronistic evaluation of Jeroboam, insisting on obedience to liturgical principles of a later age, historically-minded interpreters tend to exculpate the king. It is claimed that he was restoring an ancient tradition of Israelite worship, that the calves were pedestals for Yahweh in much the same sense as the ark was Yahweh's throne, that no polytheism was intended by shrines marking the north and south borders of the kingdom. From a literary point of view, however, none of this matters. For the Book of Kings, Jeroboam's actions were sins of the lowest order, providing a foil to Josiah, whose virtue was unparalleled. Historically the narrator may be doing Jeroboam a grave injustice; canonically the anachronistic evaluation is fully justified. Later reflections of the prophets (Amos, Hosea) make clear the theological dangers implicit in the liturgical traditions of the kingdom of Israel. The calves were all too open to misinterpretation by the unsophisticated. The plurality of shrines inevitably reflected the local multiplicity of Canaanite Baal worship, implying a Yahweh of Dan and another Yahweh at Bethel. As the Christian church itself has learned, liturgical forms are never without theological implication.

Jeroboam therefore plays the role of the king who is the author of sin, a paradigm of wickedness by which later kings are measured. In this he is the opposite of David, who is the paradigm of the pious king. Later in the book, Manasseh and Josiah will play opposite each other in analogous roles. In this, the author is following a Near Eastern ideological convention. Naram-Sin fulfilled the role of the paradigmatically wicked king in Mesopotamian literary culture for fifteen hundred years, based on his desecration of the temple of Enlil in Nippur. A later example is Nabonidus, who became a paradigm of royal impiety as a result of his interruption of the Akitu festival (ANET, pp. 312–15, 315–16).

81

The summary verse 32 and the transitional verse 33 point on to chapter 13, which will etch this sin and Bethel's ultimate fate into the consciousness of the reader. These calves will reappear as reminders of the ongoing apostasy of the North: in a judgment on Jehu in II Kings 10:29 and as a parallel to the sinful worship of Baal/Asherah in II Kings 17:16. The sin of Jeroboam will echo and re-echo through the evaluations of each king of the Northern Kingdom.

It might be tempting to read this chapter solely as a political story, as the triumph of a liberation movement against oppressive totalitarianism. That is certainly how the chapter begins. Rehoboam is the dictatorial fool who forgets that government's role is to serve its people (v. 7). Israel is standing up for a more humane position of traditional values (vv. 4, 16). Similar dramas are being played out by liberation movements around the world, often with the support of the church and its theologians.

Yet this chapter pushes beyond the political story to a theological one. The cause of this rebellion is not just human dissatisfaction with an oppressive system but the fulfillment of God's word and God's will to punish. As the story finishes, Rehoboam the foolish oppressor ends up as the obedient king. In contrast, Jeroboam the liberator of his people, who is searching desperately for religious authentication for his populist revolution, ends up as the paradigm for all royal apostasy.

Perhaps Christians who are too willing to provide religious legitimacy to an oppressive status quo ought to take the first part of this story to heart (vv. 1–20). Perhaps Christians who uncritically offer the church's blessing to all liberation movements need to remember the rest of the story (vv. 21–32). Neither group dare forget that, in the final analysis, God's sovereign will is being worked out in these historical struggles (v. 15).

I Kings 12:33–13:32
God's Word Against Bethel

The story of the man of God from Judah and the old prophet in Bethel is notoriously problematic for modern readers. The blunt designation of Josiah by name (13:2) is so obviously a prophecy made after the fact that the narrative is cast into immediate disrepute for the historically inclined. As a moral tale it is patently offensive. Trickery triumphs over the servant of God and the lying prophet is rewarded in the end. Is this a crude, insensitive God who violates our ideas of justice?

There are startling oddities in the narrative. Puzzling motives remain hidden. The bones of the man of God safeguard the bones of the prophet whose lie caused his death. The lying prophet becomes the source of a true word which in turn confirms the word of the man of God against whom it is directed. The man of God is shown to be a true messenger by events resulting from his betrayal of his calling as a prophet. This is a complex and intriguing story marked by narrative artistry (Gross, *Semeia* 15:97–135; Simon, *HUCA* 47:81–117).

The story as it stands is obviously the end product of a complex literary history. In an earlier form it may have once answered the question of why a genuine man of God was buried so conspicuously at an illegitimate sanctuary (II Kings 23:17). At the same time, it seems to be a legend on the prophetic word, motivating an unquestioning obedience to it. As an example of a prophet legend (a story told to generate respect for prophets and their word), this story stands closest to 20:35–36, sharing with it a rare expression for "by the word of the Lord" (obscured by RSV), a punishing lion, and a concern about disobeying the divine word. Motifs common to the syntax of legend are present (the withering and healing of the king's hand; death by a lion; its subsequent unnatural behavior), but these motifs are subordinate to the intriguing complexity of the plot itself.

The Bottom Line: A Word of Doom

To avoid being swamped by this complexity, the reader must search out and stick with the main point of chapter 13, as set forth in the final resolution of the story (v. 32): the word against Bethel will come true. Even early in the narrative, this central oracle of doom is already supported by two signs (vv. 4–5). The withering of the king's hand bolsters the credibility of the oracle, though not directly connected to its content. The destruction of the altar likewise supports this prophetic word and also serves as a demonstration of the altar's future fate. The final assertion of verse 32 ("shall surely come to pass") again undergirds the word of destruction and makes it clear that the disobedience of the man of God has not undercut it.

83

Like the two preliminary miracles, the restraints laid upon the man of God (vv. 9, 17) become signs that support the central oracle of doom. The messenger's alienation from Bethel and from the hospitality of those who worship there is a witness that gives power to his word. His actions are an illustration of his word, the first stage in Bethel's profanation. They make the irrevocable future concrete. For the man of God to retrace his footsteps would be to nullify his mission (cf. II Kings 19:33). This messenger of God is to keep a mysterious distance from his audience, not unlike those angels who deliver messages and then quickly disappear (cf. 13:18). These prohibitions are mentioned over and over and are clearly critical to the narrative.

The narrative uses two key words that have both spatial and ideological meanings. "Way/road" (Hebrew *derek;* vv. 9, 10 [twice], 12 [twice], 17, 24 [twice], 25, 26, 28) of course refers to the literal path of the prophet, but also to his choice of the metaphorical path of obedience or disobedience. To go with the king or the prophet would be to take the wrong "way" (vv. 8–9, 16–17). Equally important is the verb "turn/return" (Hebrew *shub;* 13:7, 9, 10, 16, 17, 18, 19, 20, 22, 23, 26, 29; the use of this verbal root in its various meanings is obscured by the English translations). To return by the same way is to retrace one's steps either to Judah (vv. 9, 10) or to Bethel (v. 17). To return with the king or prophet (vv. 7, 16, etc.) is to turn away from God's command.

At first the man of God cannot be co-opted by either the king or the old prophet, but then an unwitting act of disobedience subverts his character as a messenger and casts his oracle against Bethel into doubt and danger. His dangerous disobedience is cut short by the lion. The spectre of the potential falseness of a prophetic oracle, raised by the deceitful word of the old prophet, is banished by fulfillment of the old prophet's true word, which in turn supports the word of doom against Bethel.

Literary Structure

For all the surprises it offers the reader, this narrative is tightly structured. For example, the two prophetic titles (man of God, prophet) keep the central characters clearly distinguished, while verses 18 and 23 provide the necessary equation between the two. The repetition of key words and phrases holds the narrative together. The rare expression, "by the word of the Lord," the central concern of the unit, occurs in verses 1, 2, 5,

84

9, 17, 18, 32. Repeated also are the critical prohibitions and the duplicated invitation to a meal by first king and then prophet.

Verses 16–17 repeat verses 8–9. Both are chiasms with the word of God in their center, bracketed by a concern for the going/turning of the man of God:

> *A* I will not go . . .
>   *B* I will not eat bread or drink water . . .
>   *C* by the word of the Lord . . .
>   *B'* you shall neither eat bread nor drink water
> *A'* nor return by the way that you came (vv. 8–9)
>
>   * * * *
>
> *A* I may not return with you, or go . . .
>   *B* neither will I eat bread nor drink water . . .
>   *C* by the word of the Lord . . .
>   *B'* you shall neither eat bread nor drink water there,
> *A'* nor return by the way that you came (vv. 16–17)

Dramatic delay is created by the repetition of information already known to the reader, as in the case of verses 11*b* and 25. These verses are part of two internal transitional sections (vv. 11–14 and 25–28) which divide the narrative into three episodes: verses 1–10, 11–24, 25–32. Both these transitional sections use the sequence: bringing news, saddling the ass, finding the man of God.

> first episode—verses 1–10
>   transition sequence (vv. 11–14)
>   bringing news (v. 11)
>   saddling the ass (v. 13)
>   finding the man of God (v. 14)
> second episode—verses [11–14] 15–24
>   transition sequence (vv. 25–28)
>   bringing news (v. 25)
>   saddling the ass (v. 27)
>   finding the man of God (v. 28)
> third episode—verses [25–28] 29–32

These internal transitions slow down the action but also provide the springboard for the next episode by creating an expectation for the next move. In the second episode, the lion too "finds" the man of God (v. 24, Hebrew), offering an ironic parallel to verses 14 and 28.

The man of God and Jeroboam are the actors in the first

85

episode (vv. 1–10). Here the temptation to disobedience is presented for the first time, but rejected. This first episode moves quickly, setting up the oracle and the signs that authenticate it. The burning of ritually unclean human bones would be an effective way to desecrate a holy place. Verse 5 is awkward both grammatically and dramatically. The "ashes" are really the combination of fat and ashes from the sacrifices, which were always treated with great care but are here poured to the ground.

The motive for the king's invitation is left unexpressed. Is it gratitude, an effort to come into contact with a person of blessing, or an attempt to bribe the prophet and defuse the threat of his oracle? Of course his offer is basically just a narrative necessity to permit the man of God to turn it down, but the reader is still teased into speculation about it. Knowing that for the man of God to accept the invitation would be to go against God's command, we suspect the worst of Jeroboam. In any case, the offer is rejected, the possibility of further development along this line is aborted and the narrative must move on. Verses 9b–10 are loaded with the key words "return" and "way" and call the reader's attention to them. The reader is led to have confidence in this faithful messenger who has turned aside the challenge of disobedience, and this confidence extends to the word that he has delivered.

The second episode (vv. 11–24), concerning the man of God and the old prophet, tells of disobedience and punishment. The transitional sequence of verses 11–14 leads to a second offer, which is again refused. Yet the issue of the authenticity of the central oracle is now raised by questions which operate on two levels. Which way did the man of God go, God's way or the way of disobedience (v. 12)? Are you really a man of God (v. 14)?

The second rejection of disobedience leads to a third temptation. A new word (a lie, the narrator insistently whispers) raises uncertainty over the true status of this man of God now caught between two words and, more critically, over the effectiveness of the oracle he has spoken. The old prophet has succeeded where the king has failed. Respect for the prophetic word protected the man of God from the king, but paradoxically now makes him vulnerable to the prophet's deceit.

The question of the old prophet's motive is again left unanswered. Is he trying to short-circuit the oracle in order to pro-

86

tect his home town? Once again, the reader is faced with the demands of narrative necessity. This lie is vital to the plot. It is left unmotivated and unpunished because it is not central to the concern of the narrative, which remains the word of God against Bethel. The lie makes the third offer climactically the most attractive. It is really one of the few narrative options possible for inducing the disobedience that is necessary for the plot to continue. It is important to note that God has nothing to do with this trap. It was a lie. There was no angel and no revelation. God is not indulging in enigmatic morality, at least at this point in Kings.

Verse 23 gives the mistaken impression that the old prophet coldly finished his meal after delivering his sentence of death, but verses 20–22 are meant to be taken as simultaneous to verse 19, so that verse 23 indicates the next act in the sequence. This strange old prophet seeks to get the man of God back on his "way" (v. 23), but now matters have changed dramatically. The root *shub* is used in an active sense in this episode to characterize disobedience, and now the "old prophet in Bethel" has become the "prophet who caused him to turn back" (*shub;* vv. 20, 26; cf. 23).

In verse 24 the man of God is transformed into merely "the body." His failure has made the reader question his authenticity and even the authenticity of his oracle, for now one of the signs (his obedience) supporting it has been undercut. Yet in a strange twist, his death has now become a new sign of the power of God's word.

In the third episode (vv. 25–32), the reader's uncertainty over the authenticity and effectiveness of the word against Bethel is replaced by certainty. It "shall surely come to pass" (v. 32). Those things in the narrative which had undermined this word are reversed or superseded. Ironically, the disobedience and death of the man of God turns out actually to validate the word he betrayed. Although he has been reduced to a "body thrown down in the road/way" (vv. 25, 28) because of his "turn" from the "way," at the same time he remains a "man of God" (vv. 26, 29, 31). His degrading death proves this, because by fulfilling the old prophet's oracle of doom (vv. 21–22), it demonstrates that the prohibitions which accompanied the Bethel oracle really were from God!

The new sign bearer, the fairy-tale-like lion, refuses to eat the body (v. 28) and thus obeys the constraint the man of God

87

failed to honor! Its unnatural act emphasizes that the source of this death is God. The old prophet understands this when he first hears the news (v. 26). He is also now certain that the outrageous word against his home town is true, because its attendant prohibition has been validated by the fulfillment of a revelation he himself transmitted (v. 32).

The oracle against Bethel is also validated by his act of burial, which converts the death of the man of God into a permanent sign of the word of doom. Now the old prophet knows the truth about this man of God and the oracle he delivered, and his acts are the opposite of before. He has been transformed from an opponent of the word to a supporter. The old prophet who had caused the "turn" (v. 26) of disobedience now "returns" (v. 29) the body to his city. The first "turning" brings disaster; the second establishes the authenticity of the word of God. From deceitful hospitality, matters have changed to brotherly burial. The threat of the judgment oracle against the man of God ("your body shall not come to the tomb of your fathers") is carried out by the old prophet himself, who thus deliberately fulfills his own word. Their joint burial becomes a new sign of the truth of the Bethel oracle (v. 31). The two prophets are now brothers in the grave, servants of the same word.

Theological Implications

In the context of the Book of Kings, this narrative is the first round of God's assault on the policies of Jeroboam. Just as 12:33 provides a transition into this narrative from the sin of Jeroboam, 13:33–34 creates a bridge to the next blow against his reign. Here the word is against Bethel; there it will be a word against Jeroboam's house. There is a perhaps unconscious linkage to God's earlier dealings with Jeroboam in the use of the words "tear" and "hand" in verses 3–6 (cf. 11:31). Not being buried with one's fathers will also be a factor in the punishment of Jeroboam (14:13), so this present story illustrates what will soon happen to the king who has disobeyed. In 14:18 Jeroboam's son will be mourned and buried, as a sign of God's word of doom.

The morality of this story has offended interpreters for generations. Yet in spite of what some commentators have asserted, God is not acting in an enigmatic manner, for God is not represented as having anything to do with the trap set up by the old prophet.

The reader must note that the narrative relentlessly refuses to deal in motivations, either the king's or the old prophet's or those of the man of God. It does not matter at all that the man of God may have acted in good faith; his intentions are of no account. There is really no moral enigma. The old prophet is rewarded by the protection of his bones for his faith in the word against Bethel, in spite of his deception. The man of God is punished for violating his calling, in spite of his good faith.

God's commands have an unconditional claim to external obedience. Any subjective feeling of guilt or innocence or any pleading of good intentions are ultimately beside the point. "Lord, when did we see thee hungry . . . ?" (Matt. 25:44). " . . . I was afraid, and I went and hid your talent in the ground" (Matt. 25:25). The narrative is a lesson in obedience, for the fate of the man of God would eventually become the fate of Judah as a whole. The use of "turn/return" *(shub)* in this chapter resonates with the call for the exilic audience to repent *(shub;* 8:48).

But moral issues are secondary. This is not a story about the conflict between true and false prophecy either, for the prophet's lie is only a matter of narrative necessity. This narrative is about the word of God. It holds the word of God up as superior to its prophets and shows it triumphing over their inadequacies. Both the man of God and the old prophet turn out to be tools of God, who is striking at Bethel with the weapon of the prophetic word. This is a story about the word's power to get itself done (Isa. 55:10–11; Mark 4:26–29). The word of God changes adversaries into supporters who end up unconsciously fulfilling it (John 11:49–52).

God's word is independent, but still under the power of its messengers. It can be set back by their betrayal, but it wins out in the end. The one who blocks it is forced to advance it, albeit from motives of crass self-protection; the one who betrays it is forced to support it, even at mortal cost. Moreover, the story implies that the "way" of a servant of the word must conform to that word. The "way" from which a prophet must not "turn" is as much a sign of God's word as any of the signs and wonders described in verses 4–6. Even God's agents can become God's victims if they betray their calling. In this way the story speaks

89

directly to all who speak God's word and all who hear it.

The word of the man of God explicitly sets up the contrast, central to the plot of Kings, between Jeroboam and Josiah, the worst king and the best, the apostate and the reformer. The apparatus of apostasy is introduced here for future vilification and destruction: the houses of the high places (v. 32; back to 12:31 and forward to II Kings 17:29, 32; 23:19), the cities of Samaria (v. 32; II Kings 17:24, 26; 23:19), the priests of the high places (v. 2; II Kings 17:32; 23:9, 20). The expansion of this oracle of doom to the other cities of Samaria (v. 32) is an indication that Josiah's entire reforming career is seen as the fulfillment of the wider implication of this word against Bethel.

The shalom of the kingdom has been broken. There is a long and bitter road to follow before this word of God against Bethel will have run its course in the reforming career of the incomparable Josiah. By then it would be too late for Judah as well, and the death of a whole nation, which had turned from the way commanded of it, would serve as a sign of the irrevocable power of God's word.

I Kings 13:33—14:20
God's Word Against Jeroboam

A tragic queen in disguise, an old, blind prophet, the dying prince—what Sophocles or Shakespeare could have done with such material! Certainly, this powerful story deserves to be better known than it is. As told here, the narrative reaches a pinnacle of literary art in that the story itself echoes and reinforces the impact of the shocking oracle it encloses.

The Purpose of the Story

This story really reflects the intention of the Book of Kings as a whole: to explain the tragic events of history as God's justifiable judgment on a sinful people. More specifically, it gives the rationale for the fall of the Northern Kingdom and the exile of its people. At the same time, it proclaims a warning against apostasy from Israel's God and seeks to create confidence in the perceptive word of the prophet. Beneath it all lies the objective of eliciting a fidelity to God like David's and trust in God's word. By highlighting a story of judgment, the text seeks to create faith and repentance.

This text interprets a wide sweep of events in Kings. It is a programmatic judgment on the dynasty of Jeroboam and the whole kingdom of Israel. The text serves as a sort of orientation aid for the reader, as a map through the coming complexities of the history of the Northern Kingdom.

The core of this section is a prophetic legend of the sort in which some inquiry is made of a prophet. Similar stories may be found in I Samuel 9:1–14, 20; II Kings 8:7–15. As a narrative told among prophets and their supporting communities, this sort of legend would have had the intention of elevating the hearer's opinion of the prophetic word. In this example, the content of Ahijah's judgment speech has grown far more important than the narrative details, however. The prophet and his powers have been submerged to the word of God. The story now seems to exist chiefly to carry the sayings set within it, much like a New Testament pronouncement story.

In the context of the story of Kings so far, the dynastic promise to Jeroboam (11:37–38; 14:5, 7) has been abrogated because its conditions were not met. (chap. 12; 14:8). The prophetic warning went unheeded (chap. 13; 14:9). This story in chapter 14 offers the key for understanding the shape of things to come, concentrated in verses 10–11, 14–16. At short range, the curses of verses 10–11 will continue to work themselves out on the succeeding wicked dynasties of Baasha (16:4) and Omri/ Ahab (21:21, 24; II Kings 9:8–9). At long range, verses 14–16 point forward to II Kings 17, the powerful theological rationale for the fall of Samaria.

How the Story Works

The report in 13:33–34 and the concluding summary of 14:19–20 serve to frame this story, marking its borders and helping the reader with the transition into and out of the prophetic narrative. They also serve to set the evaluative context for the doom-laden oracle. The narrator in this frame agrees with Ahijah and God in the story itself that Jeroboam was totally disobedient.

The contemporary reader recognizes much in this narrative as familiar: parental concern, the psychological ambiguity of disguise, the plant images of shaking and uprooting. The literary convention of the perceptive blind person is almost a

91

commonplace (Teiresias, Bartimaeus). Other details require some explanation, however: the mission to the prophet, the threat about burial, and the concept of communal sin.

In the crisis of illness, ancient people sometimes sought out an oracle, as in II Kings 1:2–4. It was important to bring an appropriate gift (I Sam. 9:7–8). Jeroboam's present seems to be tailored to his wife's disguise and is not particularly princely (contrast II Kings 8:9). The "cakes" were special, perhaps topped with crumbs or raisins. In seeking out a prophetic word for the patient, one did not simply look for a prognosis on the course of the sickness. One sought help with the cure, hoping for a positive word which would have a positive effect on the outcome. Prophetic word was believed to be a powerful force shaping events. Ahijah was a good prophet from whom to seek such a word because of his track record (v. 2).

Proper burial, denied to the men of Jeroboam's house (vv. 11, 13) and indicated by the phrase "slept with his fathers" (v. 20) was critically important. One was willing to take great risks to provide burial for someone (I Sam. 31:10–13; II Sam. 21: 8–14; Tobit 1:18–19). It would be a horrible fate to have one's body lie unburied and unmourned, scattered and eaten by scavengers.

At first sight, one presupposition of this text seems especially far removed from the world view of today's reader. Here sin and punishment have strong communal implications. The sin of a nation can be sparked by that of an individual (v. 16). The sin of an individual can have communal effects (vv. 10–11). An innocent child receives the first installment of family-wide punishment. Yet is this so far from our experience? The social sciences have taught us much about the effect of one generation's behavior on the next and about the interaction between communities and individuals.

The raw information content of this section is carried by Ahijah's oracle. Because of Jeroboam's apostasy, God will bring his dynasty to an end. Because the whole nation has followed him in sin, Israel itself will be shaken and exiled. Yet the effect of this text is created as much by its narrative artistry as by the oracle's content. The prophet legend begins by lulling the reader into at least a mild expectation of a happy ending. Then the text turns viciously on the reader to drive home its terrible announcement of doom, sharpened by the contrast with our earlier mild hopefulness, intensified by the extension of disaster far beyond the horizon we had thought established, accented by an overwhelming barrage of metaphor and Deuteronomistic language.

The story begins by hinting at hope. We learn the son's name so we will identify with his illness and his mother's position. Jeroboam reminds us of Ahijah's original good news. He sends the mother as messenger, for she is able to draw us into the crisis more effectively than any court functionary could. The gift sounds delicious and potentially effective. Against this hopeful impulse, the disguise adds a note of tension. It reveals that Jeroboam knows all is not well between himself and God.

This disguise and Ahijah's corresponding blindness also provide space for suspense to develop. Following the description of the problem (v. 1) and the commissioning (vv. 2–3), the narrator moves us from the royal city to Shiloh in verse 4. Jeroboam's wife *goes* to Shiloh (spatial perspective of the royal city), but then *comes* to the house (spatial perspective of Shiloh). At this point the narrative action is halted with a circumstantial description of Ahijah's blindness and then a flashback (v. 5) of God's revelation to him. This further increases the narrative suspense. The divine speech carefully refrains from letting the cat out of the bag prematurely.

The story line resumes in verse 6. The emphasis on hearing is a skillful touch that communicates the point of view of the blind prophet. From the hint in verse 6 that Ahijah's commission is a heavy one, the reader is dragged down precipitously from mild hope to deeper and deeper levels of gloom. The news is worse than we ever expected. The stakes are higher than we had first been led to believe, not simply a child's life or even a dynasty's, but the fate of a nation. The text creates an expectation (vv. 1–5), then dashes it to the ground (vv. 10–14), then tramples it to dust (vv. 15–16). We had expected the oracle to be over at verse 13 or 14. We are shocked and surprised by the even deeper chasm of doom that opens in verses 15–16. The text slugs us when our guard is down!

The doom language is driven by powerful and colorful images: a dung fire, scavenging birds and dogs, a shaken reed, a plant torn up by its roots. There is assonance in the Hebrew of "bond and free" in verse 10. We are not sure what this formula means precisely ("minors and adults" perhaps) but it clearly includes absolutely everybody. The earthy language (RSV "male" equals "he who urinates on a wall"), the image of clean-

93

ing out every stinking trace of Jeroboam (v. 10), and Deuteronomistic sin language (vv. 9, 16) all underscore the doom. The contrasting mention of God's earlier grace to Jeroboam (vv. 7–8) and of David's perfect obedience have a similar intensifying effect. As the doom is announced, God is distanced from Jeroboam, who is first spoken of in the second person (vv. 7–9), then the third (vv. 10–11).

The shock of the story is even stronger because we naturally have come to identify with Jeroboam's wife. Jeroboam is mentioned in almost every verse, but she is the mainspring for the plot. She seeks news about her sick child but ends up the bearer of horrible tidings of a total catastrophe caused by her husband. She almost carries death into the house herself. Her feet (vv. 6, 12) and entrances (vv. 6, 17) make the bridge between prophecy and grim fulfillment. In verse 17 her movement again provides the spatial transition from the locale of word to the locale of fulfillment (cf. v. 4). She moves with the reader from a surface vision of the problem, through an encounter with the prophetic word, to a deeper insight into the crisis. An effective touch is the "good news" that the child will at least be mourned (v. 13). This pitiful scrap of comfort makes the bad news all the more intense by contrast. Our sympathy for her delivers the payload of doom to us more effectively than any simple citation of Ahijah's oracle could.

Audience and Text

So far we have concentrated on the text. The audience, both original and modern, also requires consideration. The audience upon whom this text first worked lived on the other side of the national catastrophe and exile threatened here. For this audience, the fate of the Northern Kingdom was already a long-fulfilled preview of their own tragedy. Themselves scattered beyond the Euphrates, shaken and uprooted, readers of the final form of Kings saw their own fate in verses 14–16 of chapter 14.

The canonizing process through which old words find new life and application was well underway. As a marker of this, the addressed community left a witness to their hermeneutical appropriation in the gloss ending verse 14: "This is the day; and what more now?" (JB footnote). The Revised Standard Version attempts to translate these words as part of Ahijah's oracle (cf. the RSV footnote), but they are better explained as a gloss, a

94

marginal comment caught up into the text in the copying process. In this gloss we have an opportunity to look over the shoulders of some of this text's earliest readers. Scripture produces the community of faith and the faith community continues to shape Scripture!

This audience itself faced temptations from foreign gods and irregular worship practices. They too faced the danger of casting God behind their backs (v. 9). This text sought to explain to them how they got where they were, far from the "good land" (v. 15). But it also would have worked to strip away disguises, reveal the critical nature of exilic temptations, warn against even further sin. On the positive side, it would have reoriented readers to the example of King David, to a whole-hearted keeping of the commandments. It evoked fidelity towards the God of mysterious motivation (v. 13) who penetrates every disguise and whose arena of action is history and dynasty (vv. 2, 7–8, 14). Check it for yourselves, the narrator urges the reader. The evidence is "written in the Book of the Chronicles of the Kings of Israel" (v. 19).

As a piece of literature, this text unmasks and reveals, preserves mystery, and calls to fidelity. First it removes masks. The story begins with pretense and ends with brutally honest vision. Jeroboam does not know where he stands, and this generates disguise and pretending. His wife is to act like a stranger (v. 5; cf. Gen. 42:7). The reader soon finds out this is foolishly inappropriate. The couple have chosen to consult a powerful prophet (v. 2), but are doing so on a basis that implicitly denies his perception! God short-circuits human pretense by revealing all to blind Ahijah. The woman never gets a chance to carry out her charade (read JB instead of RSV at v. 5) or even ask her question. As soon as she appears in the doorway, her pretense and ignorance are swamped by the revealing word. King Saul had the same experience at Endor (I Sam. 28:8–19). Both his disguise and his ignorance were overcome by a revelation of the worst possible news.

Disguise is a symptom of understanding only in a surface way our broken relationship with God. The problem is not too serious, one is thinking. It can be covered up. But human self-delusion cannot protect against the penetrating divine word. Encounters with this word can be surprising experiences, as Hazael discovered in II Kings 8:7–15.

This text does to the reader what Ahijah's oracle does to

95

Jeroboam's wife. It forces us to stop pretending about our behavior and God's reaction to it. Our illusions about our position with God are swamped by the recognition of the pit of doom yawning before us. If we have begun with the illusion that God does not have to be taken seriously, that illusion has been shattered. If we have begun with the pretense that we understand God, we are confronted instead by a God whose deep mystery is reflected by an unexplained graciousness to Abijah (v. 13).

The text reveals to the modern reader a God different from the sterile, tame, predictable god of public religion. The God of this text manipulates political events to divine ends. This God evaluates persons and nations on the basis of whole-hearted fidelity to divine commandment. This God's concern is not personal ethics, at least in this text, but idolatry or improper worship at improper places by improper priests (vv. 9, 15; 13:33). This God reacts harshly to faithlessness and rebellion, experiences anger, uses coarse language, and brings death to individuals, families, and nations. This God tears, burns, cuts off, shakes, uproots, scatters. This is not a God with whom it is easy to feel comfortable but who must be taken seriously.

This is also a God of deep mystery whose gracious motives for good are inscrutable. Although masks are removed, mystery remains. On the surface, the message of the text is clear: Sin leads to doom. Certain details, however, create an undercurrent of unease. Verse 9 seems to forget that Jeroboam has had no predecessors. Verse 12 is not literally fulfilled by verse 17 as to the exact moment of the child's death. God's affection for Abijah remains a mystery. Jeroboam's own burial (v. 20) seems to violate the spirit of the oracle (vv. 10–11), though not the letter. The interplay of grace and punishment is confusing. Grace shown to Jeroboam is at the same time punishment for David's house, but David remains the example of perfect obedience. Punishment for Jeroboam's house means raising up yet another king.

The reader recognizes that human understanding is only partial. There is more to this God than meets the eye, even after pretense has been overcome by revelation. There is also more to this God than is revealed in Ahijah's oracle, for there remains a countercurrent of mysterious grace. This is centered especially on the unanswered but inescapable questions: What now for David? and What now for the readers (cf. the gloss in v. 14)?

In this sense the text, for all its apparent closure around catastrophe and punishment, remains open-ended.

It is open-ended in the sense that the reader's future and choice remain open. The text is a call for fidelity to the God it reveals. In the same way as the exilic readers, we face choices of fidelity to the God of the Bible. The dangers are no longer foreign gods, but other, more contemporary idolatries. This text reorients us toward a whole-hearted keeping of faith with the real God it has unmasked for us. It evokes fidelity towards the God who punishes infidelity, whose gracious choices are mysterious, and whose arena of action remains the real world of the political, the economic, the historical.

I Kings 14:21—16:34
Paradigmatic History I

The author of Kings is often criticized for not having written the sort of history of the monarchy that scholars wish they possessed. Modern readers tend to find fault with its undervaluing of Omri's importance, clearly evidenced in extra-biblical sources. We are frustrated with the paucity of information about the fracas involving Zimri, Tibni, and Omri. Was there a division between the militia (Omri) and the chariotry (Zimri)? Did Tibni represent some third group?

The author of Kings assumed, however, that readers would have available for ready reference accounts of the two kingdoms, full of interesting and impressive royal deeds: the cities Asa built (15:23), the "might" of Baasha (16:5) and Omri (16:27), the conspiracy of Zimri (16:20). These "Chronicles of the Kings of Israel/Judah" appear to have been popularized summaries of each king's reign, culled from archival and inscriptional sources. The practice of "footnoting" these two sources was intended to build the reader's confidence in the basic accuracy of Kings and to deflect just those questions of historical detail that so intrigue the modern reader.

The purpose of Kings was quite different from that of the modern historian. For the Book of Kings, recounting history was an exercise in theological instruction, an opportunity to

97

explain the past and present according to Deuteronomistic principles. Past events serve as opportunities for evaluative judgments. The critical questions for the implied reader are: How did we get where we are today? Why did the destruction of Judah and the exile happen? The answer, insists Kings, reaches back into the rhythms and structures of the national story. Sin and apostasy are the recurring themes of this story, resulting inevitably in deserved punishment. Reform and repentance happened as well, particularly in Judah under the Davidic kings. Kings must be read as it was intended to be read, primarily as a theological work. It is only secondarily a source for information of the sort appreciated by modern historians.

In retelling the national story in the theological grammar of Deuteronomy, the author felt no need to censor or rewrite history according to some mechanical principle of retribution. The potential offense of Maacah's marital history (15:2, 10; is this some sort of error or misunderstanding?) or Asa's bad feet are allowed to stand, without the pedantic rationalizing of the Chronicler or the Lucianic recension (cf. at 15:23) of the Septuagint. Sometimes events which fit into the theological schema are presented without comment (Shishak, Asa's call on Benhadad, the division between Tibni and Omri). The assumption is that the reader can draw the proper conclusion without intrusive guidance. At other times the theological connection is made explicit. For example, Zimri's death is blamed on the sin of his seven-day reign (16:19).

Structural Techniques

In 14:21—16:34, the basic structure presenting the reigns of the kings is established and the reader is oriented to it. Turning from Jeroboam, who has occupied the narrative's attention since chapter 12, individual sections ("files") on each king are opened and closed in turn. The Ahab section remains open at the end of chapter 16, enclosing the following narratives about Elijah and the Syrian wars. Verses 21–22 in chapter 16 fall outside this system as a transition. Zimri, the seven-day wonder, gets a full-scale file; Tibni does not, although the years of his reign are accounted for in verse 23.

These evaluative regnal resumes find parallels in Mesopotamian chronicles (ANET, pp. 272–74, 564–66). The "Weidner Chronicle" even provided theological judgments something like those found in Kings. More than half of the material in this section of paradigmatic history consists of these formulaic resumes.

The synchronisms between Judah and Israel begin at this point as well. The reader is left to assume that the accession year of Rehoboam is year one of Jeroboam (comparing 14:21 to 15:1) and soon realizes that the regnal years are to be counted inclusively. For the reader inclined to check such things, the synchronisms make perfect internal sense at this point, building confidence in the accuracy of the presentation. The internal consistency of the chronology will deteriorate in coming chapters. Verse 25 of chapter 15 orients the reader to the practice of backtracking chronologically when switching kingdoms (see the introduction). The effect of this is to emphasize that in spite of the division of the kingdom this is one story of one people under the direction of one God.

Those portions of the story of Baasha that are reported outside of his regnal file (15:33—16:7) are bracketed by the repeated notice of verses 16, 32. By using this "resumptive repetition," the narrative can frame Baasha's acts and highlight them, even though they take place during the reigns of two other kings. Baasha's war with Asa and his murder of Nadab are thus held together without breaking the structural system. Another example of resiliency in employing the regnal file system is the anticipatory notice of Zimri's accession date in 16:10. Similar notices of war are used in 14:30 and 15:6, 7 to structure the relationship between Rehoboam and Abijam. The sorry course of fraternal warfare continued under the son as it had under his father.

Other structural techniques are evident. For example, the principle of analogy is at work. The covenant with Ben-hadad, followed by a report of forced labor (vv. 19, 22), is a negative analogue to the covenant of Solomon with Hiram and the forced labor that resulted (5:1–18). This event also provides a parallel to Ahaz's later request to Assyria (II Kings 16:7–9). Jezebel and Maacah (15:13; 16:31–32) provide analogies to Solomon's wives. The analogical parallel between Nadab and Elah is underlined by verbal similarities. They both serve as examples of the ephemeral nature of a potential dynasty under God's judgment.

Another organizational principle, the pattern of apostasy and reform, is set in motion by Asa, the first of several reforming kings. Many scholars suspect that these notices of apostasy (14:

23–24; 16:32–33) and reform (15:12, 14) were not really present in the author's sources, but were produced on the basis of notices involving later kings or as a result of the author's own free elaboration.

Another important structural theme is the rhythm of the prophetic word and its fulfillment. This was established by 2:27; 12:15; 13:2, 32; 14:18. Here it is carried forward by Baasha, who is both an agent of the divine word (15:29) and its victim (16:2–4, 7, 12; cf. the man of God in chap. 13).

A History of Sin

This section, 14:21—16:34, is paradigmatic history. The behavior of these kings and the history of their reigns tell the broader national story in miniature. Both Judah and Israel had the ingrained habit of sin. Although the people of Judah as a whole are blamed for this in 14:22, it is clear that the kings of Judah shared the responsibility as well (15:3, note that both Abijam and Rehoboam are faulted). In Israel, the focus of disobedience is always the king. Whoever he was, he inevitably followed in the sin of Jeroboam and as a result caused the people to sin as well. This judgment makes perfect sense in the context of the ancient Near East, where kings took an active leadership role in religious affairs, initiating observances, building and rebuilding sanctuaries, and dedicating new images.

This penchant for sin gets worse and worse as time goes on, especially for Israel (16:25, 30, 33), but in the short term also for Judah (14:22). The paradigmatic nature of this section makes it the center of a network of negative evaluative judgments. Compare 15:30 to 21:22 and II Kings 23:26; 16:7 to II Kings 17:17; 21:6, 16; 22:17. In this section 16:2, 13, 26, 33 connect generally with 14:9, 15; 22:53; II Kings 17:11; 23:19. The "idols" of 15:12 link to 21:26; Deuteronomy 29:17; II Kings 17:12; 21:11, 21; 23:24.

David provides the measure of proper conduct for Judah (15:3). The paraphernalia of sin (14:23–24) included the traditional (3:2) high places, the pillars revered since patriarchal times, and the tree-like Asherim. While any condemnation of the first two of these is certainly anachronistic and historically unfair, it was perfectly justified for the narrator in light of Deuteronomy 12:3, 5–7; 16:22. The mocking reference to every hill and green tree recalls Deuteronomy 12:2 and will be used again against Ahaz in II Kings 16:4.

100

Among these "abominations" of the Canaanites, which Judah practiced, in grim fulfillment of the warnings of Deuteronomy, were cult prostitutes (v. 24; cf. Deut. 23:18). The word probably includes members of both sexes here (against the RSV). Hosea 4:14 is evidence that the sex act sometimes played a part in sacrifices, no doubt in order to promote fertility. These cultic functionaries will be removed by Asa (15:12) and again by Jehoshaphat, the next reforming king (22:46), and yet again by Josiah (II Kings 23:7).

In 15:13, the narrative uses the unparalleled phrase "horror for Asherah" (RSV "abominable image"). Whatever this may have been, the narrator's disgusted feelings about it could not be clearer. Judah's sin with foreign gods is a continuation of Solomon's infidelity (11:4–8). The double mention of Rehoboam's Ammonite mother (14:21, 31) underlines the origin of this apostasy.

Whereas in Judah the focus is on syncretistic practices, for Israel the sanctuaries of Jeroboam at Bethel and Dan receive the brunt of the criticism. Each king's sin is equated with that of Jeroboam (15:26, 30, 34; 16:19, 26). Although this sin was triggered by the kings, the people themselves were also involved. The kings made Israel sin (16:2, 13, 19). Presumably the narrator is thinking of the golden calves when referring to idols (16:13, 26). The expressive term "vanities" (RSV "idols"), used of Elah (16:13) and generally in 16:26, will be repeated at II Kings 17:15.

Israel's loyalty to its God reaches a low point in King Ahab (16:30–33). The making of an Asherah is a common enough crime in Deuteronomistic evaluative language (Deut. 16:21); but Ahab goes further, reflecting Solomon's apostasy by building an altar and temple for Baal for his infidel queen. Historians have pointed out that such a religious center in the new capital of Samaria would make a great deal of political sense as a unifying focus for a mixed kingdom of Canaanites and Israelites. Yet none of this matters to the narrator, who cites this as evidence that Ahab was the worst Northern king so far (16:30).

An important evaluatory theme centers on Samaria. What is just a preparatory note in 16:24, becomes an open-ended indictment of the Omri dynasty in 16:32. Its Baal temple will hang suspended over the Northern kings until its destruction by Jehu in II Kings 10:18–28. Its offensive presence shadows the narratives about Ahab and Elijah which follow. Samaria as a district name will also provide the geographical designation for the Northern Kingdom when it is the object of the narrator's evaluative wrath (13:32; II Kings 17:24, 26, 23:19) and as a standard of judgment for Jerusalem (II Kings 21:13).

A History of Punishment

God's reaction is described in human emotional terms: jealousy (14:22) and anger (15:30; 16:7, 13). God's jealousy is described by the Song of Moses (Deut 32:16, 21) and in Psalm 78:58. The sexual side to this emotion is evident in the use of the noun in Proverbs 6:34 and Song of Solomon 8:6. Anger is likewise a very human passion. Here it implies vexation, grief over shabby treatment (Prov. 17:25; 21:19; I Sam 1:6–7).

The result of God's emotional reaction to apostasy is a series of disasters for Judah and Israel. Shishak's general invasion of Palestine is represented here as an attack centered on Jerusalem. Bronze replaces Solomon's gold as Judah falls into a state of decline, underlined by the durative verbs of 14:28. Baasha's coup was the outcome of Jeroboam's sin (15:29). Zimri's spectacular death was caused by his apostasy (16:19). The need to make these connections between sin and disaster is so strong that the narrator simply ignores the question of how Zimri could have had much opportunity for apostasy in his seven-day reign.

The ongoing border war between the two kingdoms is used by the narrator to emphasize this generally unhappy state of affairs (14:30, 15:6, 7, 16; with 15:32 as an oddly placed repeat of v. 16). Do not forget, the narrator repeats, this war was not over yet. It is finally brought to a decisive conclusion by the pious Asa, but he must use the worldly tactics of bribes and fortress-building to do so. The gifts just brought into the temple (15:15) have to be given away (v. 18). Ramah was only eight kilometers north of Jerusalem, and its critical strategic location is noted in 15:17. Asa is able to push the border even further north. The nominal sentence, 15:19a, may mean that there already had been some sort of treaty between Ben-hadad and Asa.

The prophetic word provides interpretations of and warnings for these reactions of an angry God (16:2–4, 7). This is a word which the reader can count on coming to pass (15:29;

16:12). Baasha is caught in history's trap, doomed for his actions as a tool for God's will (14:14; cf. Mark 14:21), but for his own sin as well (16:7), the generalized and unspecified "work of his hands."

The fulfillment of the word against Jericho reminds the reader that this restricted presentation of paradigmatic history remains part of a much larger structure of sin, warning, and punishment (16:34). With 14:24, this notice provides a sobering reference to the conquest under Joshua, which gave the people the land of promise, now divided, polluted, and the target of Egyptian and Syrian invaders.

Nevertheless Judah remains special to this angry God, although Israel too is still termed "my people" (16:2). Jerusalem was chosen by God (14:21; 15:4; cf. 8:16, 44; 11:13), although it is not inviolable. We know from his own inscription that Shishak did not actually divest Jerusalem. Historically, the temple treasures must be considered tribute from Rehoboam, but the narrator leaves us with the impression that the Egyptian Pharaoh ransacked the temple himself. "He took away everything" (14: 26).

The house of David is another focus of God's favor. God made an eternal covenant with David (15:4–5) because of his unparalleled obedience. Judah's dynastic continuity is highlighted by the contrasting penchant of the Northern Kingdom for conspiracy and regicide. The dynasties of Israel are short-lived. Nadab and Elah are jokes from a dynastic viewpoint. In parallel acts of political violence, 15:29–30 and 16:11–13 show the fulfillment of God's will, both examples of the form-critical genre "throne conspiracy report."

In contrast, the Davidic king Asa provides a focus of obedience (15:11). He is willing to depose the queen mother (15:13), an important office in Judah. His heart is "wholly true" (15:14) as Solomon's was not (11:4). He can give gifts to the temple which parallel Solomon's (15:15; cf. 7:51). By the reform of 15:12–13, he undoes the apostasy of 14:23–24. Asa thus becomes the first in a series of cultic reformers, to be followed by Joash, Hezekiah, and Josiah.

From a structural standpoint, this section provides a transition from the important King Jeroboam to the similarly important Ahab, whose notoriety prepares the reader for the prophetic stories about Elijah to follow.

103

A Theological Paradigm

The intention of this section of Kings is to characterize this period of history by means of a theological paradigm, in which apostasy and reform provide the chief variables. The narrative offers the reader a quick overview of this period of history, densely packed with theological judgments. The roots of the situation in which exilic readers found themselves go far back in the national history of disobedience.

The concept of paradigmatic history is not a strange one to the modern Western reader. Both Herodotus and Thucydides, to say nothing of Toynbee, have taught us to look for the larger patterns implicit in a restricted slice of history. Nor are we unfamiliar with the concept that a nation's fate and character are shaped by its early experiences. We expect a nation founded on black slavery and the expropriation of native land to have ongoing problems with racism and economic oppression. However, the modern reader does not feel at all comfortable with this insouciant linkage of a people's fidelity to God and the history they experience, so characteristic of Deuteronomistic theology.

Kings as canonical Scripture insists that the real fabric of history is not the interplay of economics or the march of national destiny but the issue of faithfulness to God. Although Kings displays none of the doctrinaire and mechanical theory of retribution evidenced by the Chronicler and some modern Christians and Jews, the book unambiguously coordinates national sin and national tragedy with a canonical confidence its readers dare never match. The intention of this coordination is not to inculcate self-righteousness or pride among those whose histories are temporarily unmarred by disaster but to call forth self-examination and repentance from every reader or group of readers whose "hearts are not wholly true to the Lord" (15:3; cf. Luke 13:1–5). There is a warning here for apostates, but also hope for repentant reformers.

Thus Kings offers the history of Judah and Israel as a paradigm of return, reform, and the consequent benefits. Exilic readers were provided with a prescription for their present situation. There remained a thin possibility that God's favor might still return to the people of Judah, even in exile. David's son remained their king; Jerusalem was still home, emotionally at least.

For the Christian church hope still rests on God's eternal promise to the house of David (15:4–5), fulfilled in Jesus the son of David who, like Asa, cleansed the temple in a public claim to royal status (Luke 19:45–46). The will of a jealous and angry God to punish sin with suffering and tragedy finds its ultimate focus in the cross upon which this "king of the Jews" was killed. These chapters remain a paradigm of the message the church offers the world. Those who have forgotten God must be warned, for "God is not mocked . . ." (Gal. 6:7). Those in exile who still long for "Jerusalem" are to be challenged with a call to reform and to renewed trust in God's promises.

PART THREE

Israel Under the Prophetic Word

I KINGS 17——II KINGS 8:15

I Kings 17
Life in the Midst of Death

The good news of the Bible is that God offers life in the midst of death (a sampler: John 5:21; Rom. 4:16–25; I Cor. 15: 20–22, 42–44). Elijah the prophet is abruptly introduced by three interlocking stories which tell of God's gift of life: from the brook and ravens in the desert (vv. 2–7), through the power of God's word and the grace of human interaction (vv. 8–16), and by the power of prayer over mortal illness (vv. 17–24). After a look at how these three stories have been interlocked, we shall consider the literary structure of each in turn. We shall then turn to the relationship these stories have with their immediate context and to biblical theology as a whole.

Three Interlocking Stories

These three stories are clearly intended to be read together, for they are held together by interlocking themes and movements. For example, the threat of drought (v. 1) points to Elijah's need to hide, first in the desert and then in a foreign land. Drought also points to a shortage of food, the theme of verses 2–6 and 7–16. Drought dominates the narrative. Elijah drinks from the brook (vv. 4, 6), but it dries up because there is no rain (v. 7). He asks water from the widow (v. 10). The miracle of meal and oil will continue until the rains come (v. 14).

The commands of God initiate Elijah's movement (vv. 3

107

and 9*a*) and the nourishing role played by the ravens and the widow (vv. 4, 9*b*). The response of Elijah and the widow to God's word is expressed by the same formula: "and he/she went and did" (vv. 5, 15). The word of God in verse 1 is confirmed by the widow's confession in verse 24.

The three stories are dominated by issues of life and death. The first story, brought to a quick close by the dried brook, introduces the issues of food and water, providence and life. The woman, swearing by the God who lives, knows she and her son will soon die (v. 12). He does die (v. 18), but lives again (v. 23). The connection between the first and second stories is much closer than the link to the third. Besides the common theme of life and death, the third story shares with the second only the figures of the son, the widow/woman, Elijah, and "his" God (vv. 12, 20, 21). The drought temporarily drops from view.

Form critically, these three stories are prophet legends, told to extol the admirable qualities of the prophets and to inculcate proper attitudes toward them and the power they represent. All three use miracles to describe the triumph of God's power. The problem they have in common is death; the resolution, mediated by a miracle, is life.

The legend of the never-failing jar and cruse authorizes the prophetic word in general. It is a word full of power. The focus is on prophetic power rather than on the fulfillment of an oracle (cf. II Kings 2:19–22 or 4:42–44). In the third story, as in the case of II Kings 1:2–17 and 6:8–23, the power of a prophet's prayer is emphasized. The legend of the revived son legitimates specifically Elijah as a man of God, rather than prophets in general. In this it resembles II Kings 2:1–18, which does the same thing for Elisha.

Taken together, these three legends present problems of increasing difficulty. God triumphs over the intensifying death grip of famine and then over death itself. For Elijah, these stories serve as a private period of preparation (cf. the temptation of Jesus). Elijah moves from passive to active readiness. In the first story he simply obeys and is fed. In the second, he reports what God will do. In the third, he takes an active role, and the Lord listens to him. These deeds are his credentials; his prophetic legitimacy is established. He is under God's protection and is an agent of God's power. The confession of verse 24

108

signals that he is now ready to go on the offensive and meet Baal in public combat.

Elijah and the Ravens (vv. 1–7)

The first verse of chapter 17 introduces the main characters in the coming conflict (chaps. 18—19, 21): Ahab versus Elijah. Elijah is introduced as a figure of mystery. He appears suddenly out of nowhere; his background is described in an obscure way. His oath (v. 1), the same one used by the widow in verse 12, introduces the drought that holds together chapters 17 and 18 and points forward to the coming test with Baal and the return of the rains.

This drought is presented implicitly as God's reaction to Ahab's policies favoring Baal. Once more there is a prophetic challenge to royal apostasy (cf. Ahijah, the man of God in chap. 13, Shemaiah, Jehu the son of Hanani). The title used by Elijah in verse 1, "the Lord, the God of Israel," ties back directly to God's anger over Ahab's sins in 16:33 (cf. 15:30; 16:13, 26). The announcement of a drought is a challenge to Baal, a direct blow at Baal's role as a vegetation and rain god. According to Canaanite myth, Baal was dead during the dry season. When rain eventually does come, the Lord will be the one to send it (v. 14), not Baal. This implicit challenge to Baal's status will become explicit in chapter 18.

The story of Elijah and the ravens (vv. 2–6) reflects the common folktale motif of the hero being fed by beasts and reminds the reader of the canonical traditions of wilderness feeding. (The LXX caught this implication and makes specific reference to Exod. 16:8, 12.) Meat twice a day would be rich fare in ancient Palestine. "From here" (v. 3) links back to Samaria where Ahab was presumably addressed in verse 1. Elijah must hide to protect God's purposes, for he is the one who will speak the word that will bring rain. The narrator emphasizes that the word of God is the prime mover in this story; Elijah is passively obedient (vv. 2, 5*a*).

Elijah and the Widow's Hunger (vv. 8–16)

The second story (vv. 8–16) takes Elijah deep into Baal's home territory, to Zarephath in Sidon. The reader remembers that Jezebel, Baal's champion, is also from Sidon (16:31). Yet the dead Baal cannot help; the vegetation god cannot feed. The

109

famine is so severe it has brought death near even for a woman well-off enough to own a house with an upper room (reading in context with vv. 17, 19).

The reader and Elijah know that this woman has been commanded by God to feed him, but she gives no hint of this herself. She is presented as a most inadequate source of support, scraping together a few sticks near the city gate. Elijah's round-about request, almost painfully polite, underlines her inade-quacy and builds tension. Caught between the demands of ancient hospitality and the harsh reality of famine, she reacts with an oath and fatalistic resignation. Verse 12 brings into view the jar and the cruse, important factors in the coming resolu-tion, and her son, a link to the next story. After she gathers a couple of sticks, the inevitable course of her fate is predicted in a brusque chain of Hebrew narrative verbs: I will go, I will prepare it, we will eat it, then we will die. The language of minimalism—a little water, a morsel of bread, a handful of meal, a little oil, two sticks, a little cake—provides a sharp contrast to the rich meals brought by the ravens and to the dependable sufficiency of verses 14–16.

Elijah's "fear not" is a common prelude to God's saving action (II Kings 6:16). "Faith tests" are not uncommon in mira-cle stories (cf. II Kings 5:10–14), and the woman's goodness and faith pass muster. In a sense this story is an improved, moraliz-ing edition of II Kings 4:1–7. There is a distinct didactic, horta-tory flavor. As Elijah's word is done by the widow (vv. 13a, 15a), so God's word is done (vv. 14, 16b). The word in question (v. 14) is close to being a magic formula or incantation (cf. II Kings 4:43), with God referred to only in the third person. The mira-cle itself is undramatic, the result emphasized by repetition. The meal continues to suffice; the level of oil in the cruse does not go down. The Lord God who lives (v. 12) grants life in the midst of death.

Elijah and the Widow's Son (vv. 17–24)

The story of the revival of the woman's son exhibits a dou-ble movement: The boy moves from death to life, the woman from disbelieving hostility to a confession of faith. Certain ir-regularities indicate that this story once had a history separate from the previous legends. The drought has been forgotten and the woman's social status seems to have improved. In the pres-

110

ent context, however, she is now to be taken as the same woman.

After the introduction (v. 17), the shape of the narrative is a balanced "sandwich" of three scenes:

> scene 1—Elijah and the woman
>   *A* the woman remonstrates with Elijah (v. 18)
>   *B* Elijah's speech and action (v. 19)
> scene 2—Elijah and God
>   *C* Elijah's query and petition (vv. 20–21)
>   *C'* God listens to Elijah (v. 22)
> scene 3—Elijah and the woman
>   *B'* Elijah's action and speech (v. 23)
>   *A'* the woman acknowledges Elijah (v. 24)

To modern readers, the narrative does not seem to be forthright as to whether the boy was actually dead or not (v. 17). Although to us this would make a critical difference, it would not to the original audience. There was no sharp line between life and death in Old Testament thought. Sickness or old age brought one down to the realm of death even while one was technically alive (Ps. 18:4–5; 116:3), and corpses were not considered to be "totally" dead for a couple of days (John 11:6, 17). For this ancient narrative, modern medical categories are beside the point. The boy was as good as dead. His mother, quite reasonably from an ancient point of view, blames Elijah. "What made you interfere?" she demands (v. 18 NEB). The presence of this prophet in her house has drawn God's attention to her so that her general sinfulness has registered on the divine consciousness. Punishment has followed as a matter of course.

The miracle takes place in private (cf. Mark 7:33; 8:23). The movement from public to private to public ("he carried him up," v. 19; "he brought him down," v. 23) focuses the reader's attention on Elijah and his dealings with God. This reversal of direction highlights the move from death to life. This structure also allows a climactic return scene which emphasizes the fact of the son's life, not the quasi-magical technique of transfering life force by contact (cf. II Kings 4:34–35; Acts 20:10). Elijah's deed is more a matter of prayer (vv. 21*b*–22) than of magic. The woman's climactic confession (v. 24) has a double thrust: Elijah is indeed a man with divine power, and he really speaks the

111

word of the Lord, including the word controlling drought and rainfall (v. 1).

The Context, (Chapters 17—19)

These legends ought not be read apart from their larger literary context. These are only preliminary rounds; the main bout with Baal will follow in chapter 18. The issues of who sends rain, gives food, and raises the dead are only preliminary to the central question to be decided on Mount Carmel. Is Yahweh God or is Baal?

Looking backward, verses 17–24 offer a sharp analogical contrast to the death of Jeroboam's son (14:1–18). Looking forward, these adventures of Elijah will be paralleled by stories told about his successor, Elisha (II Kings 4:1–7, 18–37).

With chapters 18 and 19, these three stories are part of a larger plot movement (Cohn, JBL 101:333–50). Chapter 17 tells of waiting, hiding, and preparing, along with implicit victories over Baal. Chapter 18 moves to a public challenge in which God's victory is explicit. Chapter 19 speaks of Elijah's retreat and attempted resignation and points on to a future shaped by Elisha, Jehu, and Hazael.

Chapter 17 creates narrative psychological space for the drought announced in verse 1 to reach its third year (18:1) and describes its increasing effect. This gap creates tension in the reader's mind over Ahab's possible reaction to Elijah's announcement. The theme of hiding (vv. 3, 9a) hints at Ahab's hostility and prepares for Jezebel's persecution of Elijah (18:10; 19:2). The woman's experience of the ambiguity of God's power (v. 18) parallels Ahab's (18:17). Her confession (v. 24) prepares for that of the people (18:39).

The three chapters share a similar structure which cuts across the linear flow of the story, creating an even stronger sense of unity:

> —In each, an announcement triggers a crisis. In 17:1 and 18:1 this announcement centers on rain (using a different Hebrew word from that employed in the stories themselves) and the crisis is resolved by 18:41. The announcement of Jezebel in 19:2 sets up a new crisis.
> —Each chapter is initiated with a journey by Elijah: from Ahab (17:1–3), then to Ahab (18:1–2), and finally away from the threat of Jezebel (19:3). God controls the first

two of these movements and then reasserts control over Elijah in 19:15.

—In each, Elijah experiences a double encounter which creates suspense by delaying the resolution. The first encounter is only a partial solution to Elijah's problem (ravens, Obadiah, first angel); the second (widow, Ahab, second angel) is needed for full resolution. These encounters all involve the theme of feeding in some way (17:3–4, 9; 18:5; 19:5, 7).

—Miraculous wonders resolve the problems. God responds to death with resurrection, to the question of who is truly God with fire, to Elijah's complaint with a theophany. Each involves a threefold act (17:21; 18:33–34; 19:11–12—the triple quasi-theophany), and God's response is progressively more direct each time.

—Each concludes with a conversion: by the woman (17:24), Israel (18:39), and Elisha (19:20–21).

A Matter of Death and Life

The three narratives of chapter 17 take the reader to the heart of life's deepest mystery, death. Although the woman thinks of death in traditional categories as a punishment for sin, the narrative itself offers no explanations. Even the implied connection between the death-dealing drought and Ahab's sin is left wide open. If anything, death is a reflection of the ambivalent implications of God's power and presence. The power and the word of the God who lives (v. 12) brings both death (vv. 1, 18, 20) and life (vv. 14, 22). Is Elijah a curse (v. 18; cf. Ahab's comment, 18:17) or a blessing (v. 24)? Is God's presence itself a curse (v. 20) or a blessing?

God is the prime mover in these stories, even to the point of being the author of death and famine, but the power of God is ultimately on the side of life. God commands the ravens and the widow to give life-giving food and provides miraculous sustenance. In the secrecy of the upper chamber, through the prayer of one deeply anguished by divine ambiguity, God raises the dead to life.

To a modern world caught fast in the grip of death from endemic famine, the terrorism of governments and their opponents, and the hydrogen bomb it would be good news indeed to hear that God is in charge and that God is on the side of life. To believe that would be to gain the courage to face the Ahabs

113

and Baals of our world and to engage them in mortal combat.

This God who comes down on the side of life is a universal God, who offers life even to a distressed widow of an alien people, of Baal's people, in fact. Jesus is reported to have suggested chapter 17 as a model for his own universal ministry (Luke 4:25–26), which included the gift of healing for at least one pagan woman (Matt. 15:21–28).

The common three-year lectionary pairs the story of the miraculous jar of meal and cruse of oil with Mark 12:41–44, the story of the widow's mite (Twenty-fifth Sunday after Pentecost, Year B). This underscores the exemplary nature of the widow of Zarephath, who passes the test of faith and was given the gift of life.

The lectionary also pairs 17:17–24 with the story of the raising of the son of the widow of Nain (Luke 7:11–17; Third Sunday after Pentecost, Year C). In telling the stories of Jesus' deeds of power, Luke intentionally drew parallels to verses 17–24 at several points (Luke 8:28 to v. 18; Luke 8:55 to v. 22; cf. also Acts 9:37 and 20:10). The lectionary parallel is sharpened by a direct quotation of the Septuagint of verse 23 by Luke 7:15. The miracles in these two stories are not ends in themselves but lead to confession and faith (v. 24 and Luke 7:16, cf. 18–22).

In the New Testament it is Jesus who becomes the focus of the ambiguity of God's power for both death and life. In his ministry he offered life in the midst of death by providing food, healing the sick, and raising the dead. On his cross he came under the power of that death whose ultimate author is God. By his resurrection he proclaimed that the God of the Bible is the God who wants to give life to all.

I Kings 18
The Lord, He Is God!

This is one of the most dramatic stories in biblical literature, the contest between Yahweh and Baal on Mount Carmel. This battle between two gods, fought out in the arena of human events, has captured the imagination of writers and artists.

The evident complexities and irregularities of this chapter

are the result of a complicated history of transmission about which scholars have come to no clear consensus. There are several loose ends. What happens to the carefully introduced Obadiah or the four hundred prophets of Asherah? How could Elijah be the only Yahweh prophet left if Obadiah has saved a hundred? Nevertheless, the narrative hangs together remarkably well (Childs, *Interp* 34:128–37; Jobling, *The Sense of Biblical Narrative*, pp. 63–88).

Elijah Confronts Ahab (vv. 1–20)

Verse 1 sets up an irony which permeates the coming narrative. We know rain is on the way; Obadiah and Ahab do not. Verses 2–16 describe how it happened that Elijah obeyed the command to show himself. The story is advanced more by dialogue than by action. Following the ancient literary convention that only two characters can occupy a scene at one time, Obadiah and Ahab go their separate ways for individual encounters with Elijah. This stage business and the conversation between Elijah and Obadiah slow the narrative down to retard the meeting commanded in verse 1.

At the same time, space is created for Obadiah to object to Elijah's commission (mentioned three times: vv. 8, 11, 14) with his fear of death (also three times: vv. 9, 12, 14). Here Obadiah encounters the ambiguity about Elijah's presence already experienced by the widow (17:18) and soon to be felt by Ahab (v. 17). Obadiah's conflict of loyalties is expressed by his use of the courtly "my lord" for both Elijah and Ahab (vv. 7, 10) and the frantic repetition in his speech. His greeting (v. 7) provides a contrast to Ahab's and foreshadows the people's reaction in verse 39. The concept of transport by the spirit of the Lord (v. 12; cf. II Kings 2:16; Ezek. 37:1; Acts 8:39) underscores Elijah's status as a powerful prophet. Elijah responds with a calm, impressive oath which contrasts with Obadiah's flustered fears and reasserts Elijah's position of courtly service to God (v. 15; cf. 17:1 and II Kings 3:14).

These interlocked Ahab/Obadiah and Obadiah/Elijah scenes do not really advance the action. At verses 15–16 we are still where we were in verse 1. Both the seriousness of the drought and the danger of Israel's apostasy have been made clear, however. Moreover, the necessary background of hostility has been established by verses 4 and 13. Obadiah has hidden prophets from the wrath of Jezebel. The violence Obadiah an-

115

ticipates against himself parallels Jezebel's murderous violence against the prophets (vv. 12 and 14 envelop v. 13). Whereas Obadiah has fed the prophets of Yahweh, Jezebel feeds the prophets of Baal (v. 19).

In verses 17–20, any ambiguity about Ahab is cleared up. The reader is not sure until this point where Ahab stands. He has been seeking Elijah for some unspoken purpose. The anti-prophet violence has been blamed on Jezebel, not Ahab. Yet Ahab's priorities are clearly askew (horses and mules instead of Yahweh's prophets). Elijah's counter accusation finally reveals that Ahab is a villain, although he remains a passive one throughout the narrative. The word "troubler" (vv. 17–18) is used in oath contexts, especially for someone who makes a foolish oath or breaks an oath (Achan, Josh. 6:18; 7:25; Jonathan, I Sam. 14:29). Elijah's oath (17:1), judged to be foolish by Ahab, makes him Israel's "troubler" in Ahab's opinion. But Elijah reverses the accusation, tarring Ahab with the "troubler" brush because he has broken the covenant relationship with God (Dozeman, *Studies in Bible and Theology* 9:81–93).

By making explicit the connection between the drought and apostasy (v. 18), Elijah transforms the conflict between Ahab and Elijah into a contest on a higher level. Ahab is accused of following the local baals. Whether the contest to follow is with the Canaanite high god Baal (Hadad), the local baal of Carmel, or the foreign god imported by Jezebel (Melqart or Baal Shamem) is totally immaterial in this context. Apostasy is apostasy no matter what the details. Indeed, the narrative's refusal to be precise is itself testimony to the worthlessness of all other gods. They are lumped together and dismissed. To specify precisely which Baal failed at Carmel would dilute the sweeping condemnation of them all. Israel is gathered to witness the contest (vv. 19–20), for it is their exclusive loyalty to Yahweh that is at stake (v. 21).

The Contest (vv. 21–40)

The Carmel ordeal moves from preparation (vv. 21–24) through the contest itself (Baal, vv. 25–29; Yahweh, vv. 30–38) to the consequences of Yahweh's victory (vv. 39–40). A time scheme structures the flow of events from noon (vv. 26–29) until the time of oblation (about 3:00 P.M.; v. 29) to the time of oblation itself (v. 36).

Another way of looking at the structure of verses 21–40 is to consider the five proposals made by Elijah. The proposal of verse 21 to the people is aborted when they do not answer. The second (vv. 23–24) is accepted, and the contest to determine which god will "answer" (v. 24) begins. Verse 25 is a proposal to the prophets of Baal which goes nowhere because there is no answer (vv. 26, 29). In contrast, Elijah's prayer proposal to Yahweh receives an answer (v. 37) which proves Yahweh is God. The prophet's last proposal to the people is accepted, as demonstrated by their actions (v. 40).

The exact translation of Elijah's accusation (v. 21) remains unclear, but the meaning is clear. The people must choose. To limp along undecided is in effect to choose to dance with Baal's prophets (v. 26). The refusal on the part of the people to answer pushes the narrative into conflict. In verse 24, Elijah assumes that the people are on the side of Baal ("your god"), as in fact they are. By refusing to choose, they have chosen Baal by default. The altar of Yahweh inevitably falls into ruin (v. 30*b*) in a syncretistic environment.

The contrast between the Baal prophets and Elijah could hardly be sharper. Their preparations are sketchy, their prayer abrupt, their liturgical action frantic. Nothing happens. Elijah's preparations are methodical and correct. His prayer is impressive and dignified. He does nothing; God alone acts. Things are made as hard for Yahweh as possible. Elijah is one prophet against four hundred and fifty (v. 22). Baal's people get first choice of a bull and get the chance at a preemptive victory by going first. Water poured all over Elijah's altar loads the dice against Yahweh. As a storm god, Baal ought to be able to produce lightning if he can do anything.

The narrative uses bitter, mocking humor to diminish Baal in the reader's opinion, although the details of Elijah's insults are no longer completely understood. Probably "he is musing, or he has gone aside" (v. 27) ought to be combined as synonyms into simply "he is busy" (cf. the Hebrew and Greek of Sirach 13:26), although the common suggestion that "he has gone aside" refers to Baal's being preoccupied with a bowel movement certainly captures Elijah's insulting tone! Although the idea of a busy or sleeping god would not be shocking to an ancient reader (cf. Ps. 44:23), Elijah is probably making sly references to Baal's mythological adventures and his annual

117

death sleep during the dry season, preserved for us in the Ugaritic texts. Whatever the details, Elijah is emphasizing the emptiness of Baal. He is no god; he is a joke!

The prophets of Baal unconsciously join in the joke by taking Elijah's mocking advice and crying all the louder. In what was probably a funeral rite for the temporarily dead Baal, they gash themselves to demonstrate their commitment and to attract their god's attention (cf. Jer. 41:5). Nothing happens.

The time notices (vv. 27, 29) emphasize how long the Baal prophets are at their fruitless orgy and hint proleptically that Yahweh will emerge victorious. Yahweh's liturgy (Exod. 29:39; Num 28:3–4, 8) sets the chronology, and the time for the oblation has arrived!

The description of Elijah's preparations and prayer slows the narrative and prevents the climax from coming too quickly. The excitement builds slowly; every detail is savored. There is a decided contrast between the excesses of the Baal devotees and the measured preparations and dignified prayer of Elijah. The building (or rebuilding) of the altar is described twice (vv. 30b, 31–32a). The prayer goes over the same ground twice (vv. 36b, 37). Elijah pulls out all the patriotic stops: twelve stones, twelve jars of water (four jars poured out three times), reference to the change in Jacob's name (Gen. 35:10), and the patriarchs. The nation as a whole is being recalled to its national God. Although we no longer understand the reference to seed (v. 32), it may have something to do with fertility. In any case, the trench holds twelve jars of water to increase the impressiveness of the upcoming miracle.

Elijah's prayer clarifies the stakes: The people must come to know that Yahweh is God (v. 37). It is only at verse 36 that Elijah is termed a prophet (cf. v. 22), emphasizing his authority at this moment and underscoring the emptiness of the claim of the Baal prophets to that title. Verse 37b is both intriguing and ambiguous. The people will learn that it is Yahweh who has turned them around in an about face. While the natural assumption is that this means God will have turned the people back to fidelity, it could also be taken as an assertion that God had previously caused their apostasy to Baal.

118 The dramatic descent of fire from heaven raises the narrative to its climax (v. 38). This is no ordinary lightning, for the sky is still clear. It is the weapon of Yahweh the divine warrior (Lev. 9:24; 10:2; Num. 16:35; cf. Judg. 6:21; 13:20), consuming not

only the sacrifice and the wood, but even the stones, the dust, and the water which had soaked it all. This is not just a miracle but a perfect whole burnt offering. The destruction of the altar solves the problem any deuteronomistically inclined reader may have had with this non-central sacrifice.

The consequences of this climax are twofold. As the fire fell (v. 38), the people fall (v. 39) and confess that Yahweh is God. They respond with a repeated acclamation formula from the liturgical tradition (Ps. 95:7; 100:3; 105:7) which is in perfect harmony with Deuteronomistic ideals (8:60; Deut. 4:35, 39; 7:9). The prophets of Baal are slaughtered in accordance with Deuteronomistic principles (v. 40; Deut. 13:13–15) and to offset Jezebel's murder of the Yahweh prophets. This plot line will carry on into chapter 19, where Jezebel's reaction is described (19:1–2).

Rain (vv. 41–46)

The issue of drought and rain (cf. the repetition of "rain" in vv. 41, 44, 45) has been in the background of this chapter beginning with the promise of imminent rain in verse 1. This verse points back to 17:1, which hinted that this drought was God's punishment for the apostasy of Israel. The interchange between Ahab and Obadiah, in addition to providing a way to get Ahab and Elijah together, served as an opportunity to report on the devastating effects of this drought (vv. 2*b*, 5–6). Ahab's intensive search for Elijah (v. 10) and the explosive nature of his potential reaction to a failure to find him (vv. 9, 12, 14) communicated just how frantic the king had become over the absence of rain. The Mount Carmel contest, as Elijah's prayer pointed out (vv. 36–37), forced the people to choose Yahweh over Baal and to turn their backs on the apostasy that occasioned the drought.

Alone again for a great act of prophetic power (cf. 17:19), Elijah assumes the posture of humble, intense prayer. The lad who appears out of nowhere is simply a narrative necessity to permit the spotting of the cloud while Elijah remains absorbed in prayer. There is a certain amount of confusion involving "going up" on the part of the characters, but the course of the action is perfectly clear.

Elijah is one step ahead of the rain at all times. He orders Ahab's celebration (eating and drinking as a contrast to the hunger and thirst brought on by drought) of the coming storm even before there is a cloud in the sky (v. 41). He instructs Ahab to flee, anticipating the coming impassability of the roads before a single drop has fallen (44b). The climax comes in verse 45 with a colorful description of the storm's sudden onset. The dramatic tension drains away in the denouement of Elijah's spirit-driven twenty-five kilometer run to Jezreel (v. 46). Once more, Ahab, who has been either passive or absent during much of the chapter, simply reacts to events.

Theological and Contextual Implications

The contest on Carmel deals with a critical ideological issue in Kings. Yahweh is truly and exclusively God. God punishes apostasy, in this case by drought; but God also rewards fidelity, as evidenced by the rainstorm that follows the people's return to faith.

In relation to the context of the Book of Kings, chapter 18 takes Elijah's ministry out of hiding (17:3) and moves it into public ("show"; vv. 1, 15). The themes of persecution and isolation (v. 22) will find further place in the next chapter (19:2, 10, 14), where Elijah attempts to resign his prophetic office. Fire from heaven will continue to blaze through his career (II Kings 1:10, 12; 2:11; cf. Sirach 48:1, 3b). His slaughter of the Baal prophets will find its more successful counterpart in Jehu's bloody reform (II Kings 10:7, 14) and the inevitable fall of the house of Omri. An analogous story of the one true prophet standing up against hundreds of raving false prophets follows in chapter 22.

This narrative reflects a variety of intentions. It seeks to evoke loyalty to Yahweh as the only God. It engages in mocking polemic against other gods. It demolishes any attempt at syncretism. It convinces the reader of the power of God's word to structure history. It provides an example story which calls the unfaithful to repentance.

This narrative spoke clearly to the exilic community in Babylon, faced by a temptation to syncretism or apostasy. The point of the narrative is not just that Yahweh is the God of Israel, but that Yahweh is God, period. It might look for now as though the Babylonian god Marduk has beaten Yahweh in the arena of history, but the contest on Carmel is a reminder that this cannot be so. Marduk is a non-entity, just as Baal is. Yahweh does not lose in the contest of history. Yahweh's word makes history happen.

120

As a paradigm of apostasy (16:30), Ahab turns out to be more of a bystander than an instigator. He remains essentially passive throughout, making no decisions, blandly accepting Elijah's suggestions (vv. 20, 42, 44*b*) just as he does Jezebel's (cf. the Naboth story in chap. 21). His villainy seems to rest in his refusal to make choices of any kind. This is a searing condemnation of any reader who seeks to hide from God's demand for commitment behind the screen of non-involvement, apathy, or the daily struggle to find grass for the horses. The New Testament reflects a similar distaste for a lukewarm response to God's call (Rev. 3:16).

To Yahweh alone belongs the attribute "God" (cf. I Cor. 8:5–6). What seems at first to be a battle between two competing gods turns out instead to be a contest between God and an empty delusion. The details of the liturgical practices of the Baal cult are mocked as empty efforts worthy only of scorn. The definition of divinity is relentlessly practical, bypassing all mythological constructs and philosophical argumentation. To hear prayer and to act in public is to be God. To control nature by the power of the word is to be God. The God of the Bible insists on exclusive loyalty (vv. 18, 21) from those who share in the divine promise (vv. 31, 36). Indecision or agnosticism will not do; to fail to choose is to choose Baal (v. 24*a*).

This narrative dynamically illustrates the process of coming to faith and our ability to make a choice for God. Human faith depends on God's prior willingness to succeed in the contest and to turn hearts around by this success. God is the author of faith, for without fire from heaven, no credal acclamation could follow (v. 39). Elijah sets this out clearly in his prayer (v. 37). In this sense, faith is not a matter of free human choice but is coerced by God's public act. In the aftershock of God's fiery blast, the people had no more choice about believing than did Mary or Thomas or the other witnesses to God's public act of Easter resurrection.

Yet the story of faith does not begin with verses 38–39, but with verse 24*b*. At first the people are simply unwilling to make any choice at all. Their silence in verse 21*b* rejects Elijah's insistence that they cannot serve both Baal and Yahweh. In verse 24*b*, they have moved to a willingness to choose. They accept the incompatibility of divided loyalties. To accept a contest is to acknowledge that there will be a winner and that the winner is to be the object of exclusive faith. To be willing to

121

choose is in some sense an act of faith in itself. To opt for a decision in place of syncretism, apathy, or agnosticism is really to opt for the God of the Bible, for that God cannot lose in any contest. Although the people did not know it yet, the scales that were equally balanced in verse 21 have begun to tip toward Yahweh in verse 24. In verses 38–40 they tip all the way.

The people, who already had that sort of preliminary faith which is the volition to make a choice, received proof that their choice must be for Yahweh. On the one hand, the people have chosen the option of faith freely, uncoerced by any proof. On the other, their choice of Yahweh has been forced on them by the evidence of fire from heaven. Their choice to choose was a free one and was confirmed later by experience, but their hearts were actually turned around by God (v. 37b). Fire coerced their choice and left them without option. Is faith a matter of free human choice or is it an irresistible gift from God? This narrative illustrates this interplay more clearly than any amount of theological discourse could.

God uses human instruments like Elijah to offer this challenge of decision and to convert the faithless. Elijah is God's servant (vv. 15, 36) in this narrative, not a wonder-working hero. He offers prayer (vv. 36–37, 42) rather than the performance of miracles. He is the opposite of the striving Baal prophets. The climactic acclamation is not that Elijah is a man of God (cf. 17:24) but that Yahweh is God.

God uses human instruments like Obadiah to preserve the faithful (vv. 4, 13) and to take the risks of obedience (v. 16a). The reader cannot miss the implication of the meaning of his name, "servant of Yahweh." Just as the reader is intended to follow the example of the people and acclaim Yahweh as God alone, so too the narrative coaxes obedient service along the models of Obadiah and Elijah from the reader who has decided to choose Yahweh.

I Kings 19
Elijah Burns Out and Is Recommissioned

Readers generally focus on the wrong element in this story, on the "still small voice" in contrast to the natural manifestations of wind, earthquake, and fire. In this way, Elijah's experience on Mount Horeb is read as a statement about the nature of revelation. God is not revealed in the fireworks of nature, but in a quiet word:

> Speak through the earthquake, wind, and fire,
> O still small voice of calm!
> —John Greenleaf Whittier

This is a serious misreading of the narrative. The story is really about Elijah's attempt to relinquish his prophetic office and God's insistence that he continue. Elijah and his mission are the focus, not God's presence or absence.

The genre of this narrative can be designated generally as legend, but it is not helpful to be more specific. It resembles a prophetic call narrative in several ways, but the intention is rather to describe the recall and recommissioning of a prophet. It shares in the spirit of Jeremiah's complaints to God and the responses he received (Jer. 11:18–23; 15:15–21; cf. Exod. 33).

First the "still small voice" must be put into proper perspective. Then the story of Elijah's burnout and recommissioning will be analyzed in regard to plot and narrative movement. Finally we shall explore the implications of this story for the Book of Kings and for its ancient and modern readers.

A Still Small Voice

The intent of chapter 19 cannot be grasped until the reader has worked out the implications of verses 11–12, the wind, earthquake, and fire, followed by the "still small voice." A multitude of possible meanings have been proposed:

—A rejection of the violent methods of 18:40.
—Revelation is to be found in the ordinary course of life, rather than in the spectacular manifestations of nature.
—The three violent events foreshadow the three violent figures of Hazael, Jehu, and Elisha, while the quiet theophany presages the remnant of seven thousand.
—The intelligible small voice of Yahweh's word transcends the thunder of Baal.
—The prophetic word is more trustworthy than what is seen and heard in the liturgical ceremonies of worship.
—The small voice is a private, personal revelation to Elijah, assuring him that he remains God's prophet.

123

—This is a comic touch in that the theophany offered to Elijah (the comic foil of Moses) turns out to be only the sound of silence, with no presence of Yahweh at all in the theophanic manifestations.

One cannot help wondering if some such obscure point was intended why the text could not have pointed it out more plainly! The position taken here is that this vivid scene has an important function in the plot of the story but carries no deep "theological message."

These verses use the traditional language of theophany, the natural events that heralded the coming of Yahweh in war and worship: *storm* (Ps. 18:12–14; Nah. 1:3*b*); *earthquake* (Judg. 5:5; Ps. 68:8; Nah. 1:5); *fire* (Isa. 30:27). The full impact of this theophany language can be experienced by reading Psalm 29 or Habakkuk 3:3–12. These images were often associated, as in this narrative, with the voice of God in the revelation on Sinai/Horeb (Exod. 19:16; 20:18; Deut. 4:11; 5:24). The assertion that Yahweh was not "in" the wind, earthquake, and fire is no great surprise, for the Old Testament was usually careful to separate the divine presence itself from its outward manifestations. Nevertheless, God is not completely absent in regard to these manifestations either. God does "pass by" in association with these impressive occurrences, and the wind does its damage "before" God (v. 11; ahead of God? in God's presence?).

The unwary reader tends to assume that, in contrast to the first three theophanic manifestations, God is really meant to be present in the enigmatic small voice. This is a completely unwarranted assumption, however. Nothing at all is said about God's presence in regard to this fourth event. The fact is that while God is associated with the first three events (though not "in" them), nothing relates the fourth event to God one way or the other. The actual contrast is between the fireworks of God's theophany and the quiet calm that followed, not between God's presence and absence.

The variety of translations offered for this fourth event indicate how poorly we actually understand it. Some take it to be a voice, presumably God's: "a still small voice (RSV)," "a gentle whisper (NIV)," "the soft whisper of a voice (TEV)." Others imply a more generic sound of some sort, implying a fourth natural event: a low murmuring sound (NEB)," "the sound of a gentle breeze (JB)." In any case, hearing this sound

124

or voice draws Elijah out of his cave after wrapping himself up, either as protection against the divine presence or as a sign of guilt (Esth. 7:8). It is important to the plot, but not theologically loaded.

The key to understanding these verses is the recognition that they fail to make any difference in Elijah's situation. Elijah is in exactly the same place after the theophany as before, complaining in exactly the same words (vv. 10, 14). Seen in this way, the impressive wind, earthquake, and fire are simply failed attempts by God to get Elijah out of his cave (v. 11a) and out of his depression (see below). The Lord passes by in theophanic grandeur, not "in" the wind, earthquake, and fire but certainly associated with them. But it is only when the thunderous noise has died down, to be replaced by a contrastingly quiet murmur, that Elijah is drawn out of his hiding place, still feeling just as sorry for himself as ever. His expected recommitment to the prophetic office fails to materialize at this point. The puzzling and overly famous "still small voice" is thus nothing more than a signal that the theophanic excitement is over and that Elijah can emerge so that God can try something else.

Narrative Movement

The basic shape of the narrative is provided by successive journeys made by Elijah which divide the chapter into four episodes:

1. to Beersheba—flight (vv. 1–3)
2. to the wilderness—depression (vv. 4–8)
3. to Horeb—recommissioning (vv. 9–18)
4. to Elisha—obedience (vv. 19–21)

Jezebel's messenger (v. 2) provides a contrast to the two angels (vv. 5, 7; the Hebrew word is the same) and unifies the first and second episodes. The theme of feeding provides unity both internally between episodes two and four (vv. 5–8; 21) and with the previous two chapters (17:2–6, 9; 18:4, 19). The repetition of "kiss" (vv. 18, 20) creates unity between episodes three and four.

What is at first flight motivated by Jezebel's oath soon changes into movement directed by God. Within this journey structure are set a series of manifestations of God: the angels (vv. 5, 7), the word of God (vv. 9, 13), and the theophany of verses 11–12. The first angel creates delay and suspense that is

125

resolved by the second angel, who moves the plot forward again by surprising Elijah (and the reader) with the reason for eating—a further journey.

Elijah has had enough (v. 4, *rab*), but instead of being permitted to die is sent on a long (again *rab*) journey. This provides the tension that shapes the narrative. Elijah is a burned out prophet. Will he continue to hold his prophetic office or will he give it up and die as he wishes? This tension will be resolved when it becomes clear that God refuses to let him go.

Elijah "sees" (v. 3, MT; RSV "was afraid") the implications of Jezebel's threat and goes to the safety of Judah, where Jezebel will not get credit for the death he desires. The narrative has Elijah divest himself of his servant (v. 3) so that he can be alone for the coming encounter with God and so that Elisha can eventually take his place.

Elijah is pictured as a broken, disappointed man. The picture of Elijah moping under an isolated, solitary tree (vv. 4, 5: "a single broom tree"; not expressed in the English versions) is a careful psychological touch. While guessing at the psychological motivations of characters in narratives is usually a serious exegetical mistake, in this case the reader has been provided with so many explicit symptoms that the "psychologizing" process becomes inevitable! The narrative shows deep psychological insight in describing the generalized depression that sometimes results from stress, in this case the stress of fear coupled with the stress brought on by victorious success. The person suffering from depression sits alone, contemplating the idea of death.

Psychologists tell us that such depression does not necessarily make logical sense. Elijah forgets Obadiah's hundred prophets; he ignores the great conversion on Carmel. Jezebel disappears as a villain and the whole people take her place. The burned out prophet can see only the darkest side of the situation as he voices his ego-centered complaint to God (cf. the grammatical emphasis on "I" in vv. 10, 14).

In response to this despondent complaint, God commands Elijah to come out of his cave to witness a theophany. But as we have seen above, the pyrotechnics of theophany fail to make any difference. Elijah does not come out of his hiding place until it is all over and he hears the soft murmuring sound. Although he has always claimed to stand before the Lord (17:1; 18:15; cf. 19:11), he fails to obey this time. He is unimpressed by the show and his complaint remains exactly the same as before (v. 14).

Depressed persons cannot usually be talked out of their gloom. What does sometimes help is a sense of purpose, and that is exactly what God provides with a new commission. The failed narrative pattern is complaint answered by theophany (vv. 9–12). The successful pattern is complaint overwhelmed by a new assignment (vv. 13–18). God simply will not permit Elijah to give up his office.

God's new commission for Elijah is set forth in metaphorical language which cannot be pressed too literally (vv. 15–17). The reader of Kings will discover that Elijah directly fulfills only one of these, but even then does not literally "anoint" Elisha. Furthermore, Elisha himself is only indirectly responsible for the anointing of Jehu and Hazael's murder of his predecessor. Again, although Jehu and Hazael do plenty of killing, Elisha does not literally "slay" anybody.

Elijah's complaint that he is the sole worshiper of Yahweh left (vv. 10, 14) is flatly contradicted by the heartening news that a faithful remnant of seven thousand remains (v. 18). To "bow the knee" (v. 18) means to worship (8:54). The kissing of an image is reflected in Hosea 13:2. Elijah's departure on the return journey (v. 19) signals his acceptance of this new commission and the end of his personal crisis.

On his way to the "wilderness of Damascus" (v. 15), Elijah fulfills the first part of this commission. Finding Elisha in charge of a crew of twelve men plowing together in a row (an indication of fantastic wealth), Elijah strides by and throws his mantle over him. Elisha requests a moment to say good-bye to his parents "that I may follow you" (v. 20). Elijah's response is enigmatic. Is it a rebuke in the spirit of Jesus' sayings in Matthew 8:21–22 and Luke 9:62? Does it mean simply: Go ahead, there is no problem (cf. NEB "What have I done to prevent you")?

Within the context of this narrative, Elijah's question is a way of focusing the reader's attention on the call while still leaving Elisha's response open. In the context of Kings as a whole, it preserves the mystery of the future. What has Elijah done, really? Has he anointed Elisha as his successor (v. 16*b*) or simply as a replacement for his servant (v. 3)? We must wait for II Kings 2 to find out. Elisha boils up the twelfth pair of oxen

127

in a communion sacrifice, thus marking a complete break with his former life (cf. "they left their nets . . . ," Mark 1:18).

Contextual and Theological Implications

Chapter 19 is linked to its immediate context. Once more an oath (v. 2; 17:1; 18:15) sets in motion a new series of events. Elijah's cave reminds the reader of Obadiah's (18:4, 13). Elijah's complaint (vv. 10, 14) points back to the previous chapter with its altars thrown down (18:30), the slaying of Yahweh's prophets (18:13), the forsaking of the covenant (18:18*b*), and the claim that Elijah stands alone (18:22). Chapters 18 and 19 exhibit an effective use of contrast, in this case between public, national victory and private, personal depression. The mantle (vv. 13, 19) will return as a prop when Elijah and Elisha next appear together (II Kings 2:8, 13, 14). The narrative points forward explicitly to the rise of Hazael (II Kings 8:7–15) and Jehu (II Kings 9).

The context of the Old Testament as a whole points strongly to an intentional comparison between Elijah and Moses. It is possible that the Pentateuchal presentation of this aspect of the Moses tradition received its shape from this Elijah legend, although scholars have usually assumed that the direction of dependence runs the other way. Moses too grew so despondent that he wanted to die (Num. 11:15). "Forty days and nights" sounds classically Mosaic (Exod. 24:18; 34:28). The clearest parallel is to Exodus 33:12–23; 34:33–35. Moses, disheartened about his position, asks for a special revelation of God's glory. God "passes before" (verse 11; Exod. 33:19; 34:6) Moses, showing him divine glory, God's back but not God's face, hiding Moses in a cleft in the rock and protecting him with a hand. As a result of this experience, Moses had to hide his shining face behind a veil (a parallel to v. 13?). Elijah falls distinctly short of Moses, however, by failing to respond to the personal revelation offered him.

In the New Testament, Jesus responds to a young man who has a request similar to Elisha's (Luke 9:61–62). This parallel is recognized by the ecumenical lectionary (Sixth Sunday after Pentecost, Year C). Those committed to discipleship cannot have second thoughts. The disciple of Jesus must make the same ruthless break with the past that Elisha did in verse 21, putting forth one's hand "against" (not "to"; cf. the other N.T. uses of this expression) the plow (to burn it?) without looking back.

128

Thus the Elisha episode can be seen as a call to a commitment which burns all bridges to other loyalties.

This narrative also explores the mystery of God's activity in history to punish and protect the elect. Elijah's recommissioning sets a long chain of events in motion, so that he can be said to "anoint" each of the three instruments of God's plan. In some mysterious way, God's will stands behind even such butchers as Jehu and Hazael. Somehow it is possible to equate the ministry of a prophet like Elisha with the swords of these two violent kings. On the one hand, they execute God's punishment for apostasy upon Israel. At the same time, their violence means protection for the faithful remnant of seven thousand. For the original exilic audience, who surely thought of themselves as the remnant (Jeremiah's "good figs," Jer. 24:4–7), this story must have been both a comfort and a warning.

This narrative explores the interplay between human despair and God's call in a way that speaks to exiles of any age. God can be counted on to provide in the wilderness (vv. 5–7). This theme is picked up in the lectionary pairing of this feeding story with the Johannine discourse on bread from heaven (John 6:41–51; Twelfth Sunday after Pentecost, Year B). However, the providence of God turns out to be insufficient for the human servant, prone to despondency and depression which neither logic nor the showiest theophany can cure. But God, sovereign over both nature (vv. 11–12) and history (v. 17), refuses to accept Elijah's resignation as prophet. God induces Elijah to get back to work by giving him more to do. God shrugs off Elijah's complaints and commissions him for further tasks. There may be no theophanies in Babylonian exile (or in the modern reader's own wilderness of Damascus), but there is certainly plenty to do.

God's command to Elijah is both a commission and a promise of future victory (cf. Matt. 28:19–20) in the shape of Jehu's conquest of Baal (II Kings 10:28), Elisha's ministry, and God's strange work through Hazael (II Kings 10:32–33). God's therapy for prophetic burnout includes both the assignment of new tasks and the certain promise of a future that transcends the prophet's own success or lack of it. In the light of such a future, life is worth living after all. And for the present there are tasks to be done, away from the womb-like security of a cave at Horeb, tasks which demand of us journeys deep into the wilderness of Damascus.

I Kings 20
Ahab Violates the Ban

The historian will read this chapter with a mind-set different from that of one who reads it as canonical scripture and as literature. Because these events do not fit with what we know from elsewhere about Ahab's relationship with Syria, they probably date from a later period, perhaps the reign of Jehoahaz. The historian must puzzle over the locale of these events (does v. 12 refer to "booths" or Succoth? which Aphek?), the strategic situation, and the implications of the eventual treaty. We may set these issues aside to ask how this narrative functions as literature, what effect it has upon its readers, and what theological themes it advances (see Long, *VT* 35:405–16). To do so we shall first investigate the overall narrative shape of this chapter, then follow the story itself carefully from start to finish. We shall conclude with some observations on the theological themes it raises.

This king of Israel is unambiguously Ahab (vv. 2, 13, 14, 34) whatever the historical facts might be. Ahab's antagonist Elijah has temporarily dropped out of sight, to be replaced by the anonymous prophets who populate this narrative. He will do so again in chapter 22. This is a literary reflex of the tradition of Elijah's pattern of intermittent appearances (18:12; II Kings 2:16). Elijah's absence from chapter 20 will make Ahab's words in 21:20 all the more dramatic.

Narrative Structure

The narrative makes effective use of the technique of what literary critics call the "aborted initial plot sequence." Simply stated, the plot starts in a given direction for a bit, then stops and backtracks to the beginning for a second try which advances the story line. Other examples of this are 17:2–6 and 7–16; 19:5–6 and 7–8. Ben-hadad's first demand on Ahab (vv. 2–4) goes nowhere, but his second demand (vv. 5–6) moves the plot forward with its new element of insulting unreasonableness. The first battle is indecisive; the second introduces the new element of Ben-hadad's insult to God and leads to his capture. The first prophet fails to strike, and his fate becomes a reminder of the power of prophetic threat. The second prophet moves the story forward.

The plot moves through a triple rise and fall of narrative tension, followed by a surprising twist. The narrative tension is provided by Ben-hadad's oath (v. 10). Will it prevail? The problem of Ben-hadad's aggression at first seems to be resolved by the climactic verses 20–21, but the tension is soon restored by a new complication: the predicted return of the Syrian army and the insult offered to God by verse 23. A second climax in verses 29–30 again sets up a new narrative tension. Will Ben-hadad escape with his life? Verse 33 resolves this question, and the narrative winds down into the details of treaty negotiations. Then comes the sudden twist introduced by verse 35.

The stories of the two battles, fought so that God might be known as the Lord (vv. 13, 28), are enclosed by negotiations, which at first seem to be completely secular and non-theological in outlook:

negotiation (vv. 1–11)
    battle (vv. 12–21)
    battle (vv. 22–30)
negotiation (vv. 31–34)

Then comes the surprising twist: Ahab's act of merciful diplomacy turns out to be a violation of the holy war ban. These secular negotiations are suddenly thrown into a theological framework. The chapter finds its overall unity in the prophetic word of verse 42, which provides evaluative guidance for understanding both the battles and the agreement that resulted from them.

In addition, internal narrative parallels create unity and invite the reader to reflect on what is happening. There are two consultations made by each king (Ahab: vv. 7–8, 14; Ben-hadad: vv. 23–25a and 31). The two battles are told in a parallel manner, describing first the preparations (vv. 12–15 and 22–28), then the battles themselves (vv. 16– 20 and 29–30), and finally the results (vv. 21 and 31–34).

Reflecting the genre of the prophetic battle story (cf. II Kings 19), this narrative evokes the archaic atmosphere of holy war. Tactical guidance is provided by a prophet (I Sam. 14: 36–37; 23:1–5, 10–12). The traditional formula promising vic-

131

tory is offered (Judg. 1:2; 4:7; II Sam. 5:19). The contrast of warfare in the hills versus that in the plains echoes the ancient concerns of Judges 1:19. Victory comes by surprise, and panic against hopeless odds. The wall of Aphek falls Jericho-like on the enemy. The narrative's hidden trump card of the ban (v. 42; "devoted to destruction") recalls the fate of Jericho and Ai, the story of Saul and Agag (I Sam. 15), and the crime of Achan (Josh. 7).

Preliminary Negotiations (vv. 1–11)

Verse 1 is the exposition of the central problem, with verses 2–11 offering complications. These complicating negotiations are presented in three exchanges permeated by the verb "send": verses 2–4, 5–9, and 10–11. The negotiating postures deteriorate from submission on Ahab's part through increased demands from Ben-hadad to an exchange of insults. Ben-hadad first requires verbal assent to the normal formula of vassalage (v. 3), and Ahab submits as a proper vassal should ("my lord," v. 4).

The second message of Ben-hadad contains the further demand that Ahab actually deliver up what he had theoretically proffered in agreeing to the vassal relationship. The usual English translations obscure this. Ben-hadad's increased demand is clearer if we translate as follows:

> (5) I am sending to you to say, "Deliver to me your silver and gold, your wives and your children," (6) for if I send my servants to you at this time tomorrow, they shall search your house . . . and lay hands on everything you delight in and take it away."

Ben-hadad insists that Ahab actually turn over what the standard formula of vassal submission offers, including members of the royal family as hostages. He threatens practical steps to enforce his demand if it is not met in twenty-four hours. Ben-hadad is thus presented as arrogant. His demands are outrageous.

The reader's sympathies are fully with Ahab as he refuses to submit to these extortionate demands or this humiliating search. Ahab had not refused the usual formulas of vassalage (v. 7), but this goes too far. The reader agrees with the elders and all the people: "Do not listen to him; you must not consent" (NEB). Even so, Ahab is still restrained and polite in verse 9

132

(Ben-hadad is still "my lord"), but Ben-hadad repeats Jezebel's oath (19:2) to announce the beginning of hostilities with an insulting example of ancient psychological warfare. Ahab returns a concise four-word proverb, similar to the Akkadian "he consecrated the temple before he started it" (ANET, p. 425) and our own "don't count your chickens before they hatch."

In a few verses the narrative has been able to reverse the reader's sympathies away from the antipathy for Ahab inherited from the previous chapters to a positive identification with him. Ahab's actions in the coming battle, in contrast with Ben-hadad's, continue to attract the reader's sympathies. His pious and correct preparations for holy war are enclosed by descriptions of Ben-hadad's drinking bout (vv. 12 and 16). Ahab's obedience contrasts sharply with the foolish sloth and arrogance of Ben-hadad (v. 18), who fails to see in this small band of young men much of a threat to the great army he has bragged about in verse 10.

Two Battles (vv. 12–30)

The usual translation of verse 14*b* makes it hard for the reader to follow the course of the first battle. The sequence of events to follow make it clear that Ahab does not "begin the battle." The verb means literally "to bind" and ought to be translated "clinch the battle," or in idiomatic English, "wrap up the fighting." Admittedly, this translation will not work for II Chronicles 13:3, where the verb is used in a similar context, but it does correspond to what Ahab actually does here (v. 21).

The "servants of the governors of the districts" were a special forces unit composed of young, unmarried men. They left the city around noon (v. 16), hardly a normal time for attack but a narrative necessity to permit Ben-hadad time to get drunk. They went out first (v. 17), lulling Ben-hadad into a false sense of confidence; then the army proper followed to capitalize on the initial shock (v. 19). Each soldier killed his opponent; the Syrians broke and ran (v. 20). Finally, King Ahab led a third group out to mop up (v. 21) in accordance with the advice of verse 14.

The perspective rapidly flips back and forth from the Israelite advance to scenes in the Syrian camp: verses 16*a*, 16*b*, 17*a*, 17*b*–18, 19. This is a narrative technique for describing simultaneous action found elsewhere in the Hebrew Bible and is not unknown in modern film and television editing.

133

This first climax, however, does not resolve the central problem, for Ben-hadad escapes (v. 21). The prophet underscores this (v. 22). When the campaigning season returns (cf. II Sam. 11:1), Ben-hadad will be back. A chiastic pattern is visible in verses 22–27:

> A advice to Israel (v. 22)
> > B advice to the Syrians (vv. 23–25)
> > B' mustering of the Syrians (v. 26)
> A' mustering of Israel (v. 27)

In the second battle, the situation is much the same as before. Ben-hadad replaces his army exactly as it was (v. 25); Israel is badly outnumbered (v. 27). Yet a new complication is offered by Ben-hadad's advisors, for their analysis of the situation involves an insult to God (comparable to the insult offered by Sennacherib, II Kings 19:16–19). The prophet carries the same message as before to Ahab, but now a reason for the coming victory is offered. God intends to make it clear that Yahweh is not simply a god of the hills (v. 28).

After a seven-day delay (which prevents the plot from rushing too quickly to its conclusion, cf. 18:43–44), God avenges this insult by a stunning victory involving tremendous casualties. In a reprise of the conquest of Jericho, for which the reader has been prepared by 16:34, the wall of Aphek falls on the remnants of the Syrian army. The Israelites may have had the technical expertise to undermine the wall in a siege operation, but the narrative intends for the reader to think of divine intervention. Again, the narrative is left open-ended by the possibility that Ben-hadad will escape once more (v. 30b).

Surrender Negotiations (vv. 31–34)

A shift in narrative tension is set up by verse 31. Will Ben-hadad escape with his life? In an ironic reflection of Ahab's proverb of verse 11, the servants of the Syrian king gird on sackcloth, putting their hope no longer in their military forces (as in vv. 24–25), but in the reputation for mercy attributed to the kings of Israel. The narrative moves back to the dialogic movement with which it began.

Once more there are three exchanges (vv. 32, 33, 34), only now the negotiating postures have been reversed. Now Ben-hadad uses the vassal language of "your servant" (v. 32). Now

134

Ahab is the active party. Ahab refers to Ben-hadad as "brother." The Syrian king's servants quickly react, and this becomes the basis for the climax reached in Ahab's instructions, "Go and get him" (v. 33). The messengers disappear as Ben-hadad is brought up into the royal chariot as an equal. The negotiations run their course face to face. Lost towns are returned. Israelite merchants are provided space in Damascus for shops and residences. Ahab lets Ben-hadad go on the terms of this treaty.

There are no surprises here for the reader who has come to sympathize with Ahab, now characterized as a "king of mercy." These negotiations are in line with the realities of international politics. All kings are indeed brothers. Death is only for the soldiers in the ranks. Ben-hadad's humiliation is a satisfying conclusion, an appropriate punishment for his arrogance and impiety. Here endeth the lesson. But then comes the twist. Ahab has been set up, and so has the reader!

The Surprise Twist (vv. 35–43)

Just where the narrative is moving with verse 35 is not immediately apparent to the reader. At first this new episode seems to be a digression. We may ask, Why must the prophet actually be struck and wounded? Why not just wear a bandage as a disguise and as support for his claim to have just come out of the battle? The answer is one involving literary effect. The "aborted initial plot sequence" (see above) does more than offer an excuse for a bandage; it provides the reader with interpretive guidance for understanding what is to come. The reluctant prophet is set up just as Ahab will be! It is just as outrageous to strike a fellow prophet as it is to slay a brother king, but the consequence for disobeying either command of God is death.

The disguised prophet tells Ahab a "juridical parable," intended to cause the king unwittingly to pronounce judgment on himself. Other examples may be found in II Samuel 12:1–4 and 14:5–7. That the large sum of a talent of silver (v. 39) was to be the restitution seems to indicate that the prisoner was of high status. Or is this a realistic touch portraying a poor man trying to gain the king's sympathy? "So shall your judgment be," replies Ahab, "you yourself have decided it" (v. 40), but these words turn out actually to apply to himself, for he has judged his own fate.

135

The climax comes in verses 41–42. How Ahab recognized

the other man as a prophet is important for a historical understanding of the prophetic office, but immaterial to the narrative
itself. The focus shifts quickly from the concept of being responsible for a valuable captive entrusted to one's safekeeping to a
much more serious crime, violation of the holy war ban. The
reader is surprised by this sudden escalation of the stakes. God
reveals that Ben-hadad is literally "the man of my ban" (v. 42;
Hebrew *herem*), whom Ahab has let slip from the hand into
which God's holy war victory had delivered him (vv. 13, 28).
What seemed at first to be reasonable behavior between kings
has turned out to be an offense against the law of Deuteronomy.
Ahab and his people must take Ben-hadad's place under the
deadly ban, life for life, people for people. Verse 43 provides the
denouement.

Theological Themes

The intention of chapter 20 is generally the same as its
immediate context. Ahab's "resentful and sullen" attitude links
this narrative to the one to follow (cf. 21:4), just as the anger of
God, mentioned first in 16:33, will push on to Ahab's death
(22:20) by way of a second prophetic threat (21:19). Chapter 20
offers another negative evaluation of Ahab as a violator of Deuteronomic law.

Its special effectiveness results from the twisting reversal in
its plot. The text begins by heroizing Ahab, selling the reader
on his cool response to crisis (vv. 7, 9, 11, 22), his scrupulous
adherence to holy war procedure (vv. 14–15, 19–21), his mag-
nanimous mercy to a defeated foe (vv. 31–33). Then the narrative takes a twist and turns against king and reader. The
bandaged prophet leads both down a seemingly innocuous
byway, then surprises both with an oracle packed with deadly
threat. Ahab's well-meant deal turns out to be a violation of
God's law, for which he and his people must die.

On the surface of things, Ahab knew nothing about this
application of the ban to Ben-hadad. Neither did the reader.
The king seems to have been set up by a divine ruse, mirrored
in the bandage that hid the prophet's features. God will play a
second, deadlier trick on Ahab in chapter 22. Yet on another
level, both king and reader should have known about this ban
all along. The narrator has played fair. That this was holy war
has been obvious since verse 13. The reader should have

136

remembered the analogous story of Saul and Agag (I Sam. 15). The collapse of Aphek's wall alone should have been hint enough that the full ban was in force, that its inhabitants, like Jericho's, were devoted to destruction. The law of the ban is unambiguous (Deut. 20:16–18).

Upon fuller reflection, the reader must agree that Ahab was just as culpable as the hapless clown in the prophet's parable, who "was busy here and there" and became guilty of sin through sheer inattention and misplaced priorities.

For exilic readers living in an environment in which accommodation to the surrounding culture was a fact of life, this narrative was a call to reexamine their behavior in light of God's law. What on the surface might seem an acceptable and even enlightened action, could on deeper reflection turn out to be a fatal betrayal of their religious identity (cf. the legends in Dan. or I Cor. 8). Ahab was acting according to the enlightened morality common to kings of all ages, but this did not save him from the deadly effects of misplaced priorities and the failure to pay proper attention.

How much more effective than any Deuteronomistic sermon this is! Biblical narrative sometimes sneaks up on the reader to deliver an unexpected blow. The parables of Jesus often depend on surprise to produce their effect, sometimes one of shocking condemnation. The man without a wedding garment (Matt. 22:1–14) is a functional parallel to chapter 20 in several respects. In both texts the reader is invited to self-examination by means of a surprise ending.

Whether this narrative can still deliver its punch to a modern audience is an open question. The holy war ban is alien and unacceptable to most readers. Religiously sanctioned genocide is light-years distant from what we have come to expect of God. The modern reader is likely to leave the narrative just as Ahab did, "resentful and sullen." Yet if the reader can get beyond this barrier, the call to reexamination and reevaluation is still a valid one. What betrayals and violations of God's will are hidden in the everyday morality of our modern lives? What vital loyalties to God are missed when one is "busy here and there"? What seemingly enlightened actions of mercy (v. 31) or shallow "brotherhood" (v. 32) may actually turn out to be betrayals of our faith and identity as God's people? At this point the preacher and teacher must take over as the exegete falls silent.

137

I Kings 21
Royal Tyranny and Prophetic Condemnation

The tale of Naboth's vineyard illustrates two well-worn bywords. One is cynically political: "Power corrupts" (Lord Acton). The other is a statement of faith: "Though the wrong seems oft so strong, God is the Ruler yet" ("This Is My Father's World," M. D. Babcock).

After attempting to clear up a couple of puzzles involving geographic and legal issues, we shall examine the literary artistry of the chapter as a whole, then look more closely at the episodes of royal tyranny (vv. 1–16) and prophetic condemnation (vv. 17–29).

Puzzles

Before the reader can consider the shape and effect of the Naboth story, there are several puzzles to be solved. One concerns locale. The action begins in Samaria, according to the context (20:43), and ends at the vineyard (21:18). All sections of the text agree that Naboth's vineyard was in Jezreel, unless one insists on reading verse 18b in a way that puts it in Samaria. Jezreel is precisely where one would expect to find a Jezreelite's ancestral inheritance. Ahab thus has two palaces, one in Samaria (v. 4) and one in Jezreel (v. 2). Although several commentators have read II Kings 9:25–26 as suggesting that Naboth died on the site of his vineyard, the passage does not explicitly say this. Nevertheless, chapter 21 leads the reader to assume that Naboth's condemnation and trial took place in Jezreel, "his city" (vv. 8, 11).

So far so good, until 22:38 is reached. This locates the deaths of both Naboth and Ahab in Samaria. This irregularity is likely due to some oversight in the redactional process, but it now causes a transfer of the locale of verses 11–13 to Samaria. The thought of the elders and nobles of Jezreel holding court in Samaria is awkward, but the alternative is to read 22:38 as a mistake in prediction or sloppy fulfillment on God's part, possibilities which hardly fit with the overall intention of these narratives. The effect on the reader when 22:38 is reached, therefore, is to cause a reinterpretation of chapter 21 in light of chapter 22, the death of Ahab brought on by God's ruse. This reinterpretation is likely to involve more than just geography.

A second puzzle involves legal issues. We do not really understand the mechanics of land tenure and sale in Israel. The "levirate law" (Deut. 25:5–10) indicates that it was critically important for inherited land to remain in the family. Leviticus 25:23 seems to prohibit any permanent sale, but such transactions certainly did happen (Micah 2:2)! Comparative materials from Mari and Ugarit indicate that land transfer was under strict control, but that legal fictions could be arranged to permit it. If there really were no possibility of such a sale, why would Ahab have asked? How could his sulky reaction to Naboth's refusal be explained? The real sticking point is not any legal barrier, but that Naboth had put himself under an oath not to sell (v. 3).

The text never indicates that Jezebel is operating out of a different (Canaanite) legal tradition. She is simply appeasing her husband's desire for the property. She does not so much bypass the law as bend it to her own ends. Royal confiscation of the inheritance of executed criminals was unknown in Israel's law, although there is at least one foreign example (Alalakh, 17).

An Artistically Told Story

This is a "story" in the literary sense of the word, consisting of episodes reflecting plot and characterization. The situation is presented in verses 1–2. A complication is offered by verses 3–7 in the shape of Naboth's refusal, which threatens to bring the story to a premature end. Jezebel's plot leads to a penultimate climax in verse 16, but the reader knows that things cannot rest here. The moral tension produced by this injustice must be resolved. The true climax comes only with Elijah's sweeping condemnation of Ahab and Jezebel. The repentance of Ahab releases the tension as a sort of denouement, and the resultant delay of punishment permits the larger story to flow on to chapter 22.

The plot line for Ahab reflects a misleading upward movement in each half of the story. In verses 1–16 he moves from non-possession to possession. In verses 17–29 he moves from a sentence of death to a new chance at life. However, the gift

139

Jezebel gives him in the first half turns out to be a source of death for him, and the promise of life at the end still includes a heritage of death for his sons.

The chapter is held together by the themes of eating and fasting (cf. chaps. 17—19). Ahab reacts to Naboth's oath by refusing to eat (v. 4). Jezebel insists that he do so (v. 7), while instigating a fast. The dogs will lap up Ahab's blood and will eat Jezebel's body, while both birds and dogs will devour the rest of Ahab's family (vv. 19, 23–24). Finally, Ahab reacts to this announcement by fasting (v. 27). Although Jezebel is the prime mover in the narrative and Ahab is the center of attention, Naboth is strongly present as well. His name is mentioned as often as the other two put together, including six times after his death.

From another perspective, the narrative can be said to shift gears between verses 1–20a and 20b–29. The language used by Elijah, God, and the narrator becomes Deuteronomistic. The horizon expands from the narrow concerns of Ahab's career to a wider panorama through oracles pointing back to Jeroboam and forward to Jehu, a concern to explain the further continuance of the Omri dynasty, and verbal links to the evaluations of the Northern kings (cf. 16:31–33). The smooth sentence flow becomes awkward and irregular. Although historical critical explanations have been advanced to explain this transition, there has been no agreement on details. In any case, this change creates a textual unit that operates in two modes to effect a negative evaluation of Ahab and Jezebel. The first mode (vv. 1–16) makes this point through an artistically told story. The second mode (vv. 17–29) makes it by heaping up successive condemnations by the prophet, God, and the narrator.

Royal Tyranny (vv. 1–16)

Verses 1–16 are shaped as dialogue punctuated by action. The dialogue between Ahab and Naboth results in Ahab's sulk (vv. 1–4). This leads to the dialogue between Ahab and Jezebel that results in her plot (vv. 5–14), the successful completion of which leads to the final scene between king and queen and Ahab's move to take possession (vv. 15–16). In a bracketing movement, verses 1–4 are related to verse 16 (Ahab and the vineyard) and verses 5–7 link to verse 15 (Jezebel and Ahab). Together they enclose Jezebel's successful plot (vv. 8–14).

After an awkward linkage to chapter 20 (which the RSV moves to v. 2), the reader is informed about the existence of Naboth and his vineyard and Ahab's offer to buy it (vv. 1–2; exposition). Ahab is identified as "king of Samaria" in line with the viewpoint of the later Judean narrator (cf. II Kings 1:3). The request to "give" opens the negotiations for purchase, as in Genesis 23:4. There is no royal pressure. This is an uncomplicated business proposition backed up by the fair offer of a better vineyard or money.

However, Ahab's proposal to use the vineyard as a "vegetable garden" is a hint that something deeper is going on. This seems to be an ironic reference to Deuteronomy 11:10, which contrasts the vegetable garden of Egypt to the land of promise. The reader may be intended to remember at this point that Israel is pictured as a vineyard under God's care in the Old Testament metaphorical tradition (Isa. 3:14; 5:1–7; Jer. 12:10). Other indications in the narrative point to the theology of the land as the ideological background: Naboth's use of the loaded word "inheritance" (v. 3), Jezebel's use of "take possession" (v. 15; a Deuteronomistic code verb for the conquest; cf. Deut. 15:4 for both words together), and the explicit evocation of God's gift of the land in verse 26. If the "portion of ground" *(heleq)* is to be restored in the text of verse 23, as is usually done, this offers yet another contact to Deuteronomistic land theology (Deut. 12:12; 14:27).

The plot complication is introduced by Naboth's oath. He will not have the vineyard God gave to his ancestors turned into an Egyptian-like vegetable garden. Ahab is stymied by this adjuration in Yahweh's name and goes home to sulk, his actions being external clues to his psychological state.

Then Jezebel takes the initiative. In this narrative, as in others, Ahab is presented as a character who reacts to the initiatives of others. Ahab remains fixated on Naboth's refusal (vv. 4, 6), as though that were the end of things, but Jezebel knows how to turn the oath that has stopped Ahab cold to the advantage of the royal house. Her words to Ahab (v. 7) may be a rhetorical question (RSV), a sarcastic indicative (JB: "You make a fine king of Israel!"), or a comforting prediction ("Now you will exercise royal authority in Israel"). Perhaps reflecting a foreign opinion on limitless royal authority, she will succeed where Ahab has been blocked (note the grammatical emphasis

141

on "I"). Jezebel will "give" the vineyard which Naboth would not (cf. vv. 2, 6).

Literally taking over the royal authority, she addresses a letter (just one in the Hebrew idiom, cf. II Kings 19:14) to two groups in Jezreel predisposed to support the king. The "nobles" are thought to be those holding land grants from the royal bounty. The repetition of the contents of her letter is a narrative technique communicating precise fulfillment. All goes according to plan. Verse 11 makes Jezebel's responsibility as instigator totally clear by repetition. Naboth's death is encompassed by her involvement (vv. 11 and 14).

Her call for a fast may be a response to Naboth's alleged offense against God or simply a suspension of regular business to permit a court session. Naboth is sitting in the first rank of the people (not "on high" as RSV) in order to make the contrast of his fall more impressive. The event at first seems similar to the land tenure hearing of Ruth chapter 4, but the required two witnesses (Deut. 17:6; 19:15) soon turn it into a trial for blasphemy and lèse-majesté (Exod. 22:28; Lev. 24:14–16). The last words of verse 10 make the purpose of this legal charade clear: "that he may die."

The two witnesses apparently distort the oath of Naboth's refusal into an abusive use of Yahweh's name. Such distortions are a common enough legal ploy (Matt. 26:61). Another possibility is that they are alleging that Naboth had backed out of a sale agreement guaranteed by an oath in Yahweh's name. The thought of cursing God's name is so offensive that the narrator (or some later scribe) cannot be brought to say it, so the Hebrew literally reports that Naboth "blessed God and the king." The mention of stoning becomes almost a refrain (vv. 10, 13, 14, 15). In the last two of these verses, the verb is thrown into the passive by the elders, as if to wash their hands of the crime.

In Jezebel's cold communication to Ahab (v. 15), Naboth is reported as simply dead, as if to suggest that Ahab is being shielded not only from actually committing juridical murder but even from any knowledge of it. Yet the narrative implicates Ahab in the crime anyway by beginning verses 15 and 16 with the same words: "as soon as Jezebel heard" / "as soon as Ahab heard." The chain of responsibility is unbroken. Jezebel may have "incited" Ahab (v. 25), but his move to take possession is one unified act with her murderous plot, as Elijah states clearly (v. 19a).

Prophetic Condemnation (vv. 17–29)

In verses 17–29, two private divine communications to Elijah (vv. 17–19 and 28–29), each beginning with identical words, bracket the confrontation between Elijah and Ahab (vv. 20–24). Ahab enters this confrontation under the domination of Jezebel, but leaves it under the domination of Elijah and the word of God. The actual delivery of the first oracle to Ahab (v. 19*b*) is not reported, but the reader may assume it was (cf. 16:3–4). The final word of delay (v. 29) is never reported to Ahab either, because this oracle is for the eyes of the reader, who needs it to interpret coming events.

Both the accusation and threat of verse 19 receive strong emphasis by full commission and messenger formulas. The effect is solemn and ominous. The reader has not been prepared for the assertion that dogs have licked Naboth's blood, which adds to the brutal shock of this prediction. Verse 19 concludes with a strong grammatical emphasis on "your own blood." Verse 20 recalls the dramatic meeting of 18:17.

Deuteronomistic language takes over in strident, unambiguous condemnation. Because Ahab has done "evil," God will bring "evil" on him (vv. 20–21). Elijah's words merge into God's at verse 21 and then into the narrator's by verse 25. The placing of quotation marks becomes a vexing problem for translators. The prophet, God, and the narrator all agree in a single Deuteronomistic chorus. The offense of the royal couple is not presented as a crime against Naboth or the ideal of justice so much as an offense against God.

Ahab's repentance reflects his crime. "As soon as he heard" (v. 27) points the reader back to verses 15 and 16 (the similarity is clearer in the Hebrew than in RSV). Again there is a fast, a real one this time, not a sham. This episode takes the literary pattern of the "schema of reprieve" (cf. I Sam. 15:24–31; II Sam. 12:13–14). As such, it is an analogous narrative to the report of Josiah's repentance (II Kings 22:11, 18–20). It is a central mystery of the Book of Kings that Josiah's pious turning back to God will lead to no greater reward than does the repentance of Ahab but to a mere delay in judgment for a generation.

Larger Connections

143

The parallel to Josiah is just one of several connections to the larger sweep of Kings. This narrative is built strongly into its context by a network of doom oracles upon Ahab and his family that interlock at this point. The most important of these concerns the end of the Omride dynasty, verses 21–22, 24. It is nearly identical to the oracle against Jeroboam's house (14: 10–11) and close to the one for Baasha (16:3–4). This dynastic doom is delayed (v. 29) until the reign of Ahab's second son, to be explicitly fulfilled in II Kings 10:17 when Jehu kills all the males of the royal house.

Two other oracles promise doom to Ahab (v. 19b) and Jezebel (v. 23). Ahab's blood is licked by the dogs in the place of Naboth's death in 22:38 (there Samaria). Jezebel's doom is enveloped by that of her husband in the text. The ancients viewed the loss of a body before burial with great horror. This oracle is fulfilled exactly by II Kings 9:36. The addition of extra details by II Kings 9:37 suggest that the narrator's attitude towards prophetic fulfillment was not a mechanical one. II Kings 9:25–26 reports a parallel doom oracle, said to have been overheard by Jehu.

The Naboth incident reflects the character of a didactic moral tale, the sort of cautionary story one uses to back up ethical instruction. Do not oppress your weaker neighbor, for divine punishment falls on those who pervert justice for their own ends. Naturally such a warning is relevant to any century and all forms of human government.

The God of the Bible brings down kings who act unjustly, for they rule only by God's mandate (Rom. 13:1–7). Along with Isaiah 5:8 and Micah 2:2, this story is a reminder that offenses against the heritage of the defenseless are offenses against God, not just against some abstract principle of economic justice. It may once have been told to uphold the traditional property laws that shielded the heritage of the poor from the greed of the rich and powerful. In the context of Kings, it serves to illustrate the generalized accusation against Ahab made by 16:30, 33 with a vivid, personalized crime that has the power to outrage the reader and motivate repentance and action.

This sort of thing has happened throughout history (Napier, *Interp* 30:3–11) whenever vineyards are within range of a more powerful party's covetousness. The argument of what Napier calls "adjacency" has justified United States foreign policy in Latin America, to say nothing of Hitler's in Poland or that of the ancient Persians in regard to Greece. Some Naboths give in. Others refuse, and then "adjacency" leads to betrayal and

144

death. The community which accepts this story as Scripture must read its newspapers and then ask itself hard questions. Who are the Ahabs and Jezebels? Who are the Naboths? What is the shape of the conspiracy this time?

Piety often cloaks oppression. The invocation of God is the center of Jezebel's scheme (v. 10). The community of faith must always ask if it is functioning as Elijah, bearing the word of God to governments and corporations. Or is it playing Ahab's role, sharing in Jezebel's responsibility by permissive silence and quietism? Read this way, the word of God in this story may turn out to be the "enemy" (v. 20) of a complacent church. Like Ahab, the church is not just under Jezebel's influence, but under the power of the word from God as well.

I Kings 22:1–40
God's Ruse Against Ahab

A great deal of effort has gone into understanding the origin and growth of the story of Ahab and Micaiah, although there has been little scholarly agreement. This highly complex narrative has as its base a "battle report" (cf. the two examples in chap. 20), but this has been drastically modified for artistic effect, enriched with a variety of prophetic genres, including the holy war "conveyance formula" (Judg. 1:1–2), two "vision reports" (cf. Amos 7:1–6 and especially Isa. 6:1–10), and the motif of symbolic action.

Whatever its origins, however, the present text works perfectly well as a narrative. Although historians have convincingly suggested that Ahab's campaign against Syria actually took place a generation later in the reign of Jehoahaz, Kings sets this account unambiguously into the career of Ahab. It closes his "file," opened in 16:29. We shall look first at the overall patterns and connections reflected in this story, next at its narrative flow. Finally we shall search for meaning.

Patterns and Connections

A literary reading of this chapter means reading it under the influence of its context. Verse 1 ties this chapter tightly to chapter 20, and verse 38 explicitly links back to chapter 21. The

145

reader has been "pre-instructed" by context to have certain expectations of the story as it unfolds. Because it follows two successful military efforts against the Syrians involving prophetic aid, the reader has expectations of a third victory, at least up through verse 15. On the other hand, this chapter also follows oracles threatening Ahab with death and the people with some unspecified disaster (20:42; 21:19, 21), so that the reader begins this new story with some doubts about the outcome, even before verse 17 reveals Ahab's fate. The disguise of the trickster prophet in 20:38 and the lying ruse of 21:9–13 prepare the reader for another subterfuge. This story is also linked to the Edomite campaign of II Kings 3:4–27, especially by the similar role of Jehoshaphat (cf. verses 4, 5, 7 to II Kings 3:7, 11).

In the larger context of Kings, two other royal deaths resonate with that of Ahab. The death of his son Jehoram, which will bring the dynasty of Omri to an end, also involves an arrow, Ramoth-gilead, and the kings of both Israel and Judah. The latter is carried back for burial in a chariot (II Kings 9:21–28). The second parallel is the death of Josiah, which takes place in a similar atmosphere of predicted peace (II Kings 22:20) and violent death (II Kings 23:29), under a pattern of a delay in divine punishment (cf. 21:29). A chariot takes Josiah's body back for burial.

The reader is confronted by a rich narrative texture exposing tensions at several levels. Jehoshaphat is both willing to fight (vv. 4, 29) and hesitant (vv. 5, 7). At points the conflict is that of king versus prophet; at other times it is prophet versus prophet. Much narrative effort is expended to confront Ahab with the oracles of Micaiah, but they seem to have little actual effect on the course of events. The story touches on the interplay of human intentions (vv. 4, 30), divine plan (v. 20), and sheer accident (v. 34). It starts as a story about a military plan, but ends with its focus on the death of Ahab, not the failure of his strategy. The people who were to have gone home in peace (v. 17) end up fleeing before the Syrians (v. 36).

The contrasting patterns woven by lies and the truth are especially intriguing. God sends a lie to the four hundred "false" prophets, who speak the "truth" as they know it. Micaiah, the true prophet, after an oath to tell the truth (v. 14), tells a lie instead to support God's ruse (v. 15). Ahab, who wants to hear the lie, still demands the truth (v. 16). Then Micaiah reveals the

146

truth (vv. 17, 19–23), but this too advances God's plan. Both lie and truth drive Ahab into battle, setting up the pivotal test of Micaiah's word in verse 28 and Ahab's deceptive attempt to evade his doom (v. 30). The wounded Ahab, propped up in his chariot, continues the theme of deception. Even the final notice of fulfillment (v. 38) contains a geographic surprise for the reader, who had expected this event to take place at Jezreel (21:19), not Samaria. The prophetic word does not come "true" in a literalistic sense.

Tracing the Narrative Flow

The plot of the narrative is basically that of a battle report. The early sentences (vv. 1–6) of the narrative start on a positive note and move along briskly. The exposition consists of verses 1–2 (introduction of characters, general situation) with an unsurprising complication offered by verses 3–4 (How can we get Ramoth-gilead back? Will Jehoshaphat go along?). The reader is led to agree that Ahab's cause is just; the border city of Ramoth-gilead belongs to Israel. The prospect of Israel and Judah uniting in free (if not equal) alliance to reach a shared national goal sounds ideal. Certainly God ought to support such a venture! The expected practice of obtaining an oracle is followed (20:13–14, 28; I Sam. 23:1–4) and the same message is received as in the last two thrusts against Syria (20:13, 28). This scrupulous piety and prophetic assurance tempt the reader to expect a positive outcome.

Jehoshaphat's unmotivated request for a second opinion introduces a second complication (vv. 7–15). The expected movement of the plot is held up and replaced with another direction. The haste to get to war, implied by the rapid pace of the narrative so far, now slows down into a leisurely exploration of prophetic conflict. A new concern is introduced, the validity of the prophetic word. The seeking and finding of Micaiah brackets the scene of verses 10–12, which is marked grammatically as something that happens at the same time as the search. While Micaiah is sought out, the four hundred prophets further support their earlier positive word. Zedekiah, introduced as their single representative in order to function in the later conflict with Micaiah, seconds their word with a symbol of invincible aggressiveness (v. 11). Their second oracle (v. 12*b*) is an advance on verse 6, an even clearer promise of victory. There

147

is no hint yet that the reader is supposed to suspect these four hundred or discount their word, except perhaps Jehoshaphat's reluctance.

At first the consultation with Micaiah offers no major change in the course of the plot. Basically it is a replay of the consultation with the four hundred, with the same request (vv. 5, 7), the same question (vv. 6a, 15a), and the same answer (vv. 6b, 15b). However, verse 8 introduces antagonism between the king of Israel and Micaiah (cf. v. 18) and divides the prophets into two camps, those who prophesy good and those who speak evil. The messenger's caution (v. 13) seems to reflect Ahab's suspicions and provides Micaiah with a chance to place himself in the category of a prophet who speaks only what God says. The reader is thus led to expect that his word will be evil (v. 8) and the truth. But Micaiah's word (v. 15) turns out to be unexpectedly positive. Verse 14 indicates that this is truly God's message, but it has not yet been revealed to be a lie also. With the prophetic assurance seconded by both Zedekiah and Micaiah, the story finally seems ready to move on to battle and victory.

Then comes a third complication (vv. 16–23) which derails the battle report's forward movement, reinforcing the antagonism between Ahab and Micaiah and establishing an antagonism between Ahab and God. Now the king, who knows from experience (v. 8) that something is wrong, insists on the truth in order to prove to Jehoshaphat that Micaiah is an enemy of the state. A back and forth movement between Ahab and Micaiah (v. 15b to 16 to 17 to 18) sets up the contrast between Micaiah's first word (the lie) and his second (the truth). Ahab demands truth (v. 16) and rejects the positive lie. Ahab cannot know absolute truth from falsehood any better than the reader at this point, but he does know that verse 15b cannot be the truth as Micaiah sees it.

Micaiah's vision in verse 17 (cf. Matt. 9:36) offers two items of information: the absence of the shepherd, implying the death of the king, and the contrasting return of the people in peace. For the shepherd as a metaphor for the king, see II Samuel 5:2 and Zechariah 13:7. Here the king's fate is divorced from that of the people. Micaiah (and God) may be the enemy of the state, as Ahab wished to prove, but not of the people. In a sense, Ahab has been vindicated (v. 18); what he said in verse 8 has been proven to be true. He correctly interprets this ambiguous vision

148

as evil and seems oddly pleased about it. Ironically, Ahab's victory in prying the truth out of Micaiah simply confirms his hate for the prophet, and this prejudice leads to his doom. Knowing the truth does not save him from the fate God has in store for him.

Micaiah then offers his second vision, that of the divine throne room (Job 1:6–12; Isa. 6:1–8). This heavenly plotting ironically reflects the earthly throne scene described in verses 10–12. Although the modern reader might explain the false message of the four hundred prophets as intentional deception or crowd pressure, Micaiah's vision offers instead an explanation of how the prophets could be inspired and deceived at the same time. These four hundred are not intentionally "false prophets." God still controls what they speak. They are part of God's ruse to entice or deceive (Jer. 20:7; Ezek. 14:9) Ahab that he might fall at Ramoth-gilead.

Verses 24–28 sharpen the general prophetic dispute into a personal feud between Zedekiah and Micaiah, while the antagonism already established between Ahab and Micaiah is deepened. Zedekiah slaps his rival and receives a threatening oracle in return. What he will see (v. 25) will back up what Micaiah saw (vv. 17, 19) and answer his insulting question (v. 24; cf. NEB). The implications of fleeing to an inner chamber are clear from 20:30, but the oracle against Zedekiah remains open-ended and ambiguous.

Micaiah is imprisoned, perhaps to contain a likely source of demoralization (cf. Jeremiah), perhaps to keep him handy for execution as a false prophet (Deut. 18:20), perhaps to weaken the force of his oracle. Micaiah is to be fed siege food (Isa. 30:20). To weaken the prophet is to diminish the power of his word. The circumstances of Micaiah's imprisonment are told in great detail, but the narrative does not pick up on the fate of either Zedekiah or Micaiah again. The central focus of the story is not the conflict between true and false prophecy but Ahab's inevitable death and the power of the word of God.

Ahab receives a further warning (v. 28). The king's fate is pivotal to the truth of Micaiah's word. That the king will not return in safety (that is "in peace") points back by contrast to Micaiah's first vision of verse 17, which promises that the people will.

Micaiah's final words in verse 28 are the opening words of the Book of Micah. Later readers of Kings added this gloss to point out the similarities between Micaiah and Micah, espe-

149

cially his attack on the salvation prophets (Micah 3:5). Whether this gloss actually intended to imply that Micaiah and Micah were the same person is uncertain, but the reader may treat it as a "cross reference" to another portion of the canonical context. Micah, like Micaiah, separated the fate of the people from the fate of their monarchy and capital city and was well known to the exilic audience (cf. Jer. 26:18).

The battle story finally resumes with verse 29, relieving the narrative pressure which has built up while all the polarities and antagonisms of the situation were explored. God's plan (v. 20) has succeeded. The exposure of the ruse does not matter, for the kings go up against Ramoth-gilead anyway. Echoing a common theme in classical Greek literature, Ahab attempts by his own ruse to escape the judgment which has been predicted. This subterfuge also provides a delaying element in the narrative. The tactical plan of the king of Syria (v. 31) prepares the reader for the idea that without Ahab the Israelite cause is lost. At first Ahab's deception seems successful.

The climax (vv. 34–36) shows that it is not. An archer lets fly a "coincidental" arrow. Ahab continues to perform his kingly role while dying, propped up in his chariot in a fading echo of the disguise/ruse motif. The blood flow indicates the gravity of his wound, while preparing for verse 38. There is no slaughter (contrast 20:21, 29–30) but rather a retreat. The royal plan has failed, but the people return in safety, as promised by verse 17.

The denouement of verses 37–40 highlights the fulfillment of the prophetic word and closes out the era of Ahab. The detail of the harlots was not part of the oracle of 21:19, but the narrator's concept of fulfillment is not a mechanical one. Perhaps this washing was intended to bring these women into magical contact with royal power or as a rather gruesome beauty treatment. In any case, it is intended by the narrator as an insult to Ahab's dignity.

Ahab's reign is concluded with impressive references to his exploits (v. 39). By the external standards of kingship, he was a great ruler; by the narrator's standards he did only "evil" (16: 30). Ahab "slept with his fathers," that is, was buried in the family tomb. The narrator uses this phrase to indicate the peaceful succession of a king's son, even as a result of violent death (II Kings 12:21; 14:22). This notice is omitted when a dynasty is brought down with violent death or the succession passes to a brother (II Kings 1:17).

150

The Quest for Meaning

Literary critics remind us that artistic communication takes place when the rules are violated, when an expected linguistic form is skewed to create new meaning. The story of Ahab's attack on Ramoth-gilead surprises the reader at several turns. It is as though the narrator is deceiving the reader, just as God has deceived Ahab. The story takes on a series of disguises, as it were. For example, the genre of "battle report" sets up expectations of victory in the reader which are not fulfilled.

At first the story seems to be about the contrast between Jeroboam's piety and Ahab's reliance on false prophets. But this turns out not to be the case. Although Jehoshaphat had demanded to hear Micaiah, he then ignores him and follows Ahab into battle anyway.

The introduction of Micaiah next implies that the story is really about true and false prophecy, but Micaiah turns out to be a temporary "false prophet" himself (v. 15). Neither Zedekiah nor Micaiah has his story completed. They simply drop out of the narrative. True and false prophecy is not the focus of the story after all.

The real thread of the story is the fate of Ahab: verses 17–18, 20, 27–28, 34, 37–38. Yet the narrator remains coy about this as well. The threat of doom is open and vague in verse 17. The grammar of verse 20 is ambiguous. (It could mean "fall on Ramoth-gilead" as NEB.) Even the assertion that he will not "return in peace" (v. 28) is still not quite the equivalent of a death sentence. Even after the "accidental" arrow finds its target, Ahab is still only wounded. The death scene is extended. Through it all, the narrator's ruse is played out. The truth is revealed, yet still in some ways hidden.

This text evidences a plurality of intentions. First it tells the story of Ahab's death and makes it clear that Ahab got his just desserts in satisfying Deuteronomistic fashion. For Josephus, reading from the viewpoint of classical literature, it taught that it is impossible to avoid predetermined fate (*Ant.* viii 15, 6). Ahab is presented with some sympathy as a tragic hero, a man feared by the enemy more than an army, yet fated to die because he cannot hear the truth from a prophet he hates. He is not struck down by the hand of God directly but has tangled himself in a web of his own making.

151

Second, the narrative demonstrates that the destiny of a

people can be separated from that of their ruler. It is generally expected that national religion will support national goals and that the good of the state is basically equivalent to the good of the people. The royal psalms certainly reflect this ideology, and the messenger of verse 13 advocates it clearly. Ahab's cause was a just one; and although God might be expected to support it, God has instead plotted disaster against Ahab. The destiny of state and people are separated (v. 17). Only the king is doomed; the people return home in peace. A king's defeat may mean peace for his people. The peasant who can go back to the farm in safety may not care about the failure of national strategy. Thus this narrative moves against any blank check of religious approval for national goals. God cannot be relied on to support the state but is totally free to protect the covenant people, even from their rulers.

The exilic readers of Kings had experienced this same God; one who had refused to support the royal political maneuvers of Judah's last days but was still loyal to the people themselves. These readers had suffered a defeat that separated state from people, yet discovered paradoxically that God's fidelity to them could be traced even in that defeat. Scattered as sheep upon the mountains, they yet could dream about returning home in peace (v. 17).

Third, the story vindicates the true prophets (Micaiah and Elijah) at the expense of the salvation prophets. The Old Testament reflects an ongoing theological debate over the test of true and false prophecy (Deut. 18:21–22; Jer. 28:8–9). The contribution offered to the debate by this text is in some ways the most theologically sophisticated of all. Sometimes prophecy contradicts itself, but both true and false prophets serve God's greater purpose! Both true and false prophets speak the truth as they have been given it. The fundamentalist quest for total security in God's word as an absolutely reliable source of true information turns out to be an illusory one.

Yet God's word, even if it is shown to be neither inerrant nor infallible, remains a powerful word. It still works. Neither Micaiah's word of lie (v. 15) nor his word of truth (v. 17) was believed, yet the purpose of God was effected anyway. The word of God, thus understood, transcends mere statements of propositional truth and becomes a power that accomplishes God's true purpose, never returning empty (Isa. 55:11).

Finally, at the deepest level, this story toys with the strange work of the lie of God. God is in such total control of events that not even the exposure of the divine ruse can block its success, to say nothing of human disguises and armor. God exercises control even through the most "accidental" event (cf. Ruth 2:3). The Old Testament was more comfortable with the concept that God causes all events than modern readers are (Exod. 4:21; 10:1; II Sam. 24:1; Isa. 45:7), but this narrative still must have been shocking. There is a certain hardness to this God who brushes aside ethical niceties to effect the divine purpose, who even lies for the good of the people.

Great tension is aroused in the believing reader when God is revealed as this strange and alien Other, who holds fast to the covenant through an overwhelming anger against apostate shepherds. Yet even the anger of God has a positive goal (Isa. 12:1). For God (and only for God) the ends do justify the means, for only God can foresee and guarantee the ends. How else could a cross be morally justifiable? This narrative shatters any idea that God automatically supports what seems ethical and moral from our viewpoint, but in the process forces us to faith in God for God's own sake alone.

I Kings 22:41—II Kings 1
Jehoshaphat and Ahaziah

The division between First and Second Kings is disruptive and artificial, coming in the midst of the section on Ahaziah and dividing the Elijah material. It is best to read the two books as a seamless whole.

The structured treatment of the kings continues after the close of the extended section on Ahab with "files" on Jehoshaphat (22:41–50) and Ahaziah (22:51—II Kings 1). These follow the established pattern. The narrative viewpoint backtracks to Ahab's fourth year to consider Jehoshaphat and backtracks again to deal with Ahaziah. The summary evaluation of Jehoshaphat is supplemented by a few notices of an annalistic nature. His battles (22:45) have already been covered in the file on Ahab. Ahaziah occurs proleptically in his section just as Jehoshaphat himself did in Ahab's. The incident of the ships (22:48–49) illustrates how far the fortunes of the divided nation have de-

153

clined since the glory of Solomon's kingdom of shalom (contrast 10:22), although at least now there is peace between the two kingdoms (22:44). The material on Ahaziah is enriched by a prophetic legend which provides a concrete example of the apostasy of which he is accused in 22:53.

The contrast between Jehoshaphat and Ahaziah is sharp. The first walked in the righteous way of Asa; the second in the evil way of Ahab, Jezebel, and Jeroboam. Although he did not eliminate the high places (cf. 15:14), Jehoshaphat did remove the rest of the cult prostitutes (cf. 15:12). Ahaziah, in contrast, served and worshiped Baal, continuing the heritage of divine anger from 16:13, 26, 33; 21:22. Ahaziah stands in the line of stereotypical apostasy (22:52–53); Jehoshaphat in the line of David his father (22:50). Jehoshaphat enjoyed a long life, ruled over Edom, and was succeeded by his son. Ahaziah ruled a little longer than a year, lost Moab for Israel (II Kings 1:1), and had no son (II Kings 1:17). He died ingloriously by falling out of a window.

The chronology no longer makes perfect internal sense. (Attempts to synchronize it with external events is a separate problem beyond the scope of this commentary.) II Kings 1:17 (either from some system alien to that used in the rest of Kings or a discrepancy caused by a coregency) occurs so near the placement of Jehoram's accession in Jehoshaphat's eighteenth year (22:51 and II Kings 3:1) that even the most unobservant reader is disturbed. If the intention of the chronology is to give the reader confidence in the narrative, this sort of discontinuity must shake that confidence to some degree.

The main plot of the story which illustrates Ahaziah's apostasy is simplicity itself. (On the narrative, see Begg, *JSOT* 32: 75–86.) The king dared inquire about his prognosis from a foreign god, God decreed death for him through a prophetic oracle, and he promptly died. This confrontation between Elijah and Ahaziah would not have been much of a story had it not been enlivened by a subplot involving getting Elijah down off his mountain to deliver the word face to face.

The narrative situation in chapter 1 is that Ahaziah cannot do anything about the loss of Moab because of his accident (vv. 1–2). A complication is introduced by verses 3–4. The king's messengers are set on a collision course with Elijah. Baal-zebub ("baal of the flies") may designate an oracle at Ekron where messages were interpreted from the sound of buzzing flies (cf.

154

the rustling leaves of the oracle of Zeus at Dodona), or it could be a pejorative corruption of some more noble title. In any case, for the narrator all baals are the same and all are equally worthless. The messengers of the king (vv. 2, 5) are a foil to the angel who instructs Elijah (vv. 3, 15; the word is the same in Hebrew). The narrative is telescoped to eliminate the actual confrontation between the messengers and Elijah. This is handled by their report to the king. This cuts down on the number of episodes and preserves Elijah's aura of separation and mystery.

Their report (vv. 5–8) takes the first step towards the coming confrontation by identifying the unknown man as Elijah by means of his hair garment (NIV, RSV) or his hirsute appearance (NEB). There may be a play on words here: Elijah, the "baal of hair" (v. 8; idiomatic Hebrew for a "hairy man"), set in opposition to the "baal of the flies."

The threefold episode of the captains (vv. 9–15) both introduces and completes the subplot of luring Elijah down from his isolation. It first delays the main plot of direct confrontation between king and prophet and then goes on to advance it when Elijah finally moves. The same triple pattern occurs in each scene: first the captain (vv. 9, 11, 13–14), then Elijah (vv. 10*a*, 12*a*, 15*a*), then the narrator (vv. 10*b*, 12*b*, 15*b*). The upward movement of the captains introduces each scene (making the usual textual revision at v. 11, cf. RSV note), and the downward movement of either fire or Elijah closes each one. The first and second scenes are nearly identical, although verse 11 offers a more formal presentation of the king's order and a brusque "hurry up." Repetition builds tension. Again there are some artistic touches. Ahaziah has gone up to his bed but will not come down (v. 4); Elijah goes up to his mountain and refuses to come down. The "fire of God" (v. 12) forms a pun with "man of God" in Hebrew. The man of God will not come down when summoned. Fire does instead. Elijah proves himself to be a man of God indeed. He hardly needs to be afraid of the king (v. 15*a*)!

The narrative moves to its goal in verses 15*b*–17. King and prophet meet face to face. The oracle is delivered personally with small variations to avoid monotony. "The third time's a charm," and the king dies promptly after the third repetition (vv. 4, 6, 16). The concluding formula for the section on Ahaziah serves as denouement.

155

Much of the effect of this story depends on its careful use of speech patterns (Koch, *The Growth of the Biblical Tradition,* pp. 183–95). The representatives of the king offer a rival messenger formula (vv. 9, 11) to that spoken by Elijah (vv. 4, 6, 16), underlining the confrontation between royal power and that of God's word. The prophetic accusation or "diatribe" is varied as it is fitted to each particular situation. It is first "that you are going" (v. 3) to the messengers, then "that you are sending" to the king (v. 6), and finally "you have sent" (v. 16). Elijah's oracle is constructed according to the classic prophetic pattern of diatribe ("because"), threat ("therefore you shall not come down"), and concluding characterization ("but you shall die").

The king's speech to his servants reflects the customary pattern of someone in high position speaking to an underling (vv. 2, 5). Elijah obeys such brusque imperative speech from the angel of the Lord (vv. 3, 15) but responds to the first two captains' use of this pattern (vv. 9, 11) with fire. The appropriate way to address a man of God is with the speech of someone of lower status speaking to a superior (vv. 13–14): polite address, entreaty rather than command, indirection.

Seen from the viewpoint of the king, the message of this story is a clear prohibition: Do not consult foreign gods. From this perspective the oracle represents the whole plot in miniature. The king violated this prohibition and so died. His critical injury put him deep into the realm of death, but his apostasy froze him there. Inquiry (the verb is used five times in this story) must be made of God through the prophets (8:8; I Kings 14:5). The exilic audience, cut off from the institutions of their homeland, would have been sorely tempted to search out oracles in their new foreign homes (ANET, pp. 448–51, 605–6). This story warns them not to.

From the point of view of the captains, this narrative gives instruction on how to treat a prophet—very carefully! In this sense the legend is similar to that of 2:23–24. The pecking order reflected in the speech patterns gives the key. A prophet is not inferior to the king himself.

From Elijah's standpoint, the story is a reminder for prophets to take their direction from God and not from the secular powers. The story of Micaiah and the four hundred prophets (I Kings 22:13–14) has a similar thrust. Again the speech patterns make this point. Elijah comes down from his perch, not when confronted by a show of force and royal imperative, but when commanded to do so by the angel of the Lord. A confrontation between a squad of fifty soldiers and fire from heaven is no

156

contest. The Christian church must always remember that "thus says the king" never takes precedence over "thus says the Lord" (Acts 4:19–20; 5:27–29).

Finally, this is a story about the power of the prophet and his word. The exact and immediate correspondence between what the word announces and what follows is emphasized in regard to both fire from heaven and the death of Ahaziah. "So he died according to the word of the Lord which Elijah had spoken" (v. 17). The focus is as much on the prophet's own authority as on the efficacy of the word. The revelation of Elijah's identity is an important step in the plot (v. 8), as is the demonstration that he really is a man of God (vv. 10, 12). The word of God is never a disembodied word, but is spoken through its authorized messengers (Rom. 10:14–15). The church, as a community living by and under God's word, needs to hear about the effectiveness of the word (II Tim. 3:15–17) and about the gifts of those who communicate it (I Tim. 4:13–14).

II Kings 2
Elisha Inherits the Mantle

The world of these narratives is certainly not the world of the modern reader. Water parts miraculously. Bears come out of the woods at the prophet's command. Magic ritual purifies a polluted spring. Chariots and horses of fire appear, and a whirlwind takes Elijah "up" to God.

In other ways, however, the chapter sounds oddly modern. The present-day reader fully understands the concept of loyalty to mentors and stubborn attachment to them (vv. 2, 4) and is all too familiar with polluted water causing medical problems like miscarriage (vv. 19, 21 NEB). Perhaps the reader was once told bogeyman stories like verses 23–24: Be good or Elisha will get you!

Structural clues suggest that this whole chapter is to be read as a unit. Journeys start and finish the chapter, finally returning the action to Samaria, the locale of chapter 1. The point of the chapter is focused in verse 15: "The spirit of Elijah rests on Elisha." The story of the search shows that Elijah is really gone. The stories of the purified water and the death of

157

the mocking boys confirm Elisha's newly inherited prophetic power.

A full understanding of this chapter depends on its context. It echoes with the fire of earlier Elijah narratives (1:10–14; I Kings 18:24). The fifty searchers link back to the fifties of chapter 1. The brief stop at Mount Carmel (v. 25) bridges back to Elijah (I Kings 18) and forward to Elisha (4:25 etc.). The mantle of Elijah, which has already played its part in the call of Elisha in I Kings 19:19, directs the reader's attention to Elijah's unfinished mission (vv. 15–16) to be completed by Elisha.

Plot Movements

In one sense, this chapter takes us into a world of mystery. In the chronological structure of Kings, the translation of Elijah takes place "outside of time." The "file" on Ahaziah has closed (1:18); the one for Jehoram of Israel has not yet been opened (3:1). By being removed from the established pattern of chronologically measured time, this story acquires an aura of mystery and otherworldliness. The event takes place on another plane of action.

This aura of mystery and hiddenness is confirmed by the narrative itself. The sons of the prophets are to keep silent, a motif not unlike the "messianic secret" in Mark. Elijah keeps trying to get rid of Elisha in order to face the future alone. The audience stands at a distance from the action (v. 7). The test founded on seeing or not seeing (v. 10) indicates that this event is not to be thought of as automatically visible to the ordinary eye. Even Elisha is separated from the climactic ascension by a fiery apparition. The theme of mystery is continued when the sons of the prophets misunderstand what has happened.

Thus the narrative moves from the known world to a place of mystery. Elijah leads Elisha and the reader on a pointless, roundabout journey from Gilgal, near the Jordan, to Bethel, then back to Jericho (only a few kilometers from Gilgal) and the Jordan. There is a journey, but no quest. Elijah is trying to shake off his tail in the person of Elisha. The two cross the Jordan on the "dry ground" of the exodus and conquest (v. 8; Exod. 14:21; Josh. 3:17; 4:18), reversing history as it were. They journey back in time and out of the land into a mysterious locale where supernatural translations can take place (cf. the "high mountain apart" of the synoptic transfiguration story; Matt. 17:1). After

158

Elijah has disappeared, the story takes the reader back across the Jordan into the world of the ordinary, to Jericho and then on to Bethel and to Samaria via Mount Carmel.

Alongside this move from known to mysterious to known again, Elisha's personal transformation represents a second plot development. He is a dependent protégé in verses 2, 4, 6. He silences the future and seems closed to it (vv. 3, 5). His first reaction to his master's disappearance is sorrow and despair (v. 12*b*), and in returning across the Jordan he still calls upon the "God of Elijah" and has to strike the water twice (v. 14; obscured in RSV). Yet in the search party incident, he exhibits calm confidence and soon functions as a prophet in his own right in Jericho. Elisha's growth to fit the mantle of Elijah is highlighted by a reverse process among the sons of the prophets. At first they predict what will happen (vv. 3, 5) and correctly interpret what has taken place (v. 15). However, their insistence on a search for Elijah shows they are less perspicacious at the end of the story than they were at the start.

A third plot movement is marked by the motif of testing. By requesting a double share of spirit (v. 9), Elisha is asking for the inheritance of the oldest son (Deut. 21:17). He is asking to succeed to the prophetic office of his "father" (cf. v. 12). Elisha passes a series of tests to qualify as Elijah's successor. He demonstrates loyalty to his master ("I will not leave you," cf. Ruth) and grasps the need for silence. He follows Elijah's silly journey wherever it leads. He gives the right answer to the test of a last request (v. 9; cf. Solomon) and walks together with his master right up till the last moment. Finally he passes the test of seeing (vv. 10, 12) and inherits the first son's double share. In contrast, Elijah appears distant throughout, detached as though already under the influence of his coming departure, following some compelling inner drive ("the Lord has sent me").

Narrative Flow

The translation narrative intersperses action and dialogue. Elijah and Elisha are on the move towards Elijah's ascension (v. 1). A pattern is repeated (vv. 2–3, 4–5): Elijah talks, Elisha responds, they move, the sons of the prophets talk, Elisha responds.

Verse 6 starts to repeat this pattern again, but now the plot advances a step. Verse 7 sets aside the other characters and

159

leaves the two prophets alone. The narrative tension is set up by the circuitous journey and the interplay of "tarry" and "I will not leave" along with "do you know" and "hold your peace." The reader already knows what will happen (v. 1). The real questions are How will this happen? Where are we going? Will Elisha be there? The Elijah/Elisha dialogue, repeated three times, shows the reader where Elisha stands. He knows exactly what is going on and takes a powerful oath refusing to leave (cf. 4:30; I Sam. 20:3; 25:26).

Verse 7 has the effect of separating the audience (both in the narrative and of the narrative) from the mysterious events to come. This is the proper response so far: watch and wait, do not interfere. A new dialogue (vv. 9–10) reveals a sharper point of tension. Will Elisha be the successor? Will he see or not? Verse 11a recaps what has been going on so far, the interweaving of speech and journey. Walking and talking merge.

In the middle of their conversation, the climax strikes like a sudden wind storm. A fiery chariot and its team, suggesting the fire of theophany, comes between the two men. The whirlwind of God's theophany catches Elijah up. (The common misunderstanding that Elijah rode to heaven in a chariot of fire is at least as old as Sirach 48:9.) Verse 12 is marked by its grammar as a simultaneous reaction of Elisha. He acclaims Elijah as Israel's defense against their better-armed enemies and addresses him as his father. The narrative tension from verse 10 is resolved: Elisha did see it happen. Then Elijah disappeared, and Elisha "saw him no more."

The rest of the chapter explores the results of this climactic ascension. Elisha tears his clothes right in half (an expression of sorrow and mourning) and picks up instead Elijah's fallen mantle, a sign of prophetic office (Zech. 13:4). He repeats Elijah's power deed, albeit with a little extra effort (v. 14), thus demonstrating his possession of the inheritance and returning to the ordinary world on this side of the Jordan.

The sons of the prophets now become a dramatic chorus recognizing the implications of what they have seen happen with the mantle. They do not know that Elijah is actually gone for good, however, for only Elisha witnessed his ascension. Knowing Elijah's predilection for disappearing (I Kings 18:12), they imagine that the spirit (whirlwind?) of the Lord has only taken him off and dropped him in some deserted place. The extensive search emphasizes Elijah's complete absence. As implied by verse 16, these fifty searchers are apparently a different fifty from the audience of verse 7, and they serve a different narrative function.

Two prophetic legends of a more traditional type demonstrate that Elisha is just as powerful a prophet as Elijah had been. The wonder deed of verses 19–22 is similar in effect to I Kings 17:17–24 in that both legitimize the office of the doer. The bad water may have something to do with the curse placed on the site of Jericho by Joshua (I Kings 16:34). Elisha uses a magically proper new container and the cleansing power of salt to effect the word of verse 21, which reflects the nature of a magic incantation. The etiological formula of verse 22 supports the credibility of the story. If you do not believe it, go look for yourself! Indeed, the tourist may still see today what is reputed to be this spring, with a line of local women seeking fertility from it.

The modern reader may wish that the narrator had chosen some story other than verses 23–25 to legitimize Elisha's power. It is a legend of the type that inculcates proper respect for prophets, along the lines of I Kings 20:35–36. Forty-two seems to have been a conventional narrative number for victims (10: 14). The ancient reader, untroubled by our post-industrial revolution apotheosis of childhood, doubtlessly found this a satisfying story. Those juvenile delinquents got exactly what they deserved! To insult God's prophet is to insult God.

Theological Implications

It is natural for the reader to identify with the sons of the prophets. We know the final outcome from the start just as they do (vv. 3, 5), but not its meaning. Elisha's insistence that they keep quiet restrains us from making any premature interpretation. We too watch the central action from some distance (v. 7), as observers rather than participants.

It is also natural to identify with Elisha. The text takes us at first on a pointless journey, but we are willing to stick with it. Then we are led into another world across the Jordan, into an inner circle of meaning, where the mysterious event takes place. We wish to inherit the power of this text and this Elijah whom we value highly. At the close, Elijah disappears for us as well, leaving behind some trace of his passing in the form

161

of a new outlook, a changed perspective. Identifying with Elijah himself, detached and distant from the start, is nearly impossible.

This narrative participates in the impulse of biography. One last incident of a career is related with a whole life in view. A distinct individual is the focus, not some generic prophet who represents a whole movement. The biographical question concerns how Elijah's end matched up with his career. The answer is focused on his acclamation as Israel's horses and chariotry. His ascension interprets his ministry as a defense of God's people from foreign aggression, in his case represented by Jezebel and Baal, and puts the divine stamp of approval on it. The common three-year lectionary properly compares this narrative with the transfiguration of Jesus (Mark 9:2–9; Transfiguration, Year B) which approves and authenticates him as Son, in part through the presence of Elijah.

The reader grasps the implication of Elisha's exclamation (v. 12) only as the narrative unfolds. The title, Israel's chariots and horses (RSV "horsemen"), will also be applied to Elisha at his death (13:14–21) in the context of national victory. The invisible chariots of 6:15–17 and their sound in 7:6–7 complete the picture. Yahweh is Israel's secret weapon, Israel's answer to the chariots of Syria (contrast I Kings 9:19, 22; 10:28–29). The prophet is the focus of Yahweh's word and, as the bearer of this word, is the defender of Israel, whether actually engaged in war (Elisha) or not (Elijah).

The narrator is using Deuteronomy 20:1 as an uncited text. The replacement of one word for horse (v. 11) with another (v. 12, translated "horsemen" by RSV) may point back to Yahweh's classic defense of the people in the exodus (Exod. 14:9, 17, 18, 23, 26, 28) and to the Deuteronomistic and prophetic insistence that Israel's true defense never lies in the horses of Egypt (Deut. 17:16; Isa. 31:1). Israel's secret defensive weapon was God (cf. Eph. 6:10–17; Rom. 8:37–39).

Yet this story is about Elisha as well as Elijah. Its dramatic tension is not really centered on the ascension. That is given away in the first sentence, and the narrative goes on for quite a while after it is completed. The focus is as much on Elisha's ability to see and his reaction as on the whirlwind and portents of fire. The narrative supports Elisha's authority to succeed to Elijah's office (3:11) and to complete Elijah's uncompleted mission (I Kings 19:15–16). Elisha's authorization is the wonderful

162

mantle he exhibits on his return. Elisha too will prove to be Israel's "chariots and horses" (13:14).

This story must have been told by Elisha's disciples to provide a sense of identity and reflected authority for their own ministries. Its intention would be to inculcate awe and respect for this powerful prophetic figure, along with confidence in his legitimate succession and the authority which went with it. The Christian church has its own concerns about legitimacy and authority to which this text can speak (cf. Matt. 16:16–19; John 20:22–23; Gal. 1:11–12).

Heraclitus looked down into the river and remarked, "Everything changes." Change is frightening, disconcerting. There is something within us that resists change. Like Elisha we do not want to contemplate it. We have an urge to silence the prophets. In this era of "future shock" we ride a rollercoaster of accelerating transition. Transition creates a sickening fear that without any changeless realities life has no purpose, no goal, no meaning. Both positive and negative change create stress.

Literature has always helped the human race rehearse change and come to terms with it, perhaps even find value in it. Elijah's transition from earth to heaven is a positive approval of his whole life. Elisha's transition is an inheritance of the first son's share. His ability to see the ascension and to use the mantle is his warrant for authoritative ministry. The community of believers, the sons of the prophets, discover a continuity of office which arches over the discontinuity of the passing of a generation.

Biblical literature goes even further, insisting that change is meaningful and bearable because God is the author of change. God's whirlwind blows away every love, every security, every safety. The same changeless God pushes ceaseless change on the world. Yet God's commission for ministry transcends change. Elisha picks up the mantle of prophetic office and turns the word of God loose on yet another generation. In institutions such as the canon of Scripture, in apostolic succession however understood, and in Christian mission to the world each generation of the church has discovered a continuity of divine purpose, overcoming even the discontinuity of death. In a way similar to the disciples of Elisha, the church celebrates this continuity by retelling the stories of its founder and its saints, thereby claiming an inheritance of power and mission.

163

II Kings 3
A Miracle For Moab

Near the end of his reign, Mesha, king of Moab, looked back at his nation's struggle for liberation from Israel, of which this campaign was but one incident (ANET, pp. 320–21). His interpretation of these events was that Chemosh, the god of Moab, had saved his people from their oppressors through the Moabite equivalent of holy war. For a generation Chemosh had been angry with his land, but in Mesha's day the god had given victory after victory in battles fought under divine guidance. Mesha devoted his captives to destruction for Chemosh, paralleling the ban practiced by Israel in the conquest. Now Chemosh dwelt in his own land once more.

This chapter reports a campaign of Israel and its allies that was on the face of it an Israelite victory, but ultimately resulted in withdrawal before the decisive blow could be struck. We can guess what Mesha would have said. Chemosh triumphed over Yahweh to defend his own land and people. Kings provides an alternate interpretation—or does it?

Background Considerations

Chapter 2 represented a gap in the structure of Kings. Now chapter 3 opens the file on Jehoram of Israel. Like Ahab's, it contains a mix of prophet legend and battle story. True to pattern, this file has no formal closing because the report of Jehoram's violent death serves this function (cf. Ahaziah, Hoshea, and the last three kings of Judah). The file closes implicitly at 8:15, Jehoram's death being reported in Ahaziah's file.

Form-critically, this is a "battle report" like those in I Kings 20. God provides for the army in its hour of need by sending miraculous water through the word of a prophet. God also brings victory to Israel by means of a trap, for this same water lures the Moabites to slaughter. Such stories must have been popular in prophetic and patriotic circles.

A special touch of verisimilitude is provided by careful references to the geographical situation. Presumably in order to avoid Moab's chain of defensive forts, the allies march around (v. 9) south and east to come in by the back door, the wilderness of Edom (v. 8). This makes sense of the report that the water flowed from the direction of Edom (v. 20). The allies faced west, the Moabite defenders east, so that the rising sun bounced off the water into their eyes (v. 22).

The plot moves along the lines of what one might call a "prophetic inquiry schema" (Long, *VT* 23:337–48): setting (vv. 4–10), audience (vv. 11–15), oracle (vv. 16–19), fulfillment (vv. 20–27). Other examples of this schema may be found in 1:1–17; 8:7–15; 22:13–20; I Kings 14:1–18; 22:4–18. As in other Elisha stories (2:19–22; 4:42–44; and 8:7–15), the plot movement is also defined by the pattern of crisis (vv. 4–13) met by prophetic oracle (vv. 14–19), followed by a confirmation of the oracle (v. 20) that meets the crisis (vv. 21–25).

The contrast between the characters of Jehoram and Jehoshaphat is handled in an artistic way. The narrator's judgment of Jehoram is negative, but not completely so (v. 2). This equivocal judgment is paralleled in the following presentation of Jehoram as a believer in Yahweh, but one who still falls short of Elisha's standards. Jehoram's unwillingness to consult the prophets of his parents (v. 13) becomes a specific illustration of verse 2. His half-hearted reform stands between the full apostasy of Ahab's altar and house for Baal (I Kings 16:32) and Jehu's full reform in demolishing the pillar and house (10:26–27). From this latter notice it is clear the narrator means to say that the pillar was put away by Jehoram, but left intact. The narrator sketches a portrait of lukewarm piety that holds true for the narratives of chapters 3, 6, and 7. In God's judgment, however, none of this matters, only that Jehoram continued in the sin of Jeroboam.

Elisha supports the narrator's evaluation of these two kings (3:2; I Kings 22:43) as "good" and "evil," but things are not quite so simple. Jehoram's "evil" is ambiguous, just as verse 2 suggests. Verses 10 and 13*b* are a confession of a sort of faith from Jehoram. He does not doubt God's power, only God's good will. "Even the demons believe—and shudder" (James 2:19). Jehoshaphat's faith is of a different nature—let's find out what God is up to and get guidance. In contrast to Jehoram's precipitate panic, Jehoshaphat is cool. You cannot be sure of what God is up to until you ask. That turns out to be an appropriate attitude in light of the way this story turns out!

165

INTERPRETATION

Following the Story

The narrative begins with an exposition (vv. 4–5) which sets up the necessary background and raises the central problem, the revolt of Moab and the consequent loss of tribute. Jehoram takes the expected steps in response to this crisis. He reacts immediately (literally "in that day" as though Ahaziah never existed). He mobilizes (v. 6), secures allies (v. 7), and fixes on strategy (v. 8). The main plot line is thus the battle; the central tension is the question of who will emerge victorious. This time Jehoshaphat is willing to join the campaign without further ado, but the repetition of his words from I Kings 22:4 is an advance hint that, as in the case of the story of God's ruse against Ahab, things may not be quite as they seem.

The shortage of water (v. 9) introduces a complication which could short-circuit the plot. A three-way conversation seeks a solution (vv. 10–12) and raises the issue of God's will. Is it true that God has brought Israel out to defeat them, as Jehoram guesses? In light of I Kings 22, the reader knows that this is not an unlikely scenario.

Jehoram's words (vv. 10 and 13b) bracket the further complication of finding a prophet willing and able to provide guidance (vv. 11–13a). Elisha proves to be both able (vv. 11–12) and eventually willing (v. 14). Pouring water for hand washing (v. 11) was a sign of respect and service, a way of saying that Elisha was Elijah's protegé. That the kings go to Elisha rather than summon him (contrast I Kings 22) describes their desperation. Elisha's initial brush-off (v. 13a) links back to I Kings 18:19. Jehoram's own peculiar brand of faith is evidenced by his reply: It would be inappropriate to go to another god, for Yahweh has caused this crisis. Elisha's self-identification in verse 14 repeats that of Elijah from I Kings 17:1 and 18:15, underscoring the line of succession indicated by verse 11b. His use of the title "Yahweh of Hosts" ("of the heavenly armies") is appropriate in this context.

After the subsidiary problem of finding a prophet has been disposed of, the more serious problem of the water shortage is overcome by an oracle (vv. 16–17) and its fulfillment (v. 20). Under the influence of music (a factor in the early practice of Israelite prophecy, I Sam. 10:5–6), Elisha is empowered by the "hand of Yahweh" (literally; cf. I Kings 18:46), to deliver a cryptic oracle (v. 16). Using a vivid infinitive absolute (4:43;

166

5:10), the oracle gives a powerful, abrupt description of what will happen: "making this gully full of pools!" Verse 17 interprets this mantic phrase as an imminent divine act. Without any visible rainstorm, the dry stream will fill with water to save the army. The fulfillment at dawn (v. 20) goes beyond even this, and the whole landscape becomes filled with water flowing from the direction of Edom.

There is a bonus, implicit in the Hebrew pun between "Edom" and "red" (cf. Gen. 25:30). Elisha's interpretation of the oracle (vv. 18–19) leads the narrative back to the main plot line. Verse 18 contains the traditional holy war "conveyance formula" (I Kings 20:13, 28; 22:12). Then verse 19 expands this into details of a triumphal progress through Moab. Israel will participate in the barbarism of total war, shattering the economic base of its former vassal and, in the process, violating Deuteronomy 20:19–20. The reader is still uninformed as to how this holy war victory will be related to the water miracle. The water flows in at the break of dawn, the time of the morning oblation, but also the traditional moment of holy war deliverance (Exod. 14:24; Ps. 46:5).

Holy war deliverance turns out to be what the Moabites had been hoping for also. At the break of day, they see more than just a good omen in the blood-like sheen imparted to the water by the red sun rising in their faces. They assume that a divinely induced panic, the prime weapon of holy war (Exod. 14:25, 27b), has struck the Israelite camp. In its grip the kings have turned on each other, each man in the army pulling his sword on his neighbor. For Moab this seems to be the "day of Midian" (Judg. 7:22; Isa. 9:3–4), and they rush in to loot. Yahweh rather than Chemosh turns out to be in control, however. The trap is sprung and the slaughter begins.

The engagement itself is reported in a back and forth movement (cf. I Kings 20:16–21). The perspective is first that of Moab (vv. 21–23), then shifts to that of Israel (vv. 24–25). Verses 26–27a return the reader to Moab's viewpoint, and verse 27b concludes from Israel's. In verse 24 the battle narrative reaches its climax with Israel's one-sided victory. Verses 25–27a report the results of this victory: the march to Kir-hareseth (cf. v. 19), Mesha's fruitless attempt to break out, and his final desperate act. Verse 27b follows as a classic anticlimax.

167

The desperate straits of Moab are indicated by the universal muster, from the youngest able to put on armor on up. But this is backwards! In the tradition of holy war, it is Israel who is supposed to be the underdog (Judg. 7:7; I Kings 20:27). If anyone needs divine aid here, it is Mesha king of Moab. The odds are three kings to one.

The allied advance to the enemy capital is reported with all the enthusiasm and inflation of a war-time press release. The last part of verse 25 is just as obscure in Hebrew as it is in the Revised Standard Version, but the idea seems to be that, although there was nothing but stones left in the area of Kir-hareseth, even these were taken up by slingers to batter (JB, not "conquer" as RSV) the city. The tactical situation behind Mesha's attempt to cut his way through "unto" (literally) the king of Edom is lost to us, but what is important is that it failed. Mesha found himself trapped in his capital city "like a bird in a cage," to quote Sennacherib's famous phrase about Hezekiah (ANET, p. 288). He needed a miracle. As Ahaz would do in a similar crisis a century later (16:3), Mesha sacrificed his son and heir on the wall of his besieged capital.

A miracle happened. In much the same way that Yahweh would defend Samaria from Ben-hadad (7:6–7) and Jerusalem from Sennacherib (19:35–36), the allied forces were forced to withdraw under the pressure of "great wrath." This word "wrath" is almost always used for divine anger and is certainly used that way here. Whether this was the wrath of Yahweh or of Chemosh is left open in the text. Ancient interpreters (LXX, Josephus) went to great lengths to avoid the implication that a power hostile to Yahweh was victorious here, but the text is certainly open to that possibility!

Looking for Meaning

What the reader had thought was the final word of the climax (v. 24) is unexpectedly undone by the anticlimactic verse 27b. The reader is brought down to earth with a thud and now must reevaluate the assumptions under which the story had been read up till now. The genre of "battle report" and the way the story is told up to the anticlimax suggested certain expected horizons of meaning. Here is another holy war won by divine ruse. God's prophetic word has power over events and can be relied on. God is our helper in dire distress. Verse 27b forces a second look. The holy war victory for Israel and Yahweh has been reversed at the last moment into a holy war victory for Moab and some unidentified "great wrath."

168

How does one explain the defeat of the people of God?
That was hardly an academic question for the exilic audience,
sometimes tempted to suppose that the victorious Marduk had
simply been a more powerful god than Yahweh, whose own
people now languished in exile. One classic explanation was
that God was punishing the people. A case for the "great wrath"
here being a punishment for sin can always be made, of course.
Israel was following in Jeroboam's sin (v. 3). Any attempt per-
manently to occupy Moab would be a violation of the principle
voiced in Deuteronomy 2:9 (by the Deuteronomistic Historian)
that Moab was outside the land permitted for Israel's possession.

Yet the text refuses to make any explicit connection between verse 27*b* and sin. Here the puzzle of national defeat is
left open, without any real explanation, and from this springs
the real literary and theological power of this narrative.

The reevaluation forced by verse 27*b* takes the reader
deep into the mystery of God's will and the control of history.
The question of Yahweh's will is at the center of the narrative
(vv. 10 and 13*b* versus 18). Was Jehoram's opinion all that
wrong, after all? Verse 24 fulfills verse 18 in the short term, but
the outcome of the whole campaign is another story. The original narrative problem was the end of vassalage and the loss of
tribute (vv. 4–5), yet the economic devastation promised in the
oracle (vv. 19, 25) could bring this problem no closer to solution.
The narrative fails to resolve its own tension. Moab remains in
rebellion against Israel.

The nature of the great wrath that saved the day for Moab
is left open for readers to interpret on their own. Mesha, we
may assume, would have insisted that this was the wrath of
Chemosh, moved by an awesome sacrifice to save his people.
With Jephthah (Judg. 11:24), he would have asserted that Moab
was not the land of Yahweh but of Chemosh. There Chemosh's
power ought to reign supreme.

As though suggesting that certain questions are better left
unanswered, the narrator lets us decide. In a sense, whether
this was Yahweh's wrath or the wrath of Chemosh does not
ultimately matter. Perhaps gods other than Yahweh do exist (cf.
Deut. 32:8–9; Dan. 10:13, 20), but the question of who is really
God was decided and disposed of by I Kings 18. The plot of
Kings as a whole makes it clear that Yahweh controls events
inside and outside Palestine and that alien armies and foreign
kings perform Yahweh's will for good or ill. Perhaps this text is

169

hinting that even foreign gods like Chemosh do so as well.

The anticlimax undercuts the assumptions the climax first seemed to support, the traditional religious beliefs of humanity. It undercuts the belief prevalent among the faithful, especially their leaders, that one can actually know just what God is up to in any given set of events. The reader certainly has no idea what is going on, even after finishing the story. It undercuts all nationalistic and ethnocentric religion, the eternal human assumption that "God is on our side." In this case God seems to have been on both sides, or neither. It undercuts all anthropocentric religion, the thought that God does things for our sake and not for God's own inexplicable purposes.

Yet there remains a certain comfort, as well. If even the wrath of Chemosh can be a tool for the purposes of the one true God, this could conceivably also be true of those technological, political, and military powers of wrath we fear so much today.

II Kings 4
Four Gifts of Life

This chapter consists of four prophetic miracle legends of the type centering more on the marvel itself than on the word of God (although cf. v. 44). Each moves from problem to solution via a marvelous deed: from poverty to money sufficient to pay off debts, from death to life, from poison food to wholesome food, and from hunger to plenty.

Three of the stories are simply anecdotes with the most minimal possible plot (vv. 1–7, 38–41). These are similar to 6:1–7. The second story (vv. 8–37) has an elaborate, complex plot and is more like 5:1–27 and 6:8–23. The first and second stories are linked by the figure of a woman in need (cf. also 8:1–6). The first and fourth share the process of multiplication, the third and fourth the theme of hunger. The community life of the sons of the prophets is common to the first, third, and fourth (cf. also 6:1–7). The figure of Elisha holds all four together. He is a man on the move (v. 9), first at Mount Carmel (v. 25), then in Gilgal (v. 38).

The four stories exhibit common folktale elements: the unfailing vessel, the seven sneezes, a baby as a reward for entertaining special visitors (cf. Gen. 18:1–15). The concern for shut doors and isolation (vv. 4–5, 33) reflects the world of magic. Elisha performs contact magic in the second story (life flows from him to the boy) and imitative magic in the third (the wholesome meal counters the poison).

Elisha's wonder deeds have been decorated with some theological frosting, although this does not really penetrate beneath the surface. The first story receives a theological touch in the dead husband's fear of God (v. 1). In the second narrative, God makes a sort of non-appearance in verse 27*b*, while Elisha's prayer of verse 33*b* seems to be almost an afterthought (cf. 6:18). Even the word about the coming baby is not described as Yahweh's word. The fourth story is theologized by identifying the magic formula of multiplication as God's word.

The narratives of chapter 4 are part of a larger paratactic (see p. 10) presentation of stories of Elisha's prophetic power (3:4—8:15). These stories are linked together in several ways. Verse 13 assumes that Elisha is a man of public influence, which fits with the general context of 3:4–27 and 6:8–7:20. The famine in verse 38 seems to be related to the one mentioned in 8:1. The resurrection narrative finds a sequel in 8:1–6.

There are also strong links to the Elijah stories. The multiplication of oil and bread suggests I Kings 17:8–16. I Kings 17:17–24 and verses 8–37 seem to be variations on the same legend. In addition to having the same basic plot, both involve a combination of prayer and bodily contact in an upper room and an angry, bitter mother. Another contact is provided by verse 31, which reflects I Kings 18:29—Gehazi was no more successful than the Baal prophets.

From Poverty to Solvency (vv. 1–7)

The first story (vv. 1–7) is told quite simply. The need of verse 1 is met by the answer of verse 7. The piety of the husband (v. 1) motivates Elisha's concern. Slavery for debt was part of the Hebrew legal system (Exod. 21:7), and the oppressive economic conditions that brought it about are reflected in Amos 2:6; 8:6; Micah 2:9. Verse 2 makes the widow's need even more apparent, but paradoxically the one little thing left to her will prove to be her salvation. Her act of borrowing jars is not reported, as the plot has been stripped down to its core, but a contrasting interest in the details of their filling throws the emphasis on the miraculous process itself. That

171

Elisha is absent at this point has the effect of heightening the wonder.

From Death to Life (vv. 8–37)

The resurrection story (vv. 8–37) is told with a good deal of artistry. The narrator seems to embrace what in those times might be thought to be a woman's psychological point of view in the description of the upper room's furnishings (cf. the Queen of Sheba in I Kings 10:5). There seem to be traces of Northern Israelite dialect (vv. 3, 7, 23), a bit of local color for a Judahite audience. Elisha becomes rather lyrical in verse 16. The bitterness in verse 28 is striking.

Gehazi's role as the classic sidekick (Sancho Panza, Doctor Watson) is worth noting. He functions as an intermediary to keep the woman and Elisha separate at first (vv. 12–13, 26), delaying their direct confrontation (vv. 15, 27). He is a forerunner for Elisha (vv. 29, 21), his failure increasing by contrast the wonder of the prophet's success. In verse 14 he is the source of information needed to keep the plot moving. He is simply a silent observer in verse 33.

One of the attractions of this narrative is its presentation of the woman. Her husband is described as a sort of "hollow man" whose character defects serve to highlight her virtues. His age interferes with their hopes for children (v. 14). When his son gets sick, he passes the buck to his wife and is too old (or indifferent) to carry the boy in himself (v. 19). He becomes flustered when she heads off to consult with a prophet on an irregular day (v. 23).

In contrast, she is a powerful and admirable character. She is a woman of substance (v. 8) capable of building and furnishing a substantial guest lodge. She knows how to take advantage of circumstances (v. 10). She is an independent woman unwilling to take favors, relying on kinfolk rather than powerful strangers (v. 13), not subject to unrealistic hopes (v. 16). She knows how to behave properly (vv. 15, 27, 37) and speak properly (v. 16) towards prophets. She knows the value of silence at the right moment (vv. 23, 26), but can make a convincing and impassioned appeal when the time is ripe (v. 28). She is engagingly maternal (v. 20), but in a crisis acts decisively. Revealing by her actions in verse 21 that her plan is already formed, she hastens straight to Elisha, refusing to talk to subordinates, refusing to be turned aside from what she has planned for the prophet, and in the end is proved right by circumstances. She is one of the Old Testament's most attractive characters.

The plot of this second story is complex and elaborate. First comes a prelude (vv. 8–17) in the form of a traditional birth story like those told about the mothers of Isaac, Samson, and Samuel. This prelude serves to get everyone on stage, to establish the character of the mother, and to provide her with a lever for her later confrontation with Elisha. The first of three uses of the generalized time marker "one day" (vv. 8, 11, 18) introduces an episode which brings Elisha and the woman together. By judging him "holy," she is not recognizing any moral virtue but the aura of power, perhaps even dangerous power, of one who is in close contact with God. Verse 10 emphasizes the value of her provision for Elisha. This is a solid chamber with real walls and elaborate furnishings.

A second "one day" carries the narrative on to the issue of reward and the birth of her son. The repeated verses 12 and 15 bracket an attempt to find a suitable reward, which builds tension through delay. She stands first before Gehazi, then later moves to the door for a direct conversation with Elisha. The word choice in Hebrew emphasizes the great trouble (literally "trembling") she has gone to. What could she possibly want from the commander of the army (v. 13)? Is it perhaps relief for her husband from some onerous civic duty? In any case, she self-reliantly turns the offer down. She can rely on her kinfolk who live nearby.

The time designation in Elisha's promise is hard to translate. Perhaps it is simply "this time next year," but it may be a reference to the period of her pregnancy. Literally it is "at the time of revival" which implies spring (RSV, v. 17), but which also may hide a word play on the central event of this narrative. The repetition of these words in verse 17 is a way of asserting precise fulfillment. It happened exactly as promised. The narrative seems to come to a resting place with the boy's birth, but a third "one day" in verse 18 drives the plot further. The preliminaries are over. The reader moves on to the main event.

The boy's death creates an intense narrative tension. It contrasts sharply with the idea that he is a gift child, a reward for pious behavior. The woman springs into decisive action. By taking the boy up to the prophet's bed, she reveals that her plan is already formed. By closing the door, she conceals the death as though to keep it frozen in dramatic time, to prevent the

173

death process from going any further. Her evasive reply to her flustered husband (shalom: "It's all right," NIV) forestalls his setting in motion the next stage of death, mourning and burial.

She sets out on the first half of her fifty kilometer round trip, urging the servant who leads her donkey to hurry. Brushing aside Gehazi, she heads directly for the one who can bring her hope. The aside of verse 27 prevents the reader from becoming sidetracked by any concern over Elisha's ignorance (contrast his knowledge in 5:26). The bitterness he sees is played out in the next verse. Her words are sharp, accusing, exciting the reader's sympathy. Elisha must do something!

The narrator then teases the reader with a half-measure involving Gehazi (v. 29). A staff could be an extension of a person (Gen. 38:18), a sort of magic wand (Exod. 4:1–4; 17:8–13) which might carry Elisha's power with it (cf. Acts 19:12). The motïf of haste continues (cf. Luke 10:4), but Gehazi's role is really that of a narrative delay, his failure a foil to Elisha's success.

The reluctant prophet is persuaded to go by the woman's persistent oath. She passes a narrative "test" of the same sort as in 2:4, 6. Verse 32 confirms the child's death to heighten the miracle. Once more the door is shut. Elisha crouches over the child. His act is repeated for dramatic effect (Elisha does things in doubles, cf. 2:14; Elijah in triples, cf. I Kings 17:21). The boy's climactic sneezing is physical evidence that his soul or breath has returned. The mother's reaction parallels the awe and amazement the narrative intends to instill in the reader.

From Hunger to Plenty (vv. 38–44)

The third story (vv. 38–41) returns to a stripped-down, anecdotal style. The need (famine) of verse 38 is complicated by the accident of verse 39, but a magic action sets things right. The prophetic brotherhood is sitting before Elisha, as students do at a teacher's feet. He orders a big pot of stew. The desperation of famine is underscored as one of their number goes out to gather some sort of wild plant (perhaps mallow, a shrub with edible leaves). He comes back instead with the spherical, green-yellow fruit of a wild gourd gathered into the hem of his robe and, in his ignorance, slices it into the pot. This fruit has strong laxative properties and a bitter taste. Whether the sons of the prophets mean that what they have tasted is truly poison or are engaging in hyperbole over its horrible taste does not really

174

matter. The desperately needed stew is ruined. Elisha comes to the rescue by sprinkling in meal, which like salt (2:21) symbolizes life.

The fourth story is still set in the context of famine introduced by verse 38. A supporter brings bread and grain, the first fruits of the new harvest. This was probably in the nature of a religious offering. Elisha's command is an echo of the conclusion of the previous story. The man's complicating objection underscores the wonder of the miracle. Elisha simply repeats his first order, adding as a word of the Lord a vividly descriptive pair of infinitive absolutes (cf. 3:16; 5:10): "eating and having left over." The conclusion emphasizes that this happened in accordance with the word. That they had some left is a narrative sign of abundance (cf. the baskets of fragments in the Gospel feeding miracles).

Theological Implications

Telling stories like these within prophetic communities built up a trust and confidence in the God around whose word they had chosen to gather. Here the sons of the prophets seem a disadvantaged lot, leaving their widows with unmanageable debts, gathering like hobos around stewpots. These four stories share a common theme of life rescued from death, hope from hopelessness. In each case life is threatened: by economic tragedy and slavery, by the death of an only child, by famine and poison, by a shortage of food. In each case the power of God through the prophet Elisha breaks into this hopelessness and shatters it with a word of life.

The gifts offered are notable for their down-to-earth practicality: money for the poor, a son for the childless, bread and stew for the hungry. There is none of the empty "spiritual" comfort so common to modern religion, so rightly derided by Marxist thinkers. That sort of religion whose watchword is "Go in peace, be warmed and filled," but never offers "the things needed for the body" (James 2:16) finds no support from the Old Testament. Likewise, the news about Jesus was good news for the economically disadvantaged (Luke 6:20–21). One of the startling signs of the Messianic age is that the poor hear the good news that the year has come when debts are canceled (Luke 4:18), a wonder ranked with the raising of the dead (Luke 7:22).

175

The earliest church loved to retell its memories of Jesus feeding vast hungry crowds and sometimes echoed verses

42–44 in the process (Matt. 14:16–20; cf. the barley loaves of John 6:9). Although there is plenty of room for wealthy women with big houses, the Kingdom of God which Jesus announced gives special hope to the world's poor and hungry. It is a hope based not on the fickle good will of political leaders or economic theorists but on the power of the Creator God reflected in these stories.

The first great Christian Old Testament theologian, the author of Hebrews, summarized a part of the Old Testament story with the words, "Women received their dead by resurrection" (Heb. 11:35). Stories of resurrection played a central role in the preaching of the New Testament communities. Sometimes the memory of these acts of Jesus were colored by reflections from the resurrections performed through Elijah and Elisha, especially the raising of the son of the widow of Nain (just over the hill from Shunam; Luke 7:11–17) and Peter's raising of Tabitha (Acts 9:36–41).

Death is the ultimate hopelessness. Resurrection is the most radical shattering of hopelessness possible. If the power and love of God cannot or will not raise the dead, the other gifts of life (pure water, freedom, food) are only temporary and conditioned, good news perhaps, but not the best possible news (I Cor. 15:13–19). The followers of Jesus, therefore, have put his own resurrection and the resurrection he promises to all at the center of their creeds, their calendars, and their preaching.

II Kings 5
Naaman Comes to Faith

The story of Naaman demonstrates a fruitful symbiosis between narrative art and theology. Complex on the literary plane, it leads the reader into deep levels of theological reflection in a variety of directions. [Recommended for further reading: Cohn, *VT* 33:171–84 (1983); von Rad, *God's Work in Israel,* pp. 47–57.]

The story reports two miracles, one of healing, one of affliction. The first is expected. The only question is how it will happen. The second is satisfying, but less expected. The characters are stereotypical: the good-hearted maiden, the foreign ruler who learns his lesson, the greedy assistant. The chapter starts as another uncomplicated miracle story, but the conversion of Naaman gives it an unusual twist. Then the reader is carried on to an unexpected sequel with didactic overtones. The successive surprises of Naaman's conversion (vv. 15–19) and Gehazi's fraud (vv. 20–27) force the reader to reevaluate the core story (vv. 1–14) from two new viewpoints. Thus the reader is given three different perspectives on the same basic material. Each of the three narratives centers around a meeting with Elisha (vv. 9–10; 15–19a; 25–27). Naaman's healing provides a bridge between the first and the second, and Gehazi's greed between the second and the third.

Naaman Is Cured (vv. 1–14)

The narrative situation and tension are set up by verse 1. How will Naaman's leprosy be cured? The mainspring of the plot is the tension between Yahweh's evident favor for Naaman and his leprosy. The reader's sympathies, like those of the little maid, rest with Naaman. The leprosy comes as a distinct shock at the end of verse 1 after the narrator has extolled Naaman so highly. The Old Testament classified a wide variety of skin diseases under the heading of leprosy. Naaman's was one of the more minor types which created no barrier to social intercourse.

Verses 2–5 move toward a solution, a move initiated by the little girl. Note how the intermediaries in this story function to advance or complicate the plot. The little maid attracts the reader's sympathy to Naaman. There is a pleasing contrast between the great Syrian hero who serves the king and the little Israelite captive who serves his wife. Verse 2 points out the real implication of the victory Yahweh has given Naaman. It is at the expense of Israel! Here the theme of universalism is introduced, to be picked up by Naaman's conversion.

Although the narrative does not at first reveal who this "prophet in Samaria" is (v. 3), the reader knows whom to expect from context. As it moves quickly from lowest to highest in the Syrian social system, the narrative eliminates the report of Naaman's wife to her husband. Naaman gathers a huge gift worthy of a story-teller's art, designed to get the readers' attention and develop curiosity and anticipation. Naaman's offer to Elisha was not inappropriate on the surface. Giving presents to prophets was the usual custom (I Sam. 9:7; I Kings 14:3). Naaman's gifts

177

(v. 5) not only build reader interest, but also unify his conversion (v. 15*b*) and Gehazi's fraud (v. 20) to this core miracle story.

The first complication is offered by verses 6–7, a comic detour to the king of Israel and his reaction. Verse 6 reflects a proper letter form, bringing the reader into it right where the formal pleasantries are over and the business starts (" . . . and now," obscured in the English versions). Because the king of Syria fails to mention the "prophet in Samaria" in his letter, this comic complication gives the reader a chance to have a good laugh at the expense of bureaucratic officialdom. Yet the king of Israel also inadvertently makes an important confession and provides an operative definition for the reality of God: God kills and makes alive. Whoever does this is God (Deut. 32:39; I Sam. 2:6). This prepares the ground for Naaman's confession in verse 15.

Elisha takes matters into hand and breaks through the slapstick of governmental fumbling. In verses 8–10 the action is once more on the track towards a resolution of Naaman's problem. More groundwork is laid for Naaman's conversion: The healing will happen so he will "know that there is a prophet in Israel." Naaman's horses and chariots make an implicit claim to superior status (v. 9, cf. 2:12; 6:15, 17; 13:14). But Elisha puts Naaman in his place by refusing to grant an audience. A messenger functions to keep them apart during their first interchange (v. 10), emphasizing the change that will take place in their relationship by the time of their face-to-face meeting (v. 15).

Naaman is given a classic narrative test: Go do something that appears silly. Naaman's anger (vv. 11–12) creates a second complication. It looks as though he will fail the test. He first makes an egocentric objection in verse 11. The prophet should have come out to me (the pronoun is emphasized in Hebrew) and performed the sort of hocus-pocus I expect. Then he makes an ethnocentric objection in verse 12: Our rivers are better than their river any day. Naaman's problem is shown to be more than physical. He still does not realize "there is a prophet in Israel." His servants, however, now play the role of getting the plot back on the track (v. 13). Naaman's healing (v. 14) is the climax which resolves the initial problem.

178   Naaman Is Converted (vv. 15–19)

Now Naaman and Elisha meet face to face. There is word play between verse 14 and verse 15: Just as Naaman's flesh has been "restored" *(shub)*, Naaman "returns" *(shub)* to Elisha. Naaman reacts to the climax with servant language that reverses his earlier claim to superior status and with an astounding confession of monotheism (v. 15). He has come to believe what the narrative claimed about Yahweh in verse 1. With a characteristic oath (3:14), Elisha refuses Naaman's gift. As Naaman "stands' before him in humility, Elisha himself "stands" before Yahweh (RSV translates the verb as "serve"). Reward is inappropriate for one who is God's servant. Elisha's refusal to perform the favor of taking a present (literally a "blessing") also helps advance the story in that it provides Naaman with a chance to ask for further favors. It also serves as a bridge to the Gehazi sequel.

Naaman's new knowledge that the only God is the one in Israel results in two consequences for him. First, monolatry is the natural result of monotheism. A little while ago he had despised Israel's river, now he wants the soil of Yahweh's homeland. He will sacrifice to no god but Yahweh. The two mules of Naaman's request will find a counterpart in the repeated "two's" of Gehazi's request. Naaman's piety makes Gehazi's fraud all the more sordid by comparison. His request in verse 17 is based on the idea that a god was tied to a home territory (Deut. 32:8) and that worshiping Yahweh from a foreign land might present a problem (Ps. 137:4).

The second consequence of Naaman's conversion requires a second favor. Now Naaman is a man of double loyalties, to Yahweh of course, but also to his master, the king of Syria. The niceties of the change in Naaman's position are reflected by a careful use of the language of subservience. Naaman is in a subservient relationship to the king of Syria (vv. 1, 6). This same relationship continues after his healing (v. 18). But in contrast to his earlier haughty behavior towards Elisha, Naaman's language to Elisha now reflects a lower status (vv. 15, 17, 18). In contrast, Gehazi's claim of subservience to Elisha (vv. 20, 22, 25) will be belied by his actions.

The hesitant language of a request wide open to refusal is realistically presented by verse 18, a verse with a concentric structure and a threefold repetition of the central verb "bow." Because his loyalty is to his king and not to Rimmon, as his overfull speech tries to make clear, his request does not undercut his monotheism. Can he retain the high favor he has with the king (v. 1) and continue to serve his human lord (cf. 7:2, 17)?

179

The narrative advances no rigorist or purist solution, only Elisha's non-committal, but non-judgmental, "shalom" (v. 19a) giving tacit approval to Naaman's practical compromise.

Gehazi's Fraud (vv. 20–27)

The Gehazi sequel sets Naaman's story into the perspective of the ordinary reader and universalizes it into categories which transcend leprosy and Gentile conversion. Gehazi appears out of nowhere to serve as a foil to Naaman's conversion. He is faithlessly greedy whereas Naaman is faithfully generous. Gehazi's chauvinism (cf. the belittling reference to "this Naaman the Syrian," v. 20) functions as a foil to Elisha's inclusiveness. Gehazi delivers a counter oath to that of Elisha (v. 20 versus 16). This creates a new narrative tension. Which oath will prevail?

This tension is extended by Naaman's question whether the "shalom" is still in force (v. 21) and Gehazi's insistence that it is, which actually is in itself a sign that shalom has been broken! Gehazi's faithlessness leads him to attribute his greedy lie to his master (v. 22). His betrayal is made the more sordid by the contrast of Naaman's gracious behavior. He gets out of his chariot for a mere servant of Elisha (contrast v. 9). "Be pleased" to take two, not just one (v. 23), he begs. He "urges" Gehazi, sharpening the contrast to Elisha (v. 16). He carefully "gift wraps" the silver and sends two servants off to parade in front of Gehazi.

Things soon turn sour for Gehazi. He can march importantly behind Naaman's servants but has to hide the loot away himself (v. 24). Five brusque consecutive verbs without objects describe his cover up. The departure of Naaman's servants marks the completion of the crime. Gehazi's lie (v. 25) leads to his exposure, for it runs up against Elisha's "second sight" (v. 26). The Hebrew speaks generally of "a man" (rather than the more definite "the man" of the RSV; cf. JB "someone"). This seems to imply that Elisha's preternatural vision was not sharp enough to identify the man or other details but certainly proved that Gehazi's claim to have stayed home was a lie.

Elisha harangues the unfortunate Gehazi, either exaggerating his crime for effect or spinning out some of the things that could be bought with the money. When God is working a healing and conversion, greed has no place. The narrative reaches a satisfying end. Naaman was a leper at the start, although God favored him. Gehazi is deservedly a leper at the end. The lep-

180

rosy has found a new home, and no one need fear it will return
to Naaman (cf. the literary function of the pigs in Mark 5:13).

Canonical and Theological Connections

As befits a complex tale, the narrative exhibits several
simultaneous movements. The maid's report of a "prophet in
Samaria" (v. 3) moves to Elisha's goal that Naaman might know
there is a "prophet in Israel" (v. 8) and on to Naaman's knowledge that the only God is "in Israel" (v. 15). The name of Yahweh is introduced to the narrative by Naaman, first only as
Elisha's God (v. 11), then as his own (vv. 17, 18). The character
of Naaman develops from arrogance to humility. The narrative
makes a satisfying circle from the "little maid" of verse 2 to the
"little child" of verse 14 (the masculine and feminine of the
same word in Hebrew) and another from leprosy (v. 1) to leprosy (v. 27).

This narrative is linked to its context in several subtle ways.
Naaman is a "great man" (v. 1) parallel to the "great woman"
of 4:8 (RSV: "wealthy woman"). Gehazi also provides a link,
although not a perfectly smooth one, for 8:1–6 will find him
lauding Elisha as though nothing has happened. His "white as
snow" leprosy echoes the story of Moses (Exod. 4:6; cf. Num.
12:10). Elisha remains a man on the move, now showing up in
a house in Samaria (RSV's "hill" of v. 24 ought to be translated
"citadel" with NEB). He will move on to the Jordan (6:4) and
Dothan (6:13) before appearing at his Samaria house again in
6:32. Here Elisha is on good terms with the king as in 4:13 and
8:4. Verses 1 and 7 testify in passing to the Syrian military
dominance which shadows all these chapters.

Such a complex story impacts the reader in a variety of
ways. As a prophetic legend it has the intent of evoking respect
and admiration for the power of prophets in general and the
figure of Elisha in particular. Elisha has the power not only to
heal diseases but to transfer them to another as punishment.
The comic helplessness of the king of Israel is contrasted with
the confident power of the prophet. On a didactic level, the
story condemns theft and greed. The gifts of God are not for
sale (Acts 8:18–24).

As an example story it urges the importance of obedience
to the prophetic word. Naaman is healed not by the competing
cleansing power of Syria's rivers versus the Jordan but by simple, open-minded obedience. In contrast, Gehazi is punished

181

for his disobedient attempt to undo his master's oath. The narrative also teaches the difference between the magic of a wonder-worker, with its impressive legerdemain, and the power of God mediated by a prophet. Elisha does not even have to come near Naaman (cf. Luke 7:1–10), for God is the doer of this deed, not the prophet.

Prophetic groups seem to have told this story as an exploration into human reactions to God's healing, life-giving work. Which reactions and behaviors are proper, which are not? The incident of Gehazi is a straightforward cautionary tale. Do not use the power of God or your prophetic office to secure personal gain. Naaman's reaction, by contrast, is the appropriate way to receive God's gifts. Naaman comes to faith. He is converted to the conviction that Yahweh is the only God.

This indeed was the purpose of the miracle to begin with (v. 8), the purpose that raised it above those ordinary prophetic services for which it is appropriate to pay. His healing was a free gift. Faith was not a precondition for health; health was given in order to create faith. Indeed God's gracious favor to Naaman is prior to everything else in the story (v. 1). (Contrast the order of events in this text's lectionary parallel, Mark 1:40–45; Sixth Sunday after Epiphany, Year B.)

The narrative expresses the revolutionary reorientation of Naaman's life, first by his explicit confession of monotheism (v. 15), second by his change from arrogance to subservience as reflected in his language and behavior, and third by his request for the soil of Yahweh's land. Faith and new life as a result of a bath echoes the church's experience with baptism (John 3:5–7; I Cor. 6:11; Gal. 3:27; Titus 3:5–7). Naaman's story is the story of every baptized believer (Rom. 6:1–5; Col. 2:12–14).

Exiles were troubled over their separation from the land of Israel. Could they worship God in a strange land? What tokens of the past could they treasure to support their faith? Even though he knows that Yahweh is God over the whole world, Naaman still needs his two loads of holy land. Rather than condescendingly forgiving him for his supposedly primitive conception of God, the reader would do well to consider this soil as Naaman's tangible way of making his confession effective. Human beings need insulating layers between themselves and the Wholly Other that is God. The unmediated presence of the Unmasked God is too terrible to tolerate. We need icons of the divine presence and favor upon which to focus our faith. Cer-

182

tainly the Christian faith has its own necessary loads of dirt with which God graciously insulates the faithful and which at the same time guarantee God's presence. Luther called them "God's masks."

Naaman's reaction goes one step further, into the dangerous territory of multiple loyalties. Certainly now he is loyal to his new God. Does his new faith automatically mean his death, either as a result of the jealous rage of Yahweh or at the hand of an outraged king? Naaman is a man threatened by his faith. He has no knowledge of the modern concept of an escape to an inner mind where externals supposedly do not matter. He needs pardon for a compromise he knows to be imperfect (cf. v. 18). His question was the question of Judah's exiles, living in a far land under intense syncretistic pressure, of the Corinthian Christians who agonized over eating meat offered to idols, of Christians pressured to burn incense to the Emperor Domitian, of Japanese Christians confronted by Shinto.

Which compromises are possible, which are betrayals of the faith by which we live? Every faithful person who does not simply abandon the world is confronted by the wrenching issue of divided loyalties. There is no easy answer that works every time. The rigidly pious and obsessively pure have always been outraged by Elisha's open-ended "shalom" (cf. the face-saving addition of the Lucianic recension of the LXX). Elisha's answer neither approves nor judges but simply sends Naaman forth to live his faith as best he can.

"And there were many lepers in Israel," said Jesus, "in the time of the prophet Elisha; and none of them was cleansed, but only Naaman the Syrian" (Luke 4:27). Chapter 5 offers an extraordinary description of an enemy foreigner as an object of God's favor and as a man of strong faith. The God of Israel is the God of all peoples (cf. I Kings 8:41–43), and God intends for them to know it (vv. 8, 15). Yet it is the natural reaction of religion to be exclusive rather than inclusive. As told by Luke, the reaction in the synagogue to Jesus' statement was anger. Although Naaman lost his egocentricity (v. 11) and his ethnocentricity (v. 12) in his Jordan bath, these things still clung to Gehazi (v. 20) even before his leprosy did. The story of Naaman, like those about Ruth and Jonah, fights against the tendency towards exclusiveness which infects God's people in the form of racism or nationalism (cf. Matt. 8:5–13; Acts 10:1–11:18).

183

II Kings 6:1—8:15
Stories of Prophetic Power

Before the "file" on Jehoram of Israel is brought to an implicit close at 8:15, the narrator recounts five more stories of Elisha's prophetic power, culminating in his fulfillment of Elijah's earlier commission (I Kings 19:15) to "anoint" Hazael as king of Syria. These are

> an axe head lost and floated—(6:1–7)
> the Syrian raiders stopped—(6:8–23)
> the siege lifted, the word fulfilled—(6:24—7:20)
> a woman's property restored—(8:1–6)
> God's word makes Hazael king—(8:7–15)

The organization of these stories is basically paratactic (see the Introduction), although there are some faint traces of chronological concern. Thus the two stories with the theme of Syrian military power are linked with "afterward" (6:24). The sequel to the Shunammite woman's story has been separated from 4:37 to provide for the famine of 4:38 and the passage of seven years (8:3). These, added to the years needed for her child to grow old enough to talk (4:19), advance the larger narrative to a point near the end of Jehoram's twelve-year reign.

The Lost Axe Head (6:1–7)

The story of the floating axe head (6:1–7) is something of an embarrassment for modern readers. The miracle seems both trivial and pointless. In part this is caused by our inability to empathize with a poor man's consternation over an expensive borrowed tool. Iron was not cheap in those days. The story is similar to the brief anecdotes of 2:19–22 and 4:38–41, but here there is a bit more in the way of plot. It is told with the realistic touch of long, polite speeches delivered by inferiors ("please," "your servants," "master," 6:3, 5) balanced by Elisha's curt rejoinders.

184

The narrative exposition, that is the introduction of the

characters and the problem, is laid out by a narrative rather than by the more common expedient of a summary. Thus verses 1–4 really serve only to inform the reader as to who was cutting trees for what purpose. Such a long preliminary presentation has the effect of arousing the reader's curiosity, a curiosity which is then quickly satisfied by the crisis and resolution of 5–7. Elisha is pictured here as the "abbot" of a prophetic community, in tension with the idea that he had a private house in Samaria (5:9). The problem of cramped quarters (v. 1) leads to a request of the prophet and his approval (v. 2). Permanent residence by the Jordan would be historically unlikely because of malaria, but the narrative moves there in order to provide water in which the axe head can disappear. Delay is created by a minor complication, in the form of a request that Elisha come along and his agreement. Again the effect is to build interest. We know that Elisha is not coming along just to chop down trees!

Verse 5 presents a major complication which turns out to be the central dilemma of the story. The problem of a new house has served its narrative purpose and is dropped. The Hebrew emphasizes that the lost object is of iron and leaves unstated the type of tool involved. Again the rhythm of an appeal to Elisha is repeated. The climax (v. 6) is an act of imitative magic (the iron floats like the stick), and the denouement is as brief as possible (v. 7).

At its core this narrative is what students of folklore would call a "technological myth," one told to bridge the gap between the natural and the artificial, here the "newfangled" use of iron tools. Under the holy man's power, this gap is closed by a reversal of natures. Iron floats like wood; wood magnetically attracts like iron. The story may also have been told to justify the erection of permanent structures for the sons of the prophets in the face of opposition from groups such as the Rechabites. In its present context, these functions, if present at all, have receded into the background. Now it does nothing more than emphasize the power of the prophet.

God's power invades the world of the ordinary to effect strange reversals. The lowly are raised to places of honor (Luke 1:51–53). The unrighteous are justified (Luke 18:9–14). The lost are found (Luke 15:3–10). The dead are raised. These are as much incredible reversals as is iron that floats.

185

Syrian Raiders (6:8–23)

The central problem of 6:8–23 is the incursion of Syrian raiding parties, stopped by Elisha's intervention (v. 23). This ties back to the appearance of these raiders against "the land of Israel" at the start of the Naaman story (5:2). A further connection to chapter 5 is that Elisha is now known in Syrian court circles.

Verses 8–10 introduce the main characters in turn: the king of Syria (v. 8), Elisha (v. 9), and the king of Israel (v. 10), and establishes the motive for the king of Syria's action against the prophet. The precise implications of the king's plan in verse 8 are lost to us. "I mean to attack" (NEB) is probably correct and "took special precautions" (NIV) captures the nuances of the king of Israel's response (v. 10).

After the background has been sketched in, verses 11–14 introduce the complicating problem of the army sent to neutralize Elisha. The Syrian advisors convince their lord by reasoning from greater to lesser. If Elisha knows the words that pass in the king's bedchamber, how much more will he reveal what passes in a council of war! The king's command, "go and see" (v. 13), will have ironic implications as the story unfolds. Dothan is a handy place for the narrative to locate Elisha, within reach of a Syrian strike force but near enough to Samaria. Verse 14 catalogues the important horses, chariots, and army.

The main line of the plot is put on hold with verses 15–17. This is a sort of a narrative "aside" which interprets what will come. The lad is a stand-in for the reader. When he can see that God's victory over the Syrians is really inevitable, he no longer is afraid. Syria's "horse" (a collective singular) and chariotry may surround the city, but God's horses (plural) and chariotry (cf. Ps. 68:17) surround Elisha (6:15 and 17). Verse 17 serves as a proleptic climax, anticipating the true climax of verse 20*b* with the repeated use of "opened the eyes and saw." The subject of the first part of verse 18 is probably the fiery horses and chariots (English versions otherwise, except for NEB which reflects the ambiguity of the Hebrew), since the Syrian army could hardly "come down" on Elisha who is up on a mountain (v. 17). The Syrian horses and chariots are thus defused and disappear from the story. Only the threat of infantry is left.

Elisha's prayers for first blindness and then sight bracket

186

verses 18–20*a*, as the story rises to its climax with humor and irony. The story moves from the lad's seeing to the army's blindness to the army's seeing. The Syrian troops are literally "dazzled." Elisha is fully cognizant of their orders and ironically offers to help them find the man they seek. He fulfills their mission (v. 13, "go and see") by causing them to go (forms of the verb are used three times in v. 19; RSV as "follow," "bring," "led") and then to see (twice in v. 20*b*, obscured by the RSV). Verse 20*b*, the moment of revelation, is the climactic point, repeating verse 17 on a larger scale.

Consequences and reactions follow in verses 21–23. Elisha is still in charge of events, even in the royal city. The king, who addresses the prophet respectfully ("my father," cf. 13:14), seems from the grammar of verse 21 to be anxious to kill the prisoners, but Elisha stops him. No holy war ban has been declared in this case (contrast I Kings 20:31–42), so the rules of civilized warfare apply. (NEB reads 6:22 differently to eliminate any contradiction here.) Elisha shows his power to control policy by ordering a banquet instead of an execution. Verse 23*b* makes it clear that the central problem has been solved. The raids stop.

There is certainly satire, at the expense of the ruling elite, present in this story (R. LaBarbera, *CBQ* 46:637–51), a theme which continues into the next narrative. All officials are powerless; it is Yahweh who gives victory. Elisha provides vital military intelligence. It is only when Elisha "sends" word (v. 9), that the king of Israel can "send" to protect himself (v. 10). Yahweh's chariots simply neutralize those of the Syrians. Elisha is, ironically, the true leader of the Syrians on their mission, not the king of Syria. In the end, Elisha sets royal policy concerning the captives.

This narrative makes the same point as the Book of Kings as a whole. Kings of nations, be they of Judah or Israel, Assyria or even Babylon, were never really in control of the history of God's people. Only God was. In this case God gave victory to the people. In the larger story the people were to experience total, humiliating defeat at the hands of the Babylonians, but again under the power and control of God.

The awesome power of government, be it totalitarian or democratic, is something of a joke when compared to the horses 187 and chariots of Yahweh, operative through the word of God's true spokesperson. To a world terrified by the possibility of destruction, the church continues to affirm God's power and to assert, with eyes opened by Easter's new life, "Fear not, for those who are with us are more than those who are with them" (v. 16).

The Siege of Samaria (6:24—7:20)

The report of the siege of Samaria (6:24—7:20) seems to have been molded together from three distinct stories (the lifting of the siege, the case of cannibalism, the captain's fate) into a single, artistic whole. Historians doubt that this event could have happened in the reign of Jehoram and usually place it instead in the reigns of Jehoahaz and Ben-hadad, the son of Hazael. In the structure of Kings, of course, Jehoram is unambiguously the king involved. The character of the king's faith (6:27, 33) resembles what the narrator has already presented in 3:13. He does not doubt God's power so much as God's good will.

There is a contextual relationship to the previous story. A vague chronological connection is made by the "afterward" of 6:24. Common themes are the Syrian wars in general, the supernatural weapons of Yahweh, and the impotence of royal power. Yahweh's chariots, horses, and army (7:6) balance those of Syria (6:14). In both, servants convince their king of the proper course (6:12; 7:13) and scouts are sent to "go and see" (6:13; 7:14). Seeing and eating encompass the fate of both the Syrian troops (6:20, 23) and the captain (7:2).

The narrative exposition, 6:24–25, introduces the twin problems of siege and famine. A full-scale Syrian attack replaces the raids of verse 23. The impact of the famine is underscored in an effective way by reporting the market prices of donkeys' heads and what is called "doves' dung." Ancient historians give other examples of astronomical prices for bizarre foods during sieges. "Doves' dung" was probably the popular name for some food like falafel, although Josephus suggested that actual dung could have been used as a salt substitute (*Ant.* ix 4, 4). The "locust beans" of the New English Bible (cf. NIV) is a colorless and unneeded correction of the Masoretic text.

Verses 26–31 of chapter 6 are a narrative aside (cf. vv. 15–17 in the previous narrative) emphasizing the desperation caused by the famine and provides a motive for the king's hostility to Elisha. The woman's cry for royal justice is typical enough (cf. II Sam. 14:4), but the case she presents is a horrible

188

parody of the sort of dispute between neighbors which kings often heard. It provides a grim analogical contrast to the case brought before Solomon in happier days (I Kings 3:16–28).

The king's double reply at first indicates his feeling of general helplessness (v. 27). Even before hearing her out, he knows this must be about food and that he can do nothing. The threshing floor and the wine press are Yahweh's sphere of action, or in this case, inaction. Yet in verse 28 he indicates a willingness to do his royal duty anyway. The horror which the woman reports was not unheard of in the ancient world (Lam. 2:20; 4:10; Josephus, *Jewish War* vi 3, 4). As the fulfillment of a Deuteronomic curse for disobedience (Deut. 28:53–57) it fits the narrator's larger purpose perfectly. What her story reveals is something modern readers know all too well. Famine robs its victims of their basic humanity.

His royal power blocked, Jehoram tears his outer clothes as a sign of mourning. Because of this action, and because he is up on the wall, the people can see the sackcloth he wears as a symbol of national repentance and desperate lament. This king takes his role as the people's representative before God seriously, but in his case, sackcloth evidences a desperation that will lead to attempted murder.

In a complex and confusing scene, 6:32–7:2 relates the delivery of Elisha's oracle, which sets the stakes for God and the captain and further emphasizes the hostility between king and prophet. Jehoram underscores the interpretation of events reflected in verse 27 by verse 33. God has sent this disaster. It is vain to expect divine help. Because he no longer expects anything from God, the king resolves to kill Elisha as God's representative, as one who could presumably undo the famine if he really wanted to (cf. 4:42–44).

The elders (v. 32) function as witnesses to the prophetic word, but also as a humorous signal of the impotence of royal power, thwarted by some old men holding a door shut against it! The door is apparently never opened, and the reader receives the impression of the king and his officers talking through it to Elisha. (The MT is confusing [RSV note]). Does the king ever arrive? In chapter 7, verse 17 will make it clear that he does, but the messenger seems to telescope into the king, then the captain pops up out of nowhere. The reader, perhaps by the unintentional intervention of textual corruption, is given a completely appropriate impression of confusion and meleé.

189

INTERPRETATION

The king's question of verse 33 is answered by Elisha's oracle predicting tomorrow's farm market report. God's word is launched on a trajectory that will reach its high point in the retreat of the Syrians and land with a solid thud at 7:18–20. Commentators have usually thought of the doubting captain's windows in heaven as a reference to rain (cf. Gen. 7:11; 8:2), but this famine has been caused by siege, not drought. A more appropriate reference is to the provision of manna through heavenly openings (Ps. 78:23), which would give immediate relief. The first oracle is precise, quoting exact prices and times. The oracle of personal doom against the captain, in contrast, is open-ended and vague. This tickles the reader's interest as to just how this business of seeing but not eating will work out.

The narration returns to the main plot line with 7:3–15, the story of Yahweh's victory and the discovery of the results. These lepers serve as classic go-betweens and provide an element of comic relief. They are not quite part of Samaria's society and so are well placed to make the discovery. They remain at their distance to shout up to the gate with it. The verb they use in verse 4 ("go over") connotes desertion to the enemy. The piled up consecutive verbs in verse 8 create the effect of a flurry of looting. The act of reporting (vv. 10–11) is dragged out, emphasizing the distance between lepers and king, building narrative tension. The bottom line is reemphasized by repeating the summary of verse 5 in verse 10: There is simply no one there.

Verses 6–7 of chapter 7 offer a flashback, a rare technique in biblical literature. It is bracketed by the repeated phrase of verses 5 and 8: "when they came to the edge of the camp." The use of flashback lets the narrator report a numinous event without witnesses, enhancing its mystery. The characters in the narrative see only the results of Yahweh's victory in tethered horses and jettisoned equipment. The reader, in contrast, is privileged with a glimpse into God's miracle. Here God fights a classic holy war (cf. 19:35–36). The noise of God's horses and chariots (cf. II Sam. 5:24) throws the Syrians into an irrational panic. It makes no historical sense that the Hittites and "kings" of Egypt should attack them, but that is just the point. This panic is induced by God, not logic.

190   God's holy war attack traditionally came at dawn. The lepers make their discovery at "twilight" (vv. 5, 7; in this case earliest dawn, I Sam. 30:17) and report it before full "morning

light" (v. 9). Yet it is still night for the unknowing king (v. 12) when he is first awakened.

The climax is delayed by yet another complication: the king's suspicions, the plan to discover the truth, and the scouting party's discovery and report (vv. 12–15). Both the main plot (siege) and the subplot (Elisha's oracle) come to a climax with verse 16. Then verses 17–20 report the further consequences of this climax. The fate of the captain and the oracle that predicted it are held between the bracketed repetition of verses 17 and 20: "the people trod upon him in the gate." Verses 18–19 repeat verses 1–2 with only slight variation, notably of order (what is *ABCD* in v. 1 becomes *CBAD* in v. 18). The narrator uses a sledge hammer approach to point out the fulfillment of God's word with a vengeance. Through an "end stress" positioning of this concern and thudding repetition, the ideological theme of God's word fulfilled becomes more dominant than the central narrative theme of victory over Syria.

As in the previous narrative, an important theme is the ineffectiveness of royal power. The locus of "gate," the place where the powerful and ordinary folk mingle, holds together everything from verse 1 on. Here is the market where economic dislocation is apparent and is reversed. From here the lepers begin and to here they report. Here the royal officer with his grand title ("third man on whose arm the king leans") is trampled by the common crowd. The king is the helpless opposite of Solomon. His power can be blocked by old men pushing at a door. His piety (sackcloth) is overcome by murderous despair. It is Yahweh who gives victory, not the army. Common folk from the absolute bottom of the social structure discover this victory, but the king fails to believe it. His shrewd reading of Syrian machinations turns out to be all wrong.

This story offers the perspective of history's common folk who suffer below the walls upon which kings walk, who are robbed of their basic humanity by the economic dislocations of war, for whom even donkeys' heads are out of reach. The liberation theology of this story is not Marxist, however, but oriented to the power of Yahweh. This is revolution through a holy war fought by God alone, a total economic reversal brought on by God's war of liberation. The common folks' trampling of their oppressors is only a by-product of the distribution of God's good gifts but is also an inevitable result of official disbelief. The modern implications are clear enough.

191

The Shunammite Woman's Problem (8:1–6)

The Shunammite woman returns in chapter 8 (vv. 1–6), an economic refugee familiar enough to modern readers. Verses 1–2 offer an extended background, identifying her significantly as "the woman whose son he had restored to life." The reader is not told why God had proclaimed a famine (cf. 4:38) because that is not this story's real interest. Verse 3 introduces the problem and a way towards solution. She will intercept the king with a petition (cf. II Sam. 14:4–11), literally a "cry" for justice. Her legal situation is unknown to us. Has the crown expropriated her property? Does the king hold it in trust? Her status is certainly complicated by being (presumably) a widow with a minor son. The narrative includes her son as a witness to the truth of Gehazi's tale. The grammar of verses 4–5 (subject, participle) communicates simultaneous action. The woman goes forth while the king and Gehazi are conversing and makes her appeal. What a coincidence after seven long years!

Again the narrator identifies her as the woman whose son Elisha restored to life. She carries out her plan "to appeal to the king for her house and her land" (v. 3) when these words are repeated in verse 5a. Climax comes with the revelation of verses 5b–6a. Here is the woman and "her son whom Elisha restored to life." Verse 6a is a confirmation of Gehazi's revelation, as she tells the same story (the same verb for "tell" is used in 8:4, 5, and 6). The problem is solved in verse 6b. Special royal attention to her case means retroactive restoration of "all the revenues from her land" (NEB).

This narrative has the effect of validating all the others about Elisha. It takes us back to the time when the oral tradition about Elisha was being handed down, to the embryonic stirrings of the process that would eventually result in the canonical Book of Kings. The king who wishes to hear of Elisha's great deeds merges with the readership, which also has an interest in the Elisha tradition. His reaction is to be the reader's reaction: become convinced and act on that conviction.

It is notable that in this case the action called for is an act of economic justice. The basic move of this story from problem to solution by means of an intervention is common to all these narratives. Here, however, the intervention is not by a miraculous deed or prophetic word. Here the intervention is really the oral tradition about the prophet. Here a problem of economic justice is solved by the retelling of good news about one who raised the dead, an act referred to four times in six verses. This story moves into the situation of God's people under the power of canonical tradition. Stories about past mighty deeds now produce the faith that those deeds themselves once created. For the church, the stories of Jesus, who raised the dead and was himself raised, have power in themselves to solve life's problems.

Hazael Becomes King (8:7–15)

The story of Hazael's rise to kingship (8:7–15) begins as a request for prophetic aid, similar to chapter 5 and I Kings chapter 14. It is a sort of mirror image to 1:2–16. In the larger plot of Kings, it gives Elisha the opportunity to fulfill the commission of I Kings 19:15. Read against the background of the Naaman story, the reader may be expecting a better outcome, but instead of the pattern of human need met by God's action, the reader encounters something extraordinarily different.

Ben-hadad's query (vv. 7–9) serves to bring Hazael and Elisha together. On the surface, the narrative seems to be about Ben-hadad's sickness. Will he recover (literally "live")? The reader might think this likely until verse 10 is reached. The lavish gifts point to a favorable outcome, as does Hazael's humble address ("your son Ben-hadad"). The plot is kept moving by a series of questions: Shall I live? Why does my lord weep? What is your servant that he should do this? What did Elisha say?

The story shifts gears at verse 10 to describe Hazael's coup. Elisha's first word directs Hazael to tell an outright lie—you will definitely live (RSV "recover"). Great ingenuity has been applied by interpreters (going back as far as the transmitters of MT) to exonerate Elisha from the suspicion of advocating a lie. The reader with moral scruples may wish to consider this as Elisha's first impression, superseded by the vision (cf. "shown") he next reports. But the pair of grammatically emphasized verbal phrases clearly contrast the lie ("certainly recover") and the truth ("certainly die"). The reader is reminded of the pattern followed by Micaiah in I Kings 22:15, 17.

The lie is for Ben-hadad, the truth for Hazael. Hazael's action will prevent the fulfillment of the first and ensure the truth of the second. Verse 11 is hard to follow due to confusion over the grammatical subject. The subject of "ashamed" is certainly Hazael (in spite of NEB), since the man of God is reintro-

193

duced as subject at the end of the verse. The text may be describing the physical manifestations of a second vision of Elisha. Or perhaps this is a contest of wills which Hazael loses by dropping his eyes. In any case, the verse hints that Hazael has some personal interest in Ben-hadad's death and that Elisha has something more to say.

The narrative reaches its emotional peak in the tears and terror of verse 12. Hazael's question is the reader's question. Elisha's tears provide a chance to reveal what else he knows. Ben-hadad's death means the horrors of war for Israel:

> Their forts you will ignite with fire.
> Their soldiers with the sword you will slay.
> Their infants you will hurl down.
> Their pregnant women you will rip up.

The language is stereotyped (15:16; Amos 1:13; Hos. 13:16) but no less horrible for that. What is "evil" for Israel is, in contrast, Hazael's "great achievement" (v. 13). Hazael's question provides Elisha with an occasion to explain with a second vision, introduced just as the first ("the Lord has shown me").

Hazael returns to tell a partial truth to Ben-hadad as a lie. Verse 15 reports Ben-hadad's death with a certain vagueness. One cannot be completely sure that Hazael is the subject of the verbs nor are we completely clear as to the nature of the murder weapon (coverlet? mosquito net?), if indeed murder is intended. "Somebody put something woven into water and laid it over the king's face, and the next thing you know, he was dead." Such a report gives a good impression of the partial knowledge one might have of an event which took place in the inner rooms of a far-off palace.

In sharp contrast to previous stories, here a human agency brings God's word to fruition. Historically, Hazael was indeed a usurper, the "son of a nobody" (ANET, p. 280). Neither Elisha nor God is tied directly to Hazael's succession. The prophetic vision planted a seed and became a classic "self-fulfilling prophecy." Only the context of the sin of Ahab's house and of God's long-range plan (I Kings 19:15) reveals God's hand behind Hazael's succession. This is the same universal God one has read about in 3:27 and 5:1. Once more a lie has been used to advance God's purpose (cf. I Kings 22).

194

But what a terrible purpose! God is working disaster on Israel. This story is a narrative reflex of the communal lament, which interpreted national crisis as sent by God (Ps. 44:9–12; 89:38–42). Israel has no automatic guarantee of divine favor. If there is any meaning to be found in the holocaust of verse 12, it will not become clear until the fall of the Kingdom of Israel. It is not explicitly punishment for sin, at least not yet. Here the word of God impels a wicked deed for the strange purpose of bringing doom to Israel. Yahweh is not powerless, as some exiles were tempted to conclude, but rather one whose own purposes have made it necessary to declare war on the people of promise.

PART FOUR

Israel's Last Chance and the End

II KINGS 8:16—17

II Kings 8:16—10
Fruitless Reformation in Israel (Jehu)

One could easily imagine that this is contemporary news rather than ancient history. Replace the horses with tanks, the arrows with automatic weapons, Elisha and Jehonadab with doctrinaire political theorists and one has a classic modern military coup. These chapters carry us deep into the paradox created by human and divine violence as it intersects with God's will for peace. We shall examine first the material on Joram and Ahaziah, then the prophetic designation of Jehu and the seven violent acts that result. Finally we shall search for some meaningful applications for these stories.

Joram and Ahaziah (8:16–29)

Before reporting the revolt and reformation of Jehu, the narrator opens and closes the file on Joram of Judah and opens one on Ahaziah. The organizing system required that the death of Jehoram of Israel be reported in the section on Ahaziah.

The details given for the reign of Joram of Judah are in harmony with the narrator's negative evaluation of him. Edom broke away (v. 20). Historians find this verse hard to reconcile with 3:9 and I Kings 22:47. Verse 22 seems to be contradicted by 14:22. Perhaps the author is using sources in a partisan way at this point. The details of the battle at Zair are unclear, presumably because of textual corruption (contrast the solutions of NEB and RSV). We gather that the outcome was mixed, but that it was ultimately a defeat for Judah. Edom's continued independence (v. 22) would have sounded a bitter note for exilic readers in view of Edom's recent occupation of Judah's territory. Joram's fortunes were so blighted that even a small independent city like Libnah thought it safe to revolt.

The coregency indicated at verse 16 (RSV note) was required to keep the chronology internally consistent, reconciling 3:1 and I Kings 22:41 with an accession in Jehoram of Israel's fifth year. The note in the next chapter (9:29) is a disturbing element, perhaps added through a failure to understand that Ahaziah's accession year was being counted as a whole year (vv. 25-26).

In the reigns of these two kings, the narrator insists, Judah merged with Israel in apostasy according to the pattern of the house of Ahab (vv. 18, 27). One symptom of this (according to the author's sources or imagination) was the erection of a temple to Baal in Jerusalem (11:18). This contamination is traced to the marriage alliance between the two kingdoms, an evaluative echo of Solomon's foreign wives and Ahab's marriage to Jezebel. Joram of Judah married Athaliah, the daughter of Ahab and Jezebel. The "daughter" of verse 26 should be understood generically as "female descendant." Ahaziah also had some unidentified alliance with the house of Ahab (v. 27; not the mother of Joash anyway, cf. 12:1), unless "son-in-law" is to be understood broadly as his relationship through his mother Athaliah. It is as though apostasy was a contagion spread by marriage.

Although Judah and Israel merge in sin, God has differing attitudes towards the two nations, based on God's unconditional dynastic promise to David (v. 19; cf. I Kings 9:25; 15:4). The word translated as "lamp" ought to be understood as "dominion." Thus, there is no need to change the Masoretic text as the English versions do, under the impression that David's "lamp" equaled his sons. The promise reads, "to give to him dominion for his sons for ever." The fundamental difference between Israel and Judah is not their respective behavior, therefore, but God's gracious choice of David. The narrator announces that, whatever is in store for Israel, God has no intention of destroying Judah—for now at least. Exilic readers would have known that there would be more to the story than this.

The Designation of Jehu (9:1–16)

Within the file on Ahaziah, brackets created by the repetition of most of the content and much of the language of 8:28–29 by 9:14–15 enclose the designation of Jehu. This information sets up the locale of the coming event, creates a necessary separation between Jehu and Jehoram, and shifts the reader from the annalistic to the narrative mode. In the first bracket (8:28–29), Ramoth-gilead points to the anointing scene, Jehoram's wound to verses 17–26, and Ahaziah's visit to verses 27–28.

The anointing episode itself moves from commission (vv. 1–3) through execution (vv. 4–10) to results (vv. 11–14a). Movements of the young prophet mark off these sections. Elisha instructs his protegé with a string of brusque imperatives, which then expand into the narrative of execution.

The execution section is packed with a preliminary delay (v. 5) and expansions to Elijah's oracle that point forward to what is to come (vv. 7–10). The oracle as delivered makes it clear that God (first person) is really doing the anointing. Jehu is to be king over Israel as "the people of Yahweh," a sacral term that indicates Jehu's reforming purpose and implies that Israel has become something other than this under the Omrides. The divine speech contains traces of Deuteronomistic language, reaching back to Jezebel's acts of violence against the prophets reported in I Kings 18:4. The target of God's vengeance is the entire house of Ahab. In verses 8–10 strands of prophecy come together into a nexus (I Kings 14:10–11; 16:3–4; 21:21, 23, 29), then separate again to be fulfilled in Jehu's coming actions (v. 36; 10:10, 17, cf. 30).

The results section again contains delay (v. 11). The question of "shalom" (is all well?) points forward to Jehu's encounter with Jehoram. Jehu first deflects curiosity: "You know how these prophets prattle on." Both he and his officers (with "mad fellow") deprecate the peculiar, ecstatic behavior of the prophets of their day, but a similar madness will mark Jehu's own zeal (v. 20).

In verse 11, Jehoram is still Jehu's "master," but this does not survive his revelation of the core of the young prophet's oracle: "I anoint you king over Israel." This revelation is followed by acclamation (vv. 12–13), and the conspiracy is set in motion (v. 14a). With a haste that betrays their enthusiasm, the officers shower Jehu with the traditional symbols of royalty: a carpet (Matt. 21:8) or throne made from their cloaks, trumpets (11:14; I Kings 1:34), and acclamation (I Kings 1:39–40).

The closing bracket (vv. 14*b*–16) is interleaved with transitional material (closing the city exits, Jehu's move to Jezreel) which carries the reader over to the progress of the conspiracy.

Seven Violent Acts (9:17—10:36)

The rest of chapters 9 and 10 is organized on the basis of seven violent acts. The targets are struck down in rational order:

> Jehoram—9:17–26
> Ahaziah—9:27–29
> Jezebel—9:30–37
> Ahab's seventy "sons"—10:1–11
> Ahaziah's kinfolk—10:12–14
> loyalists in Samaria—10:15–17
> the worshipers of Baal—10:18–28

The focus moves from acts against individuals to whole groups, and the reader is given the impression of that snowballing violence that is so characteristic of revolution.

In each case the climactic act itself is set up by some narrative preparation. This ranges from the elaborate delays produced by Jehoram's successive horsemen, Jehu's letters to the elders of Samaria, or the steps taken to gather Baal's faithful, to the less extensive lead-ins to the death of Ahaziah or of his relatives. Sometimes an order of Jehu precedes those killings he does not commit himself (9:27, 33; 10:6, 14, 25). In all but one of these reports, certain results of the violent act are described, for example the burial of Ahaziah or the destruction of Baal's pillar and house. Often these results are presented as a fulfillment of the prophetic word (9:25–26, 36–37; 10:10, 17), a fact pointed out by the narrator or, more often, by Jehu himself.

Elements of trickery are involved in the deaths of Jehoram, the seventy "sons," and the worshipers of Baal. The deaths of Jehoram and Jezebel are linked by the theme of "shalom" (9:17, 19, 22, 31) and the references to Jezebel in 9:22 and Zimri in 9:31. Ahaziah's death is linked to Jehoram's by his flight. The deaths of his relatives are tied to the others by the mention of the king (not RSV) and queen mother (that is, Jehoram and

200

Jezebel) and the word "shalom." The presence of Jehonadab the son of Rechab links the last two massacres.

The story of Jehu is told artistically. The dialogue is realistic and revealing: Jehu's reticence in 9:19, his reminiscence in 9:25, or the exchange with Jehonadab in 10:15. There is heavy irony in Jehu's claim to be preparing a "sacrifice" for Baal (10: 19) and lighter word play between "worshipers" and "destroy" at the end of this same verse and between "servant" and "worshipers" in 10:23. The narrator knows the value of suspense, produced by the hidden anointing of Jehu and the delay in making this act known (9:6–12) or the tension-building messengers sent by Jehoram. Chauvinist readers must have delighted in the strategem for smoking out true Baal worshipers. The artful characterization of Jehu is worthy of note. He drives like a madman (RSV "furiously") (9:20) and approaches his other actions in the same way. His letters to the elders of Samaria reveal insight into human nature. He is tricky, brutal, and cold (cf. 9:34).

At first, the narrator is in perfect evaluative harmony with Jehu. What Jehu does is according to God's revealed will, and both he and the narrator carefully point this out (9:7–10, 22, 26, 36–37; 10:10, 30). The agreement with Jehonadab (10:15–16, 23*a*) performs the same evaluative function. Yet at the end of the report, the narrator turns on Jehu with an evaluation that is at best ambiguous (10:29–31).

The episode of the murder of Jehoram (first act; 9:17–26) climbs through a long, tension producing preparation (vv. 17–21) to a climactic peak of revelation and death (vv. 22–24) and then descends through denouement (vv. 25–26). The forced isolation of Jezreel (v. 15*b*) insures Jehoram's ignorance. The narrative permits the reader to imagine that the king assumes that this rapidly approaching company brings news from the front and to appreciate the irony in the king's anxious attempts to find out what is going on. The tension builds with the repeated question, "Is it shalom?" Does all go well at Ramoth-gilead? Has war broken out? Jehu's response to the riders anticipates the one he will make to Jehoram, "What do you anti-shalom people have to do with shalom" (vv. 18–19)? Jehu, the commander himself, is tentatively identified (9:20). This can only be the best or worst possible news! Jehoram and Ahaziah ride out in separate chariots to set the stage for two separate killings and meet Jehu, as the narrator ominously points out, at the property of Naboth.

Jehu's reinterpretation of the question "Is it shalom?" signals the revelation of his true intent (9:22). The issue of true shalom runs deeper than any matter of war or peace. Jehu rides now in the service of shalom (balance, harmony) between God and the people. This sort of shalom has been destroyed by the harlotries and sorceries, both literal and metaphorical (17:17; 21:6; cf. Deut. 18:10), incited by Jezebel. At the shocking moment of revelation, the king turns to flee. Jehu grabs his bow (cf. NEB) and shoots Jehoram in the back.

It is only as Bidkar mops up that Jehu's reminiscence of an old oracle against Ahab's family explains what is going on. The reader has not encountered this particular oracle before. I Kings 21:19 was something quite different, not involving Naboth's sons, for example, and was fulfilled in the next chapter (22:38), albeit in a slightly odd way. There is no mention of how this remembered oracle was delivered or by whom. Jehu is telescoped into the spokesman for God's word and its fulfiller (9:26). To modern ears this previously unmentioned word seems a bit too convenient, flavored strongly with pretext and self-justification. Yet Bidkar is the needed second witness, and ancient readers probably would have accepted it as genuine without question.

The word translated as "requite" (v. 26) offers the key to Jehu's actions and the text's insistent repetition of "shalom." This verb is from the same root as "shalom" and means "to create balance, harmony." Paradoxically, Jehu's violence is restoring peace, the shalom between God and the people that had been destroyed by Ahab's blood guilt and Jezebel's harlotries and sorceries. "Is it shalom? Is everything OK?" Jehu's subordinates asked him (9:11). His personal answer was yes, but at a deeper level it was no. "Is it shalom? Is all well at Ramoth-gilead?" Jehu's answer was that supporters of Ahab's dynasty have nothing to do with real shalom. God is restoring shalom, strangely enough, by the murderous violence of political revolution (Olyan, *CBQ* 46:652–668).

The murder of Ahaziah (second act; 9:27–29) eliminates him as a possible source of vengeance for his uncle's death and puts Jehu in harmony with the narrator's own evaluation of the royal house of Judah (8:27). The path of Ahaziah's flight makes good geographic sense. The fate of his body resonates with

Josiah's end (25:30). Here the narrator's file on Ahaziah closes explicitly and a new one on Jehu (9:30—10:36) opens implicitly.

The liquidation of Jezebel (third act; 9:30–37) begins as she puts on eye shadow and greets Jehu with a rhetorical question. Most likely the reader is supposed to evaluate her final toilet as a reflection of her "harlotries" (9:22; cf. Jer. 4:30; Ezek. 23:40) and hear her question as a bitter and insulting reference to Zimri's seven-day fiasco (I Kings 16:11–14), with an ironic echo of the topic of shalom. An alternate interpretation is to understand her final act as a seductive, Cleopatra-like preparation for lovemaking in the expectation that Jehu would take over Jehoram's harem (II Sam. 16:21–22). Her greeting would then be teasing or taunting. In any case, Jehu orders her dropped out the window, and the horses in his entourage trample her.

His eating and drinking reflects his contempt for her and gives the dogs time to do their work. Already showing a king's solidarity with royalty (cf. Saul with Agag and Ahab with Benhadad) in ordering her burial, his evaluation, "accursed woman," agrees with that of God and the narrator. The narrative itself does not state why so little was left of Jezebel, but Jehu interprets this circumstance as a fulfillment of Elijah's prophecy. This is the second time Jehu himself has interpreted his own actions as prophetic fulfillment. The reader will find out in 10:17 and 30 that both God and the narrator agree. There is no insistence on an exact, mechanical correspondence between prophecy and fulfillment; dung was not mentioned at all in I Kings 21:23.

The fourth act (10:1–11), the elimination of the seventy (a round number to indicate many) members of Ahab's family ("sons") is prepared for by a delaying exchange of messages. Jehu sends two letters, a structural link to the two riders sent by Jehoram (9:17–19) and the double call for a convocation of Baal's worshipers (10:19, 21). Jehu's first letter to the decision makers of Samaria is quoted in midstream (cf. 5:6). He suggests that Jehoram may still be their "master," but the language of their reply denies this with "your servants" (10:3, 5) and emphasizes total submission. Jehu's second letter indicates that this is not enough; Jehoram is still their master (10:6) until they pass a test of loyalty and obedience. The call for the "heads" of the royal princes is open to interpretation, for the word "head" can also mean "leader."

The great men of the city prove themselves by choosing

203

the more loyal interpretation and pack off the heads of their former wards in baskets. Jehu imitates Assyrian practice and has them set out in public view. The next morning he skillfully uses them as a springboard to justify his murderous policies. "You are righteous" (10:9, the literal meaning of the Hebrew), he informs the populace, meaning either that they are innocent of his actions or that they are fair-minded judges. "My deeds are well known, but where have these heads come from?" It is as though they have arrived out of the blue; therefore, this must be further fulfillment of Elijah's word! Then Jehu continues the process of fulfillment with a general purge of everyone connected with Ahab's house (10:11).

The massacre of Ahaziah's relatives (fifth act; 10:12–14) comes next. Note the conventionalized number of victims (2:24). Historians have considered it an unlikely event that these folk would have been out for a visit in such perilous times. From a literary point of view, however, these are classic "babes in the woods," ignorant of what is going on. (A similar group meets a similar fate in Jer. 41:4–8.) They are on the way to Jezreel to inquire after the welfare (the Hebrew word is "shalom"!) of the royal princes, but Ahab's house has no one left there. They still speak of Jehoram as king. Their interest in shalom is as misguided as Jehoram's was. The usual identification of Beth-eked with Beit Quad puts them well off the beaten track between Samaria and Jezreel. Perhaps the reader is meant to understand that they are coming in the "back door" to Jezreel via the Jordan valley and Beth-shan, which would explain their being out of touch with the current crisis.

The slaughter of loyalists in Samaria (sixth act; 10:15–17) is prepared for by the explicit approval of the rigorist party of the Rechabites (Jer. 35). This group represented fanatical support for what they considered to be the old ways of Yahwism, symbolized by a return to an idealized nomadism. Jehonadab their "father" (Jer. 35:6) will be an approving witness to Jehu's zeal. The narrator uses this as another way of evaluating Jehu positively. Jehu's "zeal" connects with that of Elijah (I Kings 19:10, 14).

Jehu's seventh, final, and climactic act of violence is reported in 10:18–28. The Baal temple in Samaria goes back to I Kings 16:32 and is representative of the sin of Ahab's house. The preparation for this "great sacrifice" for Baal is full of doublets and redundancies. The repetition of the call for assembly in

10:19 and 21 emphasizes the completeness of the gathering. The broken grammatical construction (whatever its origin) gives an appropriate impression of confused meleé. Jehonadab is still functioning as an approving witness (10:23). Once the climax has passed, the narrative focuses on the results (10:27–28). The pillar of Baal had been stored away by Jehoram (3:2); now it is burned up (is it wood? limestone?). The notice that the Baal temple remains a latrine "to this day" is less a way of supporting the credibility of the narrative than simply a good joke.

The file on Jehu is wrapped up with an ambiguous evaluation. Pointing forward to 15:12, verse 30 reveals God's approval of Jehu's violent deeds against Ahab's family. Jehu is promised the "throne of Israel" (cf. Solomon in I Kings 2:4; 8:25; 9:5), but this very promise is an ambiguous one: four generations, but no more. Jehu is condemned for following in Jeroboam's sin with the two golden calves (10:29).

Punishment becomes evident even in Jehu's lifetime. Hazael's military successes are equated unequivocally with God's act of cutting off from Israel the entire Transjordan, described in classic Deuteronomistic terms (Deut. 3:12–13). Historians point out that Syria's victories depended on a relaxation of Assyrian pressure, but for this narrator, God's intent to punish was the causative factor. The territorial loss will be taken up again in chapter 13. The length of Jehu's reign is given at the end of his file (10:32) because there was no formal beginning to it (cf. I Kings 11:42; 14:20).

Violence and Shalom

Prophetic intervention in royal succession is nothing new to Kings (I Kings 11:29–39). Jeroboam had offered the hope of reform, but it had likewise been a disappointment. The reader has been expecting this intervention since I Kings 19:16 and can hardly be surprised that an oracle and an act of anointing could set in motion such prodigious results. The reader knows by now the power of the prophetic word.

What is new and shocking is the scope and brutality of Jehu's reforming violence. Jehu's murders at Jezreel were to become a byword, a bloody symbol of the dynasty he began (Hosea 1:4–5). Modern readers need no reminder of how easily high-principled revolutions deteriorate into bloodbaths. Jehu impresses us as one of the Old Testament's most modern char-

205

acters. What is harder for us to come to terms with is the claim
that God was behind all this bloodshed and betrayal and that
God's intention was to reinstitute shalom by means of violence.
Is it really possible to create peace with violence?

On the human level we know that this will not work. Peaceful ends can never justify violent means, because in our world
the means inevitably contaminate the ends. Our ethical decisions about violence (war, revolution, capital punishment, abor-
tion) are always a matter of compromise, leading at best to
partial shaloms, thoroughly leavened by the violence we must
employ to achieve them.

Only of God can it be thought that peaceful ends might be
achieved by violent means, for only God can guarantee the
outcome. Yet even in this narrative, the outcome is not complete and perfect shalom between God and Israel, as the final
evaluation of Jehu makes clear. Even a violence as brutal and
widespread as Jehu's could not reform Israel. Even more radical
violence would have to be employed by God, defeat at the
hands of Hazael, then the Assyrians, and finally the Babylonians.
Certainly this narrative is a warning to all who would take
lightly loyalty to the God of the Bible. It is a witness to the
power of God's prophetic word and the resolute nature of God's
action in the arena of human events.

There is a paradox here that goes deep into the nature of
the biblical God and into what a terrible, violent price that God
must pay in order to restore peace and harmony with a sinful
people. The New Testament will raise this paradox to an even
higher order of magnitude and focus it on the cross (Rom 4:25;
5:8; 8:32; II Cor.5:19).

II Kings 11—12
The Fruit of Reform in Judah (Joash)

This is not an unbiased historical report but a story told to
advance a certain interpretation of events. Read in context, the
revolution of Joash is a low-key reflection of Jehu's, which suffers
by comparison. In both, an evil queen is killed and the temple
of Baal destroyed, but here there is a contrast to Jehu's heart-
less, intemperate violence. Here all is "according to the cus-

tom," a constitutional transition of which the Judahite readers could be proud (cf. England's "Glorious Revolution" or the smooth functioning of the United States Constitution in the aftermath of Watergate).

The narrative is told in such a confusing manner that source critics have divided it into at least two and as many as five sources or layers. Their observations have often been cogent but not helpful in understanding the text as it now stands.

Narrative Concerns

One narrative concern of chapter 11 is to de-legitimate Athaliah. The time of Athaliah is treated as an interregnum by Kings. Like the ascension of Elijah, her reign and overthrow are reported outside the usual system. Jehu's file was closed by 10:36, and the section on Joash does not start until chapter 12. She is no heir of David. She is an alien anomaly. Her story is told against the background of God's eternal dynastic promise to David in 8:19, the narrator's evaluation of the contaminating marriage alliance of 8:18, 26–27, and the brutal death of Ahaziah, 9:27–28.

A second major narrative concern of chapter 11 is to convince the reader that the restoration of Joash was a popular effort. The little king himself performs only one action: He sits on the throne (v. 19). Jehoiada the priest is the prime mover in the conspiracy, but the people as a whole take over at key moments. He or those obeying him are subjects of the action from verse 4 to 12a, but an indefinite "they" join in at verse 12b. Athaliah hears and sees not just the guard but the "people" (v. 13) and the "people of the land" (v. 14). Jehoiada and his obedient captains are the subjects again in verses 15–17 but alternate with the "people of the land" in 18–19. The awkward indefinite plurals in verses 2 (RSV note) and 19 are reflexes of this same concern. Again, the cast of characters is as inclusive as possible: the captains of the Carites and the guards (v. 4), both major divisions of the guards and all three subdivisions of at least one of these (vv. 6–7)—enough soldiers to stretch out through whole temple area (v. 11), the captains of the army proper (v. 15), and the "people of the land" (vv. 14, 18, 19, 20). Contrasting emotional responses are also used to underscore the popularity of Joash's accession. The true representatives of the people blow trumpets, clap hands, shout, and rejoice (vv. 12, 14, 20). In contrast Athaliah tears her clothes (v. 14), and the

207

city, which one might have expected to support her, remains quiet (v. 20).

A third concern is to assure the reader that Jehoiada's action was legitimate. The baby is identified as the son of Ahaziah (v. 2), kidnapped by Ahaziah's own sister, who is herself a guarantee of his identity. The narrator refers to him as the "king's son" (vv. 4, 12). Joash is spoken of as king even before the ceremony, by Jehoiada in verses 7 (RSV note) and 8 and by the narrator in verse 11 (RSV note). The ceremonial shields of David (II Sam. 8:7; I Kings 14:27) and his spear (RSV makes it plural) add an air of authenticity to the ceremony (v. 10). The acclamation is by the people themselves, not just some soldiers (vv. 13–14), and Joash stands by the pillar "according to the custom" (v. 14; 23:3). A covenant is made between king and people (v. 17), and then Joash sits "on the throne of the kings" (v. 20) as their legitimate heir. The propriety of this revolution is undergirded by the care shown for the sanctity of the temple. They only set hands on Athaliah there and wait to kill her outside (vv. 15–16).

Restoration

The narrative exposition in chapter 11 is presented by verses 1–2. All seems lost in the first verse, but the rescue focuses our attention on baby Joash. The central complication is the contrast in verse 3. Two incompatible facts are coordinated by the grammar of simultaneous circumstance: The true king hides, meanwhile the false queen reigns. The presence of the nurse signals Joash's babyhood. The seventh year (traditionally the year of restoration) signals an upset in this unacceptable status quo.

Verses 4–8 present the plan. We do not yet know just who this Jehoiada is (unless like the original audience we have heard the tale before) but will find out when he is obeyed (v. 9). He is obviously in charge, taking action with a series of narrative verbs (v. 4) and initiating a secrecy that will end with verse 12.

Verses 6 and 7 are difficult to understand and have often been emended. From verse 9 it is clear that the major division in question is that between those who were going off duty and those who were coming on duty and that both halves of the total guard were to take part in the coup. It is possible to stick with the text as it stands (and NIV offers a paraphrased attempt to

208

do so). The first set of orders goes to the watch coming off duty, a group divided into thirds: those who guard the palace, those who are at the gate Sur, and those who are at the gate behind the guards. They are to guard the palace. The second set of orders goes to the watch going on duty, a group considered to be in two divisions, perhaps implying that this group is twice as large as the first watch. They are to guard the temple and the king.

Do these intricate orders create the effect of a complex plan in the reader's mind? Or of military jargon only partially understood by the layperson? In any case, some things are perfectly clear. This plan is a disturbance in the ordinary routine which takes advantage of the complexities of the special Sabbath movements of the guard. It is one which robs Athaliah of troops with which to resist. The purpose is to protect the king as he goes out and comes in, to surround him with weapons in hand and to kill any who approach.

The execution of Jehoiada's plan is reported in verses 9–11, the upshot of which is that the king is well guarded. The troops form a semi-circle around the entrance to the temple building proper and the altar out in front of it. When the king emerges, they will therefore be beside him (RSV note to v. 11).

The narrative climax comes in verse 12, and then reactions and results are reported by verses 13–20. One item in the coronation is of special interest—the "testimony" given the king. Psalm 132:12 indicates that this "testimony" was part of the coronation ideology of Judah and that it could be paralleled by the word "covenant" in the context of dynastic promise. Scholars have sometimes envisioned a scroll handed the king during the ceremony. Whatever this "testimony" may have been in actual historical fact, in the context of Kings the law of Deuteronomy is clearly intended. Deuteronomy 17:18–20 instructs the king to have his own copy of the book of the law handy for ready reference. The coming story of Josiah throws light on what is intended here.

The first results of the climactic coronation involve Athaliah (vv. 13–16). The sight of legitimacy (the people of the land, the king by the customary pillar) undoes her. Just who these "people of the land" were is a contested matter. Some have seen the expression as simply a synonym for the people in general, as the enfranchised citizens, or as property owners. The most popular opinion, supported by the contrast in verse 20, is that this group represents the rural gentry who stood solidly behind Yahweh and the Davidic dynasty in opposition to the nobility of Jerusalem. This group's ideology will show itself to be in harmony with that of the narrator. They will assist with the legitimate succession of four kings evaluated as righteous: Joash, Amaziah, Uzziah, Josiah (but Jehoahaz otherwise). "Follows her" in verse 15 is not intended metaphorically but literally. There was no general purge.

Two covenants are made (v. 17). The first is between God on the one hand and the king and people on the other. In the context of the Book of Kings, this must be understood as the covenant set forth in Deuteronomy. Its pivotal consequence is that Judah is to be the "people of Yahweh" (Deut. 27:9; cf. 4:20; 9:29; 14:2; 26:18). Certainly the dynastic promise to David (II Sam. 7:8–16) is also to be understood, given the ideological tendencies of Kings. This is a covenant of the sort that Josiah will mediate in 23:3. Jehoiada seems to be a stand-in for the under-age king as covenant mediator. This covenant links back to the "testimony" given Joash in verse 12. The king is viewed as the custodian of the law, in harmony with Deuteronomy 17:18–20. A second covenant is made between king and people, the formal statement of popular recognition for which Rehoboam was hoping in I Kings 12.

Verse 18 follows verse 17 automatically. Purification is the result of covenant renewal. The acceptance of Deuteronomy as covenant law naturally leads to the destruction of Baal's temple in Jerusalem and Mattan its priest. Both make their first appearance here just in time to become the objects of reforming zeal, and their actual historical reality has been properly doubted. This reformation is so important that it interrupts the logical flow of events, which is picked up again in verse 19. The setting of watchmen for Yahweh's temple at the end of verse 18 provides a contrast to the destruction of Baal's house. Verse 20 implies a contrast between the joy of the people of the land and the quiet of Jerusalem, where Yahwistic loyalty may have been less clear cut. Athaliah's death is mentioned once more (cf. v. 16) by way of summary. Finally verse 21 returns our attention to the age of the king, causing the reader to reflect once more on Jehosheba's providential action in verse 2 and providing a transition to the opening of a file for Joash in chapter 12.

Reformation

Chapter 12 consists of the opening (vv. 1–3) and conclusion (vv. 19–21) of the file on Joash, enclosing two reports focused on the temple. These tell of Joash's system for reconstructing the temple (vv. 4–16) and the tribute of temple treasures used to pay off Hazael (vv. 17–18). The file opens with an evaluation of Joash. The king generally did right, but failed to remove the high places. From a historical point of view, it is unfair to condemn Joash for not following the law of Deuteronomy, which would not be discovered for two centuries yet. However, Kings tells the story from an ideological perspective. Like his son (14:6), Joash has the book of the law in hand, to follow if he so chooses. Joash had been handed this "testimony" at his coronation.

The narrative exposition of the first report takes the form of the king's reforming command in verses 4–5. The word translated as "acquaintance" more likely refers to a temple official concerned with business and finance, a combination tax collector and cashier. The narrative complication is introduced by the failure of the first system to produce results (v. 6).

Verses 9–16 describe a new, successful plan. The silver would be collected by one of the three priests of high status who guarded the entrance (cf. 25:18). It would be placed in a box somewhere near the entrance. The exact placement of the box by some "altar" or other is confusing to us, perhaps because we do not know enough about the layout of the temple grounds. Commentators have had trouble with the statement (v. 10) that the officials "wrapped up" or "tied up" the money before counting it. (RSV reverses the verbs. NEB takes the problematic verb from another root meaning to "melt down.") Perhaps what is being described is bagging up the miscellaneous bits of silver and pieces of jewelry, there being no coins in circulation until the Persian period, in order to make the weighing and recording ("counting") easier. The grammar of the Hebrew indicates that a new customary procedure was established: verse 9, "used to put in" and verse 11, "would give."

The narrative presents this new plan in a positive light. First, the collection was aboveboard (cf. v. 8a). The chest was in public view and the money was counted by respected representatives of the crown and the priesthood. No accounting was needed because the distribution was done honestly. Sec-

211

ond, any direct role for the priests was eliminated (v. 8*b*). The money was paid to intermediaries, who in turn paid the workers (v. 15). Third, all the proprieties were observed. The monies under consideration, assessments and voluntary offerings, are scrupulously described (v. 4). Only repairs were paid for from this fund, not liturgical vessels. The legitimate perquisites of the priests (Lev. 5:16) were not affected. The general effect is to clarify that all was done properly.

The reader simply assumes without being told so that the second plan worked. The real focus of interest is less the repair of the temple than the wisdom of the king. The non-performance of the priests (v. 6) highlights this by contrast. Joash thus becomes a pale reflection of Solomon, a bittersweet sign of how far things have deteriorated in Jerusalem. There are parallels between the accessions of Solomon and Joash (11:12 and I Kings 1:39; 11:13 and I Kings 1:41). In this narrative, verse 13 provides a contrasting echo to I Kings 7:50. Like Solomon, Joash reigned forty years, but his wisdom dealt only with minor administrative details and his patronage of the temple involved only patching it up.

The incident with Hazael is a further sad commentary on his reign. The report in verses 17–18 moves simply from a threat to its deflection. Apparently Hazael's control of Gath, the exact location of which remains in dispute, made an attack on Jerusalem feasible. In the ancient world, buying off a stronger attacker was a standard diplomatic ploy; and the reader cannot automatically assume that the narrator implies disapproval. The use of the temple offerings of so many generations, however, shows the desperate position in which Judah found itself.

The concluding material demonstrates that even pious kings are not immune to the vicissitudes of political existence. One may contrast this more realistic view with the retelling of Joash's story by II Chronicles 24. Text corruption obscures the names of his killers and the location of the murder, but the good news is that the Davidic dynasty has returned to its automatic succession. Both temple and dynasty have been repaired by the reforming king.

Implications for Theology and Context

212

What is fascinating about these chapters from a theological point of view is that God does not seem to do anything or say anything. The prophets, so visible in previous chapters, have disappeared, and along with them the word of God which has been the prime mover of events. Instead a priest is the instigator of this revolution and the people quickly join in. A king comes up with a new administrative procedure. In place of prophetic intervention, the causative factors are the danger which threatens the Davidic dynasty, the "lamp" (dominion) of God's promise (8:19), and the disrepair of the temple. God's presence has contracted down to written law (the "testimony" and "covenant"; 11:12, 17). Yet this written law produces the fruits of reformation as effectively as the prophetic word could have, perhaps even more so. God is at work even when there is no visible evidence of God's presence (cf. Ruth or the Succession History, especially II Sam. 17:14, and perhaps Luke 11: 29–30).

Given what Kings has said about the Davidic line (8:19), these chapters begin with a threat to Judah's very existence. God's promise hangs by the single thread of a baby boy. In the larger canonical story, this had happened before and will happen again: the last minute provision of the legitimate heir (Isaac), the protection of the baby who is the key to the future (Moses), the new shoot from the chopped off stump of dynasty (Isa. 11:1–2). In the New Testament drama too, all hangs on the fate of a single baby boy, heir of David, providentially protected from the violence of threatened royalty (Matt. 2:13–15). Looking at the story of Joash from this perspective, one may be less willing to conclude that God plays no role in the unfolding of events here. Instead, the action of God has retreated behind the events of ordinary history: political revolution, the institution of kingship, obedience to the written law, and even the mechanics of fiscal responsibility.

This fiscal plan of Joash is important to the larger structure of Kings. It prepares the reader for the more important reform of Josiah. Just as there are similarities between the covenant renewal of Josiah and the events surrounding the accession of Joash (11:14, 17 and 23:1–3), the background for the discovery of the law book in 22:4–7, 9 will repeat much of the language of 12:9–15.

Chapters 11–12 (Joash) share a basic structure with chapters 9–10 (Jehu). First there is a removal of Ahab's house and the

213

restoration of an acceptable king (9:1–10:17 and 11:1–17, 19–21). This is followed by efforts at religious reform (10:18–28 and 11:18; 12:4–16). Both stories are told in the context of editorial evaluation (10:29–31 and 12:1–3) and the threat of Hazael (10:32–33 and 12:17–18).

Yet the two stories also develop a strong contrast between a fruitless reformation in Israel and the fruit of reform in Judah. Jehu's revolution was marked by widespread violence, recounted through the heaping up of murderous examples. The revolution that brought Joash to the throne resulted in only two necessary deaths, Athaliah and Mattan. Jehu was a usurper, a Zimri, whose dynasty could last only four generations. Joash was the legitimate heir of David, enthroned according to customary procedure. The public nature of his acclamation is emphasized; all the people were involved. In contrast, Jehu is anointed in secret and acclamed only by some military commanders. Jehu launched on a reform which wiped out Baal by means of crafty violence. The reform that resulted from Joash's accession involved not only the destruction of Baal but the restoration of the temple as well, and this latter not by violence but by administrative wisdom. Hazael took territory from Jehu. From Joash he took only a bribe and then went away. Jehu is judged as evil in that he followed Jeroboam; Joash is judged as righteous because he followed Jehoiada. In chapters 9–10, the prophetic word is the driving force behind events. In chapters 11–12 revolution and reform are motivated by dynastic legitimacy and God's promise, along with Deuteronomic covenant law.

The reform of Jehu failed miserably. The story of Joash is more ambiguous. Joash was able to refurbish the temple, but in the end had to rob it. Rescued from death as a baby, he was struck down forty years later by his own servants. Heir to God's gracious promise to David, he received the testimony of the law and was a partner in the covenant between God and the people. Yet he failed to live up to the precepts of that covenant. He did right, but not completely right. His accomplishments were ordinary enough, but still significant. Like all of those who read his story, he lived in the tension between gracious promise and the demands of God's law, between divine protection and the cruel reality of death. Perhaps his story is satisfying, both as art and Scripture, because it is the common biography of every believer.

II Kings 13—15

Paradigmatic History II

The chronological pace of the narrative picks up in these three chapters, covering about a century in brief summaries of the reigns of eleven kings. Once more the concept of "paradigmatic history" dominates (cf. I Kings 14:21–16:34). The kings of Israel are all evil, following Jeroboam's sins. The kings of Judah all do right, except in the matter of sacrifice at the high places. The reader, now familiar with the evaluative stance of Kings and with its organizational system, comes to these chapters with certain expectations. Some of these expectations are met, others are not.

One unexpected factor in these chapters is an increase in confusion and disorder. The impression of confusion left by chapter 13, for example, has led to numerous attempts to "improve" the order of the verses. The established structure of files on the individual kings breaks down. Two closings are offered for the file on Jehoash of Israel. The first (13:12–13) is premature, leaving the last acts of Elisha out of the system. Because it follows 14:1, the second closing (14:15–16) comes too late, leaving two files open at once.

Furthermore, the synchronic chronology, which has made reasonably good sense so far and has bolstered the reader's confidence in the competence of the narrator, now falls apart. The careful reader will be disturbed by a comparison of 13:1 and 14:23 on the one hand, with 12:1 and 13:10 on the other. Even the reader who has not paid any attention to chronology is likely to be shocked by 15:1, which conflicts by a quarter of a century with the other dates in chapter 15.

Although the strictly contrasting Deuteronomistic evaluations stand out, there is no simplistic pattern of sin punished or repentance rewarded. If anything, the events reported seem to be kinder to some of the wicked kings of Israel (Jehoash, Jeroboam) than to the righteous kings of Judah (Amaziah, Azariah, Jotham). The presentation of God's will for Israel in 13:23 and 14:27 seems to contradict the ultimate fate of Israel. In chapter

215

14, verse 28 does not make sense geographically or historically. Azariah is called Uzziah much of the time without explanation.

This confusion and disorder (whatever its origin) reflects in a literary way the breakdown of the institutions and structures of national life which these chapters report. The way in which the story is told reinforces its content.

Jehoahaz and Jehoash of Israel

Chapter 13 presents an impression of confusion if the sentences are read as though in chronological order. The root of this confusion is likely to be a textual corruption in the earliest stages of transmission. It is possible that the order found in the Masoretic text and the alternative order offered by the Lucianic recension of the Septuagint are both attempts to "correct" an original order represented by verses 1–3, 8–22, 4–7, 23–25. The hypothesis is that this original order was thrown into confusion by a corruption of Jehoash's name into Jehoahaz's in verses 4 and 7 under the influence of verse 22. To "improve" matters, the Masoretic text moved verses 4–7 to between verses 3 and 8. The ancestor of the Lucianic recension of the Septuagint moved one verse more (vv. 4–7 and 23), retaining in verse 22 some words lost by the Masoretic text. (The Lucianic position of vv. 12–13 is a separate issue.)

Canonically, however, we may feel obligated to make sense out of the Masoretic text as it stands. Since reading chapter 13 chronologically (or diachronically) is so problematic, it is better to set aside the order of presentation and read synchronically, without attention to historical order. When so read, chapter 13 exposes the interaction of human sin and divine grace worked out in a complex matrix of events.

The text instructs the reader to consider the reigns of Jehoahaz and Jehoash as a single unit. Verses 3 and 24–25 present an overview of the entire period, just as verse 22 looks back to Jehoahaz as a prelude to the exploits of his son. First Hazael, then Ben-hadad oppressed Israel (v. 3). Hazael is associated with Jehoahaz (v. 22), Ben-hadad with Jehoash (vv. 24–25). Jehoahaz is characterized by defeat (vv. 7, 22), but Jehoash achieved victory (v. 25). Defeat was caused by sin and God's resulting anger (vv. 2–3, 6, 11).

216

Victory, in contrast, was a gift of God's grace alone. The arrow of victory over Syria is the Lord's arrow (v. 17). God stuck to the covenant made with the patriarchs (v. 23). So when God, besought by the king, saw Israel's predicament, God sent a mysterious savior (vv. 3–4). Whether this is meant to be Elisha or some unnamed historical figure such as Adad-nirari III, God remains the effective force behind this savior (cf. Judg. 3:9, 15).

God's grace to undeserving Israel is motivated by the covenant made with their ancestors, Abraham, Isaac, and Jacob (v. 23). This statement of the covenantal relationship is unique in the Book of Kings (although cf. I Kings 18:36). In Kings the covenant made at Sinai is the usual basis of God's dealings with the people (17:13, 15; I Kings 8:21). The covenant with the patriarchs is bound up with the theology of the gift of the land in Deuteronomy, however, so it is a most appropriate ideological principle to raise when the loss of land and nationhood is threatened (Deut. 1:8; 6:10; 9:5; 30:20). Here Kings reflects the prayer of Moses in Deuteronomy 9:27 that God would preserve the people by remembering the patriarchs.

Yet God's grace is not unlimited, for it is modified by continuing sin (vv. 6, 11) and the king's failure to pass the test of the arrows (v. 19). A comparison with Ahab's forces at Qarqar (ANET, p. 279) shows that Jehoahaz's chariotry has been cut back to an insignificant force. The weakness of Israel's chariot forces is a motive for God's intervention through Elisha, who is Israel's effective equivalent of chariots and horses (v. 14), but it is also a sign of God's punishment for sin (v. 7, where God is the subject of the first verb; cf. JB).

The narrator reminds the reader that this is but one episode in a larger story of sin, grace, and punishment. The Asherah of verse 6 had been erected by Ahab in I Kings 16:33 and stood as a sign of the incompleteness of Jehu's reform (10: 31). It will later surface as part of the general accusation against Israel in 17:16. Manasseh will install one like it in Jerusalem (21:3) to be destroyed by the complete reformer, Josiah (23:6, 15).

Verse 23 also connects to the larger story, although its meaning is open to interpretation. Some translators (NEB, TEV, and NIV) interpret the ambiguous "until now" as an assertion that God still has not cast Israel away, even in the time when the narrator is speaking. Others (RSV) more naturally take this to mean that God had not yet cast Israel away in the past, but now has (Deut. 12:9; cf. Gen. 32:4). This certainly represents the point of view of 17:20, where the language is parallel. Israel received a gracious respite from the doom it

217

deserved. It was never God's wish to write Israel off (cf. 14:27), but time finally ran out because Israel's sin continued unabated. These words are an ominous pointer to Judah's fate as well, for they echo 8:19, where God's unwillingness to destroy Judah is stated in similar terms.

Elisha makes his last appearance (vv. 14–19). The narrative problem is stated by Jehoash in verse 14. Elisha, the equivalent of horses and chariots for Israel, is dying (cf. v. 7; 2:12; 6:10). The first episode, introduced by the command to "take" (vv. 16–17) represents the situation while Elisha still lived. Jehoash quickly obeys each imperative. The prophet's hands aid the king's. The arrow flies true, and Syria will be beaten to a decisive finish. Here Elisha engages in a prophetic act, similar to the javelin of Joshua 8:18 or Zedekiah's iron horns (I Kings 22:11). This is not just a "visual aid" for the prophetic message, but combines with a word of power (v. 17b) to set the future in motion. The arrow flies east, in the general direction of Syrian attacks.

The second episode, the description of a test also beginning with "take," (vv. 18–19), contrasts the ambiguous state of affairs following the death of Elisha. The king knows now what the arrows mean. He still responds to the imperatives but fails this test of aggressiveness. Verse 19 qualifies verse 17. In contrast to the arrow of Yahweh which would have made a decisive end to Syria, the king's half-hearted arrows will give only partial victory. What could have been will not be. This story powerfully underlines Israel's situation of crisis. The glory that was possible when Elisha lived is replaced by partial, ambiguous victories. Elisha could call on the divine power at will. This power had passed from Elijah to Elisha in prophetic succession, but no further. Now Israel must rely on lukewarm kings whose prayers (v. 4) are undercut by their obdurate sin (vv. 2, 6, 11).

The last story about Elisha (vv. 20–21) is told with his whole career in view and again reflects on Israel's situation. The chariots of Israel are gone; raiders invade without opposition. Yet the prophet whose career was characterized by the gift of life (8:4–5) still gives life even from his bones. The story is told with some humor. Read in context, the impact seems to be that there is hope for Israel yet (cf. vv. 4–5, 23), even though the glory days of Elijah and Elisha are dead and gone. Time, however, is quickly running out.

218

To summarize, chapter 13 presents no simplistic pattern of sin punished and repentance rewarded. There are some victories, but they are not complete (vv. 19, 25). Israel receives a savior, but its chariot force is decimated. The kings are supported by the prophet, but condemned by the narrator. Jehoahaz prays but is defeated; Jehoash fails his test but is victorious. God has not cast Israel out of sight yet, but eventually will. God's anger over violations of the law stands in unresolved tension with gracious compassion and divine loyalty to the patriarchal covenant. All of this is worked out in the complex patterns of real life, not in rigid Deuteronomistic theory.

Amaziah of Judah and Jeroboam II

The section on Amaziah of Judah in chapter 14 (vv. 1–22) has been prepared for by 13:12. Again the narrative proper stands in some tension with the Deuteronomistic evaluation. Jehoash is evil but victorious. Amaziah does right, obeying the book of the law (v. 6, quoting Deut. 24:16), but loses. God cannot even be counted on to defend Jerusalem and the temple (contrast I Kings 9:3; 11:36; 14:21).

The narrative exposition takes the form of Amaziah's request for a "summit meeting" (v. 8; not a challenge to battle yet, but the neutral language of "facing each other" will turn ugly in v. 11). Conflict arises with Jehoash's insulting fable (v. 9). The genealogies of the two kings are purposefully traced back to Jehu and Ahaziah (vv. 8 and 13) to expose this as a transgenerational conflict, contrary to the spirit of Deuteronomy 24:16, cited in verse 6.

The seriousness of Judah's defeat at the strategically important Beth-shemesh on the western approaches to Jerusalem is underscored by another plundering of the temple treasures, most recently cleared out in 12:18. This story offers a proleptic analogy to the crisis of King Hezekiah (chaps. 18–20) in which the city is saved, but its treasures and hostages are put in danger by royal folly.

Verse 17 reorients the reader back to Amaziah after the oddly placed conclusion of verses 15–16. Amaziah, the good but hapless king, is murdered like his father in a conspiracy which seems to reflect a tension between Jerusalem and the people of Judah (v. 19). Again, his obedience to the law of Moses does not seem to have done him much good in a political sense!

The next section of the fourteenth chapter, on Jeroboam II (vv. 23–29), is overly brief from the modern historian's viewpoint. This king was of great historical importance, reigning

219

over unparalleled economic prosperity, but the narrator's ideological stance has reduced Jeroboam to a theological paradigm. Jeroboam is used to orient the reader theologically as to how things now stand between God and Israel. Israel is in dire straits, with absolutely no one to save them (v. 26), but God is still unwilling to "pull the plug" (v. 27). The language of verse 26 reflects the idea of Deuteronomy 32:36: God, who vindicates in war, has compassion when all human power has evaporated. God's gracious favor alone saves the people, not the worthiness of their king (v. 24).

Verses 26–27 use the rich store of liturgical lament language to speak of God's motives for helping. For "see affliction," compare Psalm 9:13; 25:18; 31:7; Lamentations 1:9; and especially Deuteronomy 26:7. One's "help" (really the active participle, "helper") can be a military ally (I Kings 20:16; Jer. 47:4; Ezek. 30:8; 32:21). God is the "help" of the weak and the powerless (Ps. 10:14; 72:12; 118:7) who brings justice and vindication (Isa. 63:5). Again this is part of the language used by lament to motivate God (Ps. 30:10; 54:4). If one's name is "blotted out," one is totally forgotten. This is what happens to one who dies without a son (Deut. 25:6, cf. Ps. 109:13) and is the ultimate curse on the apostate (Deut. 29:20). It was used as a threat against the people in Deuteronomy 9:14. The verb will return later as a grim domestic metaphor in 21:13.

Thus the Transjordan was restored and the border with Moab (cf. 13:20) secured (v. 25). The kingdom returned to the idealized boundaries of Solomon's kingdom of shalom (vv. 25, 28; I Kings 4:21; 8:65). Amos reflected a more negative contemporary view of these same victories (Amos 6:13) and a less optimistic picture of Israel's potential future (Amos 8:2). The modern historian ascribes Jeroboam's success to Assyrian pressure on Syria (Shalmaneser IV, Tiglath-pileser III), but for this narrator the cause was God's favor. The theological stance is the same as 13:4, 23.

Once again, events fulfill prophecy, although the narrator can now telescope the prophetic pattern into a single sentence (v. 25) that the reader fills out from past experience. That this Jonah was a servant of God is authorization enough. What God spoke "by the hand of Jonah" (v. 25 literally), God did by the hand of Jeroboam (v. 27). This same pattern of the fulfillment of an uncited prophetic word followed by theological elaboration will return in grimmer circumstances in 24:2–4 (cf. 17:

13–18). Context makes it clear that although God's grace saved Israel for a while in the end grace ran out. God was forced to destroy and exile Israel. As a reflection of God's dilemma, the very phrase that motivates God's help ("bond or free," v. 26) also echoes God's punishment on earlier kings (9:8; I Kings 14:10; 21:21).

The Slide to Disaster

As in the case of Jeroboam II, the data given for Azariah (Uzziah) in chapter 15 are paltry compared with the king's historical importance (vv. 1–7). The narrator refuses to moralize about the king's leprosy, simply stating it as a fact and letting the reader draw whatever conclusions seem warranted. For one example of reader reaction, see II Chronicles 26:16–20.

As already mentioned, the synchronism of verse 1 makes no sense. Amaziah would have been long dead (14:23) by the twenty seventh year of Jeroboam. This notice also conflicts with verses 8, 13, 17, 23, and 27. By exercising enough ingenuity and with the flexibility provided by the variables of dating systems and coregencies, the patient reader can work out a system that hangs together, as long as certain items like verse 1 are left out or modified. (See the standard commentaries. External consistency with Assyrian data requires more extensive modification.) Nevertheless, the reader is left with the impression that from this point on, the problem of synchronism and chronology has gotten the better of the narrator.

The files on the last kings of Israel in chapter 15 open and close quickly. The judgment formulas on the kings, formerly marked by variety and flexibility in the choice of language, now rigidify into a standard refrain (vv. 9, 18, 24, 28). It is as though the story has begun to rush to its tragic ending. The narrator hammers home the point. Because each king did evil according to the sin of Jeroboam, the destruction of Israel is inevitable. The Assyrians now appear as a dangerous force, first exacting only tribute (v. 19), but then imposing exile and loss of territory (v. 29). These events point ominously to the final tragedy of chapter 17.

Zechariah (vv. 8–12) provided a chance to point out once more God's control of political history (v. 12). If Ibleam is to be restored in verse 10, there is a certain irony in Zechariah's death. The last of Jehu's line died where Jehu murdered Ahaziah (9:27; cf. Hos. 1:4–5).

Shallum's brief reign (vv. 13–16) underscores the brutality of the civil strife into which Israel had fallen. Menahem waged total war (cf. 8:12; Amos 1:13; Hosea 13:16), the sort characteristic of Assyria, against an Israelite town (but see RSV note). Tappuah became Israel's Guernica. Menahem (vv. 17–22) had to institute an oppressive tax to pay tribute to Assyria.

His son Pekahiah (vv. 23–26) fell victim to another coup, assassinated inside his own palace by fifty commandos from Gilead, apparently Shallum's home territory ("son of Jabesh," vv. 13, 14). What look like stray place names in verse 25 (RSV note) may further localize his death to a spot "at the eagle and the lion," near statues of these animals or a sphinx-like combination of them.

Pekah (vv. 27–31), whom external evidence allows a reign of only five or ten years, suffered the catastrophic effects of the Syro-Ephraimite War (v. 37; 16:5, 7–9; Isa. 7:1–17; 9:1; ANET, pp. 283–84). He too was struck down by revolution.

Nor was Judah exempt from the tremors shaking Israel, as the reign of Jotham illustrates (vv. 32–38). The onslaught of Rezin and Pekah began in his time, but the full impact would be faced by Ahaz, his successor. Once again, God was the true author of this threat (v. 37; cf. 10:32).

These three chapters (13—15) read like a review of modern history in diminished scale: war, civil strife, atrocity, revolution, governmental incompetence, displaced persons. All that the modern reader recognizes; it is as familiar as the evening news. What is unfamiliar is the insistence that God was playing some intentional role (14:25; 15:12) in all these events, which are seen through the evaluative lens of sin and divine response. God willed only good for this people Israel. God was bound to them by ties of covenant and compassion (13:4–5, 23; 14:26–27). Yet obdurate sin (13:2, 6, 11; 14:24; 15:9, 18, 24, 28) demanded punishment (13:7; 15:37).

This ideological cycle of apostasy and punishment, repentance and deliverance, reflected in 13:2–5, is that which structures the Book of Judges (Judg. 3:7–11). The theology of these three chapters of Kings is Deuteronomistic, but not mechanically so. There is nothing doctrinaire about the way events are reported. Good things happen to bad kings and bad things happen to good ones. The connections between theological patterns and real life remain general, long term rather than short term. Dogma proves to be no infallible guide to current events.

If the narrator or a prophet does not point out the hand of God, it remains invisible. Yet there remains an insistence that beneath the surface eddies of events runs a deeper current. God willed good for the people and saved them without merit, but in the end God was driven by their infidelity to punish them with the ultimate punishment.

The realization that no naive theology of retribution and reward governs events in the short term can stand side by side with the biblical insistence that God blesses obedience and punishes sin in the long term. A proper balance of these two assertions goes a long way towards dealing with the pastoral and theological problems raised by issues of theodicy. "Here is a call for the endurance of the saints" (Rev. 14:12). God's will is not very evident in the short term, but is guaranteed in the long term.

II Kings 16
Ahaz and Judah's Open Future

This chapter is one of those places where knowing too much may hinder us from experiencing the text actually before us (Ackroyd, *Svensk Exegetisk Årsbok* 33:18–54). For one thing, we have developed an opinion of Ahaz's character and the nature of his faith from Isaiah 7, and we tend to read this into chapter 16. We also tend to assume that Isaiah's outraged opinion of Ahaz's international policy is identical with that of the narrator of Kings. Our evaluation of Ahaz's construction of a new altar is contaminated by the Chronicler's assumption that it was an act of syncretism. Because of our reasonably full knowledge of the Syro-Ephraimite War (see any standard history of Israel), we may assume connections in the text that are not really present. The Book of Kings should be permitted to speak for itself.

The judgment formula (vv. 2–3) emphasizes Ahaz's wickedness. Ahaz acted like the kings of Israel (cf. 8:18). The example of David points up Ahaz's failings (cf. 14:3; I Kings 15:11). The normal positive formula has actually been converted into a negative one. In a couple of ways the evaluation of Ahaz is a reversal of the positive one which Josiah will receive (22:2):

223

> Ahaz: And he did not do what was right in the eyes of the Lord his God, as his father David had done, but he walked in the way of the kings of Israel.
> Josiah: And he did what was right in the eyes of the Lord, and walked in all the way of David his father.

The narrator then offers the evidence. The shocker is that Ahaz burned his son as a sacrifice in violation of Deuteronomy 18:10, a crime which ties him to the sins of Israel (17:17) and to the arch-villain Manasseh (21:6). As Deuteronomy 18:9 makes clear, Ahaz thus joined in the "abominable practices" of the Canaanites (cf. Deut. 20:18). This ties Ahaz to Jeroboam (I Kings 14:24) and Manasseh (21:6). Like Jeroboam and Israel generally, he contaminated Yahweh worship at the local high places with fertility religion (as implied by the shared language of 17:10 and I Kings 14:23). Ahaz is not associated with Assyrian religion in any way here. The practices he encouraged or permitted are explicitly Canaanite.

On the International Front (vv. 5–9)

There is no reason to imagine that the narrator views Ahaz's reliance on Assyrian assistance as an apostate act (as opposed to the prophet Isaiah). Calling on a larger nation's help could be a reasonable policy for a small nation. Asa did so without being condemned for it (I Kings 15:16–21), and the narrator reports without comment that both Hezekiah and Menahem bought off Assyrian attacks (15:19–20; 18:15–16). Certainly verse 17 emphasizes that this entailed the undoing of much of Solomon's glory, but Hezekiah's actions in 18:16 are quite similar.

If anything, the story here has a happy ending for Judah, at least when one considers the fate of Israel (15:29) and Syria (v. 9). Kings offers no comment on the political wisdom of Ahaz's desperation move. It may be clear to us, with the benefit of hindsight, that this was an extremely foolish step to take, but Kings operates from a completely different view of historical causality. Indeed, Kings is rather coy about the connection between the fate of Israel in 15:29 and that of Syria in verse 9. It knows of the Syro-Ephraimite alliance (v. 5; 15:37), but chooses not to associate Israel's defeat and dismemberment with Ahaz's deal with Tiglath-pileser in any way. The reader is left to make the connection.

All in all, international affairs under Ahaz are described as a mixed bag. The crisis with Edom (v. 6), which reversed 14:22, was not resolved and remained an issue even in the exilic readers' own time. Yet the far more critical problem of the attack of Syria and Israel was taken care of quite neatly. The anti-Judah coalition could not engage Ahaz in open battle (v. 5, NEB). Instead his submissive language and diplomatic "present" (NEB "bribe" is indefensibly judgmental) to Tiglath-pileser saved the day. We may speculate about other Assyrian motives, but the narrator sees verses 7–8 as the direct cause of verse 9: "the king of Assyria listened" to Ahaz.

Kings gives few details about Ahaz's foreign policy. We learn much more from the Book of Isaiah and Assyrian sources (ANET, pp. 282–84). In contrast, the following report on Ahaz's religious activities is rich in detail. It is obvious where the narrator wishes to put the stress. In a sense, the story of the Syro-Ephraimite War is actually told to get Ahaz to Damascus and thus lead into the more important narrative of verses 10–16.

On the Religious Front (vv. 10–18)

These verses offer an etiology for the great temple altar which exilic readers would have remembered. The narrative is a unified description of the actions of Ahaz, the subject of most of the narrative verbs. The Chronicler interpreted Ahaz's new altar as evidence of syncretism (II Chron. 28:22–23), and many readers have since followed suit. However, there does not seem to be any justification for this negative opinion from the text of Kings itself.

Scholars remain undecided as to whether the Assyrians ever forced religious practices on their vassals, although the drift of opinion seems to indicate that they did not. What is clear is that the Book of Kings has absolutely no knowledge of such a practice. Religious apostasy in Kings follows Canaanite models and results from a loss of loyalty to God. Political considerations or vassal status have nothing to do with the matter.

There is no hint that this was an Assyrian altar. The reader is left to assume that it was of a Syrian pattern. Ahaz went to Damascus and there saw the latest thing in impressive altars. His project is not presented as apostasy at all. He seems to have been motivated by practical and aesthetic considerations.

This new altar was bigger and better than the old one erected by Solomon. Although the actual historical facts may have been quite different, Kings knows of only one altar for

225

sacrifice in Solomon's temple, the one described as the "bronze altar" (I Kings 8:22, 54, 64). This was too small to handle the vast Solomonic dedicatory sacrifices, and overflow arrangements had to be made (I Kings 8:64). By contrast, this new (stone?) one was a "great altar" which could handle all the sacrifices required of it (v. 15). It was big enough to "go up beside" (v. 12; cf. NEB) on steps or a ramp.

Not only is Ahaz not blamed for this innovation, but everything points to it as a positive step:

—Ahaz dedicates the new altar in a way reminiscent of Solomon (v. 13; I Kings 8:62–64).
—The careful terminology for the sacrifices of verses 13 and 15 underscores their legitimacy. Uriah the legitimate priest offers traditional sacrifices to the God of Israel.
—This bigger and better altar would be used by Hezekiah (18:22) and Josiah (23:9) without comment from the narrator.
—The replaced bronze altar is itself put to a legitimate use (v. 15). Although many commentators imagine that the word "inquire" implies improper divination of some kind (cf. TEV), Psalm 27:4 offers a perfectly orthodox meaning for the verb, to inquire of God. The word is never used for divination.

The Deuteronomistic author of Kings does not seem to have been hypercritical about such worship arrangements. What mattered was the centralized location of sacrifice in Jerusalem, not those liturgical details that so concerned the priestly writer or Ezekiel. Unlike Exodus, Deuteronomy does not offer any regulations for the construction of the central altar, although it does describe one of unhewn stone at Shechem (Deut. 27:5–6; carried out in Josh. 8:30–32). If anything, Ahaz's altar would be closer to this ideal than Solomon's bronze one.

The narrator of Kings was not so rigid as to require that every action of a king judged evil had to be wrong. One need only think of the reforming actions of Jehu (10:18–27) or the prayers of Jehoahaz of Israel (13:4–5). Ahab's altar was an act of temple improvement which the narrator sees as a positive move.

Yet the two verses which follow (vv. 17–18) keep the reader from viewing things in too rosy a light. Verse 17 reminds us of the practical consequences of Ahaz's diplomatic present to Assyria. Judah moved one step closer to the undoing of Solomon's glory that would end with 25:13.

Verse 18 is almost impossible to understand:

> The Sabbath structure which they had built in the house (temple? palace?) and the royal entrance to the outside he reoriented in regard to the house of the Lord because of the king of Assyria.

Although there has been a temptation to include the new altar of Ahaz as something also done "because of the king of Assyria" along with these alterations, there is no warrant for this. Although one can hardly be dogmatic about such an obscure verse, these temple modifications are clearly a separate issue which have to do not with apostasy but with comparative royal dignity. Ezekiel 46:1–2 throws some light on this business. Perhaps Ahaz's independent royal claims had to be modified in light of his new submissive relationship to Assyria. One might compare modern questions of diplomatic precedence and protocol. To blame Ahaz for the rooftop altars of 23:12, as is commonly done, goes far beyond what Kings itself actually says.

In religious matters, then, as in foreign relations, Ahaz's reign was something of a tossup. His apostasy to Canaanite religious practices was unquestionable (vv. 3–4), yet he was also an orthodox patron of the temple, the king who installed the great altar of sacrifice.

The ambiguous figure of Ahaz, partially a success and partially a failure, sometimes faithful to God but quite often not so, reflects Judah's situation precisely. At this point in the plot of Kings, Judah's future is still open. There are still two ways before Judah, the way of obedience and life and the way of idolatrous worship and death (Deut. 30:15–20). Eventually Judah would lose this choice, and death became inevitable (21:10–15). Yet in chapter 16, Ahaz and Judah stand where the exilic and modern reader stand, at the intersection of choice between faith and disbelief, obedience and apostasy, life and death.

The all-too-human Ahaz is much easier for the reader to identify with than Josiah the saint or Manasseh the arch-villain. His final evaluation had to be that "he did not do what was right," and of the reader too it must be said that "all have sinned and fall short of the glory of God" (Rom. 3:23). Yet the future remains open-ended, dependent in the last analysis not on

227

human fallibility but on God's gracious will. That was a word of hope to the original exilic readers and a good description of the ambiguities of the Christian life of faith.

II Kings 17
God Casts Israel Out of Sight

Kings chronicles the endemic sin of the nation and the divine punishment which struck as its result. Chapter 17 plays a central role in this theological analysis of Israel's history, reflected by its dense concentration of Deuteronomistic language. A network of evaluative nerves from all over the Book of Kings gathers into a central ganglion at this point. Here there are echoes of the language used by the narrator's editorials and the judgment speeches made by the prophets and by God.

The narrator looks backward to gather together Israel's sins at the point of punishment. The narrator also looks forward to Judah's eventual fate, to other dense concentrations of Deuteronomistic judgment language in 21:3–15; 23:26–27; 24:3–5.

The Indictment of Israel

Israel's sin was abominable, inexcusable. They copied the Canaanites (v. 8; 21:2; I Kings 14:24), setting up pillars and Asherim (v. 10; I Kings 14:23) indiscriminately (16:4), serving idols (v. 12; 21:11, 21; 23:24; I Kings 15:12; 21:26; cf. v. 15 to I Kings 16:13, 26). They worshiped the stars (v. 16; 21:3, 5) and served Baal (10:18; I Kings 16:31; 22:53). They violated every part of Deuteronomy 18:10–11 (v. 17; 16:3; 21:6), selling themselves to do evil (v. 17; I Kings 21:20, 25) and provoking the Lord to anger (vv. 11, 17; 21:6, 15; 22:17; 23:19, 26; I Kings 14:9, 15; 15:30; 16:2, 7, 13, 26, 33; 22:53). A major share of the blame falls on Jeroboam (vv. 21–22; 3:3; 10:29, 31).

Israel had been warned over and over by the prophets (vv. 13, 23; 9:7; 21:10; 24:2) to repent and keep God's law (v. 13; 18:6; 23:3; I Kings 2:3; 3:14; 8:58, 61; 9:4, 6; 11:11, 34, 38; 14:8) but they would not listen (vv. 14, 40). So God removed them out of sight (vv 18, 23; 23:27; 24:3). Judah's story was not much different (v. 19), and its fate was to be similar (v. 20; 24:20).

Although permeated by homiletical concerns and editorial commentary, this chapter retains a skeletal narrative structure shaped by the actions of the king of Assyria, who "found treachery" in Hoshea, "shut him up and bound him," "invaded," "besieged," "captured," and "carried away" (vv. 4–6). After a section of theological commentary, this narrative thread resumes as the king of Assyria returns as the grammatical subject. He "brought," "placed," and "commanded" (vv. 24–27).

Narrative is followed by commentary twice:

> direct attack on Israel (vv. 1–23)
> > narrative (vv. 1–6)
> > commentary (vv. 7–23)
> indirect attack on Israel (vv. 24–41)
> > narrative (vv. 24–28)
> > commentary (vv. 29–41)

The first set of comments represents a direct attack on Israel (and by implication, Judah) utilizing outright accusation. The second set of comments supports this with an indirect attack on Israel by means of a bitter comparison with the foreign settlers brought in by the king of Assyria.

The Direct Attack (vv. 1–23)

Although verses 1–6 seem to report two invasions by the king of Assyria (v. 3 and vv. 5–6), only one is actually intended. Verse 3a is in the nature of an introductory overview: "He was the one the king of Assyria came up against." Then verses 3b–4 back up to start the story at the beginning. Hoshea had been paying tribute but then withheld it, angling for Egyptian support. The Assyrians first somehow arrested Hoshea, then besieged and finally captured Samaria. Israel was exiled and scattered among a deliberately vague and remote catalogue of places.

As if to mirror the confusion of Israel's last days, verse 1 offers the reader a disturbing chronological inconsistency (cf. 15:27 and 16:1). The presentation of Hoshea is equally unsettling. The judgment against him is mysteriously softened in a way unparalleled for any other Northern king (v. 2). Yet paradoxically, he was the one (note the emphasis in the Hebrew of v. 3) against whom the king of Assyria came. Hoshea thus antici-

229

pates the paradox of Josiah in a minor way. When the time for divine punishment has arrived, even a virtuous king cannot derail it.

The rambling homily of verses 7–23 does reflect some degree of order. A single logical move is encompassed by verses 7–18 from the "because" of verse 7 through a catalogue of offenses to the "therefore" of verse 18. (This is clearer in Hebrew than in the English versions.) The indictment cycles from the general to the specific with its central focus on the prophetic warning and Israel's refusal to listen:

A general indictment (vv. 7–8)
  B specific crimes (vv. 9–12)
    C prophetic warning unheeded (vv. 13–14)
A' general indictment (vv. 15–16a)
  B' specific crimes (vv. 16b–17)
    C' result (v. 18)

God's reaction (v. 18) provides the theological explanation for the events of verses 1–6.

This punishment is ironically linked to the exodus from Egypt, now effectively reversed by exile (v. 7) and to God's gift of the land of promise (v. 8). The kings receive a major share of the blame (v. 8) through a two-pronged direct attack on Israel's worship life. They worshiped alien gods and idols (vv. 10–12, 15–16), but at the same time worshiped the Lord in an improper manner at the high places (v. 9) and under the guise of the golden calves (v. 16; I Kings 12:28–32; 14:9).

There is a sobering word play in verse 15: They followed empty things (idols; Deut. 32:21; I Kings 16:13, 26) and became empty themselves. God gave Israel (and Judah) fair warning by the prophets, calling on them to repent (*shub;* I Kings 8:33–34), but like their ancestors they remained stiff-necked (RSV "stubborn") and refused to listen (v. 14; 21:9; cf. Judg. 2:2; 6:10). Their idol worship, their refusal to obey, represented symptoms of the most basic and fatal sickness of all, their lack of faith in God (v. 14).

In verses 19–23 the narrator coordinates Judah with Israel's experience. This was already implicit in verse 13. At this point, the narrator does not yet come right out and predict Judah's demise. There are only hints so far. Only Judah was left (v. 18), but Judah too followed Israel's lead (v. 19). Verse 20 seems deliberately obscure. The Lord rejected all the "descendants of Israel." Although the reader knows that this phrase includes Judah and that the threat of "spoilers" (RSV, "plunderers" from Judg. 2:14) will come to pass against Judah in 24:2, such open-ended language emphasizes that Judah still had a chance to repent at this point in the story.

Israel's punishment represents classic poetic justice. They had "rejected" God's law (v. 15; RSV "despised") so God "rejected" them (v. 20; cf. 23:27). Israel did not "depart" from their sins (v. 22) so God "caused them to depart" (v. 23; RSV "removed"). Israel's fate also points forward to what is in store for Judah (the parallel is obscured by RSV):

> "So Israel was exiled from its land" (17:23)
> "So Judah was exiled from its land" (25:21)

The Indirect Attack (vv. 24–41)

The narrator is not particularly interested in the narrative of verses 24–28 for its own sake, as demonstrated by the fact that the priest of the Bethel cult remains unscathed by any Deuteronomistic condemnation. The story is really told in order to provide an opportunity for a second, indirect attack on Israel's disobedience (vv. 29–41).

Although we know that this exchange of population was only a partial one (ANET, p. 284), the narrator speaks as though there has been a total replacement by foreigners. They brought with them a smorgasbord of gods from all over, with names probably deliberately corrupted to poke fun.

Much confusion has been generated by the common assumption that these foreign immigrants are somehow related to the (much) later religious community of the Samaritans (as RSV, NEB, and JB do at v. 29; TEV follows the interpretation advanced here). Such is not the case. The narrator is here simply referring to the people of the Northern Kingdom as the people of "Samaria" (used for the Northern Kingdom in 17:24; 23: 18–19; I Kings 13:32; 21:1).

Verse 29 therefore speaks of the shrines previously built by Jeroboam, by the "Samarians," being reused by the imported foreigners. Naturally later Jewish readers applied these verses to the origin of the despised Samaritan religious group (for example Josephus, *Ant.* ix, 14, 3).

231

The present-day (from the viewpoint of the narrator and original audience) syncretism of these foreigners (vv. 29–34, 41) encloses Israel's former refusal to keep the covenant (vv. 34b–40). The expressions "they feared the Lord" and "to this day" (vv. 33–34 and 41) thus bracket a retrospective review of Israel's covenant betrayal. Both Israel and these imported foreigners committed the same crime, trying to "fear the Lord" while worshiping other gods (vv. 33, 41 and 35–39). They both appointed priests in an indiscriminate fashion (v. 32 and I Kings 12:31; 13:33) for the high places. The foreigners even put images of their own gods in the "shrines of the high places" which the residents of Samaria had constructed (v. 29; literally "in the house of the high places" just as I Kings 12:31). The teaching of the priest of Bethel resulted once more in what the Bethel cult had always implied —syncretism.

These foreigners parody Israel. Trying to fear the Lord in their syncretistic way (vv. 32, 33, 41), they really do not fear God at all (v. 34), for they do not follow the law of Deuteronomy. If you want to see what Israel was like, the narrator suggests to exilic readers, go look at these contemporary foreigners who are "doing according to their former manner" even "to this day" (v. 34a) just as Israel used to do (v. 40).

Theological Implications

For the first readers of Kings, this chapter helped explain their own circumstances. The nation of Judah had followed Israel into exile because of disobedience. They had not kept the covenant either (vv. 15, 35). They too had refused to listen to the prophets (vv. 13–14, 40). They too had disobeyed the law of Deuteronomy (vv. 15–16, 34b).

The challenge now, as exiles in an alien land, was to avoid syncretism. Any attempt to "fear the Lord" while serving other gods on the side is not really fearing the Lord at all (vv. 7, 12, 15–16, 34b). Syncretism undercuts the covenant which is founded on God's law (vv. 35–38). To serve the gods of Babylon would be to descend to the level of those benighted foreigners brought in by the king of Assyria. Remember the lesson of Mount Carmel (v. 34 echoes I Kings 18:31). Serve God alone.

As exiles in an alien world, modern Christians also face the challenge of syncretism. In some place the temptation is still a religious one, especially for the younger churches, but many of the most attractive idols today are economic (Matt. 6:24) and political (Matt. 22:15–22) gods. Yet the first commandment still holds and God still jealously demands exclusive loyalty (Matt. 4:8–10).

PART FIVE

Judah: Paradox of Promise and Punishment

II KINGS 18—25

II Kings 18—19
God Versus Sennacherib

> *And the might of the Gentile, unsmote by the sword,*
> *Hath melted like snow in the glance of the Lord!*
> —Byron

Scholars have long recognized that this dramatic story of Jerusalem's dire peril and fantastic deliverance has been shaped out of a number of independent sources. Chapters 18 (vv. 13–16) and 19 (35–37) seem to tell quite different stories about the success of Sennacherib's invasion. And 18:17—19:7 and 19:8–34 appear to go over the same ground and are thought to represent parallel sources. A further line of inquiry has mushroomed out of attempts to reconstruct the actual historical facts of the Assyrian invasion and to harmonize this account with that of Sennacherib himself (ANET, pp. 287–88). Our task is to read the narrative of chapters 18—19 as it stands in the canonical text of Kings and to consider its literary and theological impact. We may therefore leave literary history and historical reconstruction to others.

Once the reader has determined to read the story as it stands, the twists and turns of the plot line make reasonable dramatic sense. As we see in chapter 18, Hezekiah was an ultra-righteous king who could count on success from God (vv. 1–8), unlike the apostate northerners whom the Assyrians destroyed

235

(vv. 9–12). Yet Sennacherib launched an attack on Hezekiah anyway, and surprisingly (from a Deuteronomistic point of view) Hezekiah was forced to pay tribute (vv. 13–16). Even then Sennacherib was not satisfied and sent a great army and the Rabshakeh to demand the surrender of Jerusalem with convincing argumentation (vv. 17–37). The narrative tension is clear enough. How could Jerusalem be in such dire straits when Hezekiah was so righteous?

As in any exciting story, however, things get even more complicated in chapter 19. Hezekiah reacted properly (vv. 1–5) and received a comforting oracle in return (vv. 6–7). Sennacherib will hear a "report" and go home. Yet the news Sennacherib did hear (vv. 8–9) had no such result. Instead a second threatening message was sent to Hezekiah, one which clarified the issues at stake and escalated the conflict into a direct struggle between God and Sennacherib (vv. 10–13). Hezekiah's response to this deepened threat was even more exemplary than his first reaction—a prayer rich in confessional trust (vv. 14–19). In turn Isaiah proclaimed even more pointed and wonderful oracles (vv. 20–34).

The awesome climax is worthy of this extensive buildup (v. 35) and the denouement (vv. 36–37) undoes Sennacherib's hostile approach (18:13) with an ignominious retreat and a delayed fulfillment of verse 7.

The Exposition (18:1–12)

The narrator praises Hezekiah's virtue without restraint, using a rhetorical hyperbole in verse 5 that ignores both David and Josiah (23:25). This positive evaluation is supported by details of an extensive reform which anticipates Josiah in the removal of the high places. Even a venerable relic of Mosaic tradition (v. 4; Num. 21:6–9) was broken up in obedience to Mosaic law (cf. Deut. 4:15–18). Both the language and the thought is Deuteronomistic: Because Hezekiah kept the commandments, the Lord was always with him and he prospered in everything (vv. 6–7). His rebellion against Assyria and conquests in Philistia are cited as examples.

The brief retelling of Israel's fate (vv. 9–12) makes the same point by contrast. Hezekiah obeyed the commandments; they had transgressed God's covenant. This section also functions to point up the serious danger of Sennacherib's coming attack by

236

means of the structural parallel between verses 9 and 13. Judah was in mortal peril.

The key word is "trust" (v. 5). This verb will serve as the focus for the Assyrian negotiating position (vv. 19–22, 24, 30; 19:10; eight times in all). The critical narrative issue is whether Hezekiah's trust in God will be justified or not. Sennacherib's victorious advance and diplomatic treachery put this into deepest doubt and seem to give the lie to the narrator's naive statement of Deuteronomistic theology in verse 7. The narrative problem is starkly clear. Hezekiah is threatened with ultimate doom for his nation, in spite of his saintly virtue.

The Complication (18:13–35)

At first it seems that another round of heavy tribute from the temple vaults will solve the problem (as I Kings 14:25–26 and elsewhere). Yet Sennacherib, after setting the terms and accepting the bullion, treacherously sends envoys and a "great army" to demand the surrender of the capital anyway. Such diplomatic chicanery should not stretch the imagination of a modern reader (Stalin: "Sincere diplomacy is no more possible than dry water or wooden iron").

The exotic titles of the emissaries add to the realism of the narrative, as do the precise details of geography (v. 17). They are met, three on three, by high Judahite officials (I Kings 4:2), whose names add further to the realistic impact, as does the authentically Assyrian "great king" of verse 19. The Rabshakeh's oration is divided into two parts by the transitional business involving language in verses 26–27.

The Rabshakeh is no mere messenger; he is a propagandist and skilled negotiator speaking the language of diplomatic disputation. His goal is to split Judah along class lines (v. 27), undermine their will to resist, and acquire Jerusalem without utilizing the "great army" he has brought as a show of force. In a speech reminiscent of those in Thucydides and Acts, he advances what seem to be four excellent arguments for capitulation:

—Reliance on Egypt is foolish and dangerous, as history has shown (v. 21).
—Reliance on your God is unwise because your king has been removing this God's holy places (v. 22).

237

—Reliance on your own military establishment would be ridiculous (vv. 23–24).

—We Assyrians are the agents of your God, charged with the mission of destroying you (v. 25).

Each of these arguments has a certain plausibility. The Book of Kings itself demonstrates that Egypt was an unreliable ally (24:7) and underscores several times the nation's lack of chariots and horses. Certainly there was no universal agreement that cult centralization was a good idea among either the subjects of Hezekiah or the exilic audience. And the claim that foreign armies can sometimes do God's will is one of the major theological foundations of the Book of Kings, advanced just a few verses earlier in verses 9–12. Rabshakeh's interpretation of events is not unreasonable, offering as it does a possible explanation for why Hezekiah's piety and reform seem to have made no difference. What the narrator characterized as trust in God (v. 5), the Rabshakeh derides as trust in "empty talk" (RSV "mere words"; v. 20).

Judah's weak position is underlined by the request to avoid Hebrew lest the common folk understand (v. 26), but that of course is precisely the Rabshakeh's intention. This episode functions as a transitional section. Rabshakeh's psychological warfare now is broadened to include those who will pay the loathsome price of an extended siege (v. 27). The second half of his speech (vv. 28–35) is designed for popular consumption.

Blame is placed squarely on Hezekiah and his claim that the Lord will deliver the city (vv. 30, 32b). Now the argument shifts ground and moves in the direction of demeaning God's power to save, not just God's will to do so (vv. 33–35). No other gods have been able to stand up against the might of the Assyrian war machine. Certainly the gods recently imported by the new settlers in Samaria (v. 34; 17:24, 30–31) have been unable to save that land from Sennacherib. Here the Rabshakeh ironically echoes Deuteronomistic diatribes against the gods of other peoples (cf. Deut. 4:33–34), but then goes on to draw the arrogant conclusion that the God of Judah too is just another helpless nonentity (v. 35).

238

Even more arrogant is the Assyrian king's claim to be what is in essence a rival god to the Lord (vv. 31–32). In what looks like a parody of Deuteronomy 8:7–9, the king offers what only God can offer: the security of vine and fig tree, a new promised land full of good things, life in the place of death. Now the real issue becomes clear. Sennacherib is in effect claiming to be God's rival for the loyalty of Judah, one who can in reality give what God is apparently unable to provide—security, land, life. As in the struggle between Pharaoh and God in Exodus or between Baal and God in I Kings 18, the stakes have reached the ultimate limit. Is the God of Israel really God alone, or can Sennacherib demote God to just another empty divinity?

The First Reaction (18:36—19:7)

The people's silence leaves the dramatic tension hanging in the air (cf. the function of such silence at I Kings 18:21) and at the same time demonstrates national solidarity (v. 36). The movement of the three officials signals the close of Rabshakeh's threat and the transition to Hezekiah's comparatively low-key response (vv. 1–4): sackcloth, a proverb about impotence in the face of crisis, a tentative expression of hope that God has noticed this mockery, and a request that Isaiah pray for what little is left of Judah.

The approach of Hezekiah's deputation initiates Isaiah's comparatively low-key oracle (vv. 5–7). God has indeed taken the Rabshakeh's words as an insult. God will put a "spirit" into Sennacherib, an inner state of confusion (Isa. 19:14) or depression (I Sam. 16:14–16, 23). The Assyrian king will hear some "report" (RSV "rumor") and return home to his death. The reader is led to expect a relatively uneventful withdrawal, at most something along the lines of 7:6–7. Instead, the narrator teases us with a false climax.

Further Complications (19:8–13)

Sennacherib, it turns out, has indeed heard a report concerning an advance by Tirhakah, but instead of withdrawing home he sends a second threat to Hezekiah in the form of a letter. In verse 9 the narrative exploits the ambiguity of a Hebrew verb to tease the reader. After hearing Isaiah's oracle we are expecting to read, "And when the king heard . . . he returned *(shub)* home." But the sentence ends a different way: "And when the king heard . . . he once more (another meaning of *shub*) sent messengers."

In his second communication (vv. 10–13), Sennacherib's arrogant attack on God is sharpened. Hezekiah is no longer the deceiver (18:29); God is (v. 10). The kings of Assyria have acted

239

like gods in placing their enemies under the holy war ban (v. 11; JB). It is much shorter because in this second round Hezekiah's reaction and Isaiah's oracles are given the bulk of the space, in contrast to 18:17—19:7.

The Second Response (19:14–34)

Hezekiah's response to this letter (vv. 14–19) is exemplary and a distinct advance over his first reaction. In accordance with the pattern laid out in I Kings 8, the king enters the temple and himself offers prayer in the classic format of invocation (v. 15), complaint (vv. 16–18), and plea (v. 19). This prayer neatly points up the issues implicit in the Assyrian crisis.

The Assyrian king's theological logic is faulty. It is true that the gods of other nations are nothing but human creations (Deut. 4:28) and that the Assyrians are unconsciously obeying God's law by destroying them (Deut. 7:5, 25). But the God of Israel is something else again. Because the Lord is God alone of all nations, creator of all, the living God, Sennacherib's insulting arrogance cannot remain unpunished. God's motive in delivering Israel is to let the nations know just who is really God in this world. In a sense we are back at Mount Carmel again, or even at the Red Sea. The stakes are the same (I Kings 18:24; Exod. 5:2). God's motive to act is identical (I Kings 18:36–37; Exod. 14:4).

Unbidden this time, Isaiah offers three oracles that represent a clear advance over the divine response of 18:6–7. The first and longest is a taunting poem exposing Sennacherib's arrogance and the folly of his godlike pretensions, contrasting his boasting with his fate (vv. 21–28). Jerusalem wags her head (Ps. 22:7; 109:25) in derision at the traditional bragging of Assyrian kings, who publicized their exploits in inscriptions. To wrestle chariots up into the mountains of Lebanon would be a feat worthy of Hannibal. If verse 24 is being read properly ("Egypt" instead of "fortress," as most English versions), Sennacherib may be making an oblique claim to something like the Red Sea miracle. It is true that Sennacherib has blighted cities like the rootless rooftop grass that withers prematurely, but "it" (v. 25) has all been God's doing and God's plan. God has been in charge all along, keeping track of every detail (v. 27). To mock Judah is to mock God (v. 22) and that is what Sennacherib's messengers have done (v. 23). The metaphorical hook of verse 28 is a humiliating imitation of actual Assyrian practice.

240

To be turned back on the way he advanced empties Sennacherib's attack of all significance (cf. I Kings 13:9–10).

The second oracle (vv. 29–31) offers a "sign" to Hezekiah, a symbolic guarantee that God's word will come true. Here the hardships caused by Assyrian depredations and natural botanical processes become pointers to a three-year recovery for what is left of Judah. Certainly exilic readers would have reinterpreted this "surviving remnant" as themselves, although in the context of the story it indicates those who have survived the Assyrian siege.

The third oracle (vv. 32–34) turns directly to the immediate crisis now that the first two oracles have explored its implications. The promise is still relatively low-key: either the present siege will end (if we assume that the "great army" of 18:17 is still around) or no siege will even take place. God will act for God's own sake and for David's sake (20:6; cf. 8:19; I Kings 11:12–13, 32, 34).

Jerusalem Is Saved (19:35–37)

The stakes are high, raised to the limit by Assyrian arrogance and God's oracles offered in response. Simply stated, the issue is whether the God of Israel is really God after all. Sennacherib's word (vv. 6, 16; 18:28) stands directly opposed to the word of the Lord. "Thus says the Lord" (vv. 6, 20, 32) cannot be true if "thus says the great king, the king of Assyria" (18:19) is permitted to stand. God's honor is at stake (vv. 15–19, 21–28). For both theological and literary reasons, an extraordinary event is called for, something perhaps of the magnitude of the Red Sea deliverance or the death of the first born.

That night (cf. Exod. 12:29) the angel of the Lord slew one hundred and eighty-five thousand Assyrians. The "great army" (18:17) was gone overnight, all dead bodies (cf. Exod. 14:30).

The rest is denouement. Sennacherib's pseudo-god "Nisroc" (a parody name for Marduk or Nusku?) cannot even protect him in his own temple. The threat of 18:7 belatedly comes true.

Theological Implications

This narrative is a call to trust God even in the face of inevitable disaster, even when all evidence and logic point the other way. The assurance that God was with Hezekiah (18:7) turned out to be true after all. Rabshakeh's tempting logic

241

turned out to be specious. Sennacherib's vaunted power evaporated into corpses. Assyria's word could not stand before God's
word.

Certainly the original exilic audience, victims of Babylon's
power, needed such a challenge to trust God. In the light of
Jerusalem's fall, God's power must have been called deeply into
question. Judah itself had joined that roll call of bludgeoned
nations (vv. 12–13; 18:34) whose gods had proved powerless to
save them. Was Rabshakeh right after all?

This narrative insists not. It is itself a "sign" for the "surviving remnant of the house of Judah" in exile. No promises are
made to these exiles in the Book of Kings, except the most basic
promise of all—God remains God, whose power cannot be undermined by any human agency, any political system, any military force. God remains God, whose word stands, who brings to
reality that which was planned ages ago. God remains God, who
will act so that all the kingdoms of the earth might know that
the Lord is God alone.

The major interpretive problem with this narrative is that
most of its modern readers will simply be unable to believe that
it actually happened. Modern commentators show their unease
by dragging in reports from Herodotus about bowstring-eating
mice and rationalizing about plague. According to his own reports, Sennacherib left Judah without capturing Jerusalem, but
few historians would be willing to credit the angel of the Lord
for a death toll of one hundred eighty-five thousand.

For those to whom Scripture can speak authentically and
authoritatively as "story" and not just as history, this dramatic
narrative can still deliver its impact, its call to trust in God when
the chips are down. See the introduction on "Reading the Book
of Kings Today."

All those who, like Sennacherib or the beast in Revelation
13, claim the trust and loyalty that belong to God alone, even
if they control "all the kingdoms of the world and the glory
of them" (Matt. 4:8), must be answered as Jesus answered
the tempter, "You shall worship the Lord your God and him
only shall you serve" (Deut. 6:13; Matt. 4:10). They may and
must be so answered because in the end God will defeat
them—Pharaoh, Sennacherib, Domitian. For Christians,
the event which makes it possible to believe such incredible
news is the resurrection of Jesus, the defeat of death itself.
All the Old Testament victories of God, both historical and

242

literary, serve as pointers to and signs of that cosmic Easter triumph.

II Kings 20
Reflections on Jerusalem's Deliverance

Two further incidents of Hezekiah's reign reflect on the wonderful deliverance of Jerusalem reported by chapters 18–19. The order here is not chronological but paratactic (see the Introduction). Hezekiah's illness and the delegation from Babylon are offered as flashbacks. The deliverance from Assyria has not yet happened (v. 6) and the royal treasury is still full (v. 13, contrast 18:15–16). The vague coordinating time references of verses 1 and 12 instruct the reader to understand these two stories as comments on or recollections of the events of the previous two chapters (Ackroyd, *Scottish Journal of Theology* 27:329–52).

These two narratives are held together by the interchanges between Hezekiah and Isaiah and by the king's illness. The first story reminds the reader that deliverance is associated with righteousness and prayer and is a sign of God's mighty power. The second story sounds a more somber note, clouding Judah's fate with a threat involving Babylon, but not yet closing off the future completely.

Hezekiah's Illness (vv. 1–11)

The first narrative is a prophetic miracle story like those found in 4:1–44. It echoes the motif of sickness and recovery earlier explored in regard to Ahaziah (1:2–6, 16–17) and Ben-hadad (8:7–10).

The central narrative problem is Hezekiah's "sickness unto death," which is reinforced by Isaiah's prognosis (v. 1). This mortal illness is not presented as a judgment on the king, simply as a fact. The crisis moves toward resolution as Hezekiah seeks privacy by turning his face to the wall (v. 2) and offers a faithful prayer in the spirit of the lament psalms. This is not a prayer of repentance, for Hezekiah is a virtuous king (18:3–6). Instead, speaking in a way common to the narrator (I Kings 2:4; 8:6; 11:38; 15:3, 14), the king begs God to remember his virtues.

243

Hezekiah's claim to virtue is in no way presumptuous; he follows accepted prayer practice in asserting his own righteousness (Ps. 17:3–5; 26:1–5). Tears underscore his sincerity and desperation (Ps. 6:6; 39:12).

Hezekiah's fate is changed by his prayer, so quickly that Isaiah has barely gotten out of the palace (v. 4). His prayer and tears have moved God to restore his health and his opportunities for worship (v. 5; again a concern of the lament psalms, Ps. 30:9; 88:10–12). There are strong hints that God's special concern for the dynasty of David plays a role here as well. Hezekiah is addressed as "prince" (*nagid;* a term rich with traditional associations: I Sam. 13:14; 25:30; I Kings 1:35), and the Lord is identified as the "God of David." More than just recovery is offered. Hezekiah will reign fifteen more years and Jerusalem will be delivered, defended for God's sake and David's sake. Instead of a report on the king's healing, the narrative uses a cake of figs (cf. bathing in a river, 5:10 and throwing meal in a pot, I Kings 4:41) to resolve the sickness plot line. In this way the story can continue on to its subsidiary narrative problem, the request for a sign.

Conversely, because there is no healing, the narrative needs the sign to be complete. Again the basic movement is prayer and God's response (v. 11). A sign was a support and guarantee for an imminent divine action (19:29; Isa. 7:11–17), but in this case the sign is far more extraordinary than the healing it presages. It is the reversal of time itself. This is clearly connected to Hezekiah's fifteen extra years of life. The symbolic logic is an argument from greater to lesser. If God can reverse time in its path, how much more can God lengthen the king's life!

Hezekiah's request for a supporting sign is not presented as illegitimate in any way, nor does it indicate a blameworthy lack of faith on the king's part. He has already been offered one sign in 19:29. His request is simply part of the story-telling pattern, part of the rhythm of oracle reception. It gives the story a chance to throw the spotlight on God's immense power to respond to prayer.

There is some confusion over Isaiah's offer. Most modern versions follow the Targum and represent Isaiah as giving Hezekiah a choice between the shadow lengthening or shortening. The narrative implicitly assumes it is afternoon, and Hezekiah chooses the more difficult option. Yet the Masoretic text also makes reasonable sense as it stands, eliminating this peculiar, non-functional business of a choice: Isaiah says, "The shadow has gone forth ten steps. Shall it return ten steps?" Hezekiah agrees, "It is nothing for the shadow to extend ten steps. No, let it go back ten." No matter which textual choice is made, however, the narrative focus remains on God's significant power, not Hezekiah's request.

The sign not only assures the king's recovery but interprets it for the reader, offering it as a commentary on the tale of Jerusalem's deliverance. Future well-being, for the exiled nation and the individual reader, depends on piety (v. 3; cf. 18:3–6) and faithful prayer (vv. 2–3, 11; cf. 19:1, 15–19). The future is secured by God's power (vv. 5b–6a, 11b; cf. 19:35–37) and good will (vv. 5a, 6b; cf. 19:34).

Like a lens, this little narrative focuses the majestic story of Sennacherib's destruction on the issue of faithful prayer. Prayer, along with obedience to the law, was the foundation of Jewish life in exile (Ezra 9, Nehemiah 9, and the prayers in Chronicles). Prayer remains the bedrock of daily Christian living still (Matt. 6:5–13; James 5:13–16). This ancient story intends to convince us that, with the God of the Bible, prayer makes a critical difference (Luke 18:1–8).

Hezekiah's Folly (vv. 12–19)

This second reflection on Jerusalem's deliverance moves from situation (vv. 12–15) to oracle (vv. 16–18) to the king's reaction (v. 19). As is the case with a New Testament pronouncement story, the narrative itself functions as a "delivery system" for the oracle, which is the real center of attention. The narrative is linked to the first story by Hezekiah's illness. Although modern commentators have speculated on various political reasons for this visit, Kings represents it as a simple courtesy call and shows no interest in the international implications.

The story functions as an analogue to Solomon's reception of the Queen of Sheba (I Kings 10:1–10), but Hezekiah's hospitality represents folly instead of wisdom. Isaiah's interrogation gives the narrative a chance to explore the implications of this folly. Repetition underscores the grim significance of "Babylon" (vv. 12, 14) and "everything" (vv. 13, 15). Hezekiah's answer (v. 14) exposes the critical point: They have come from a "far country," an ominous echo of the land of exile from I Kings 8:46.

Isaiah's oracle picks up the twin themes of "Babylon" and "everything" (v. 17), but it falls short of being an unambiguous prediction of Judah's demise. It is too soon in the plot for that! The language remains vague, Delphic. A far more limited disaster seems to be implied. All the wealth will be taken (cf. 18:15), while "some of" the king's sons will be carried off as hostages to serve as courtiers in Babylon. Actual military defeat or exile are neither mentioned nor implied. Of course when the reader reaches 24:13, 15, the catastrophic implications of this threat will become clear, but for now hope for Judah still lives, as far as the plot of Kings is concerned. It is not until chapter 21 that doom becomes inevitable. The narrator refuses to let the cat out of the bag prematurely.

Yet this narrative provides a vital corrective to any overly-optimistic reading of chapters 18–19. God delivered Jerusalem from Sennacherib, but this does not mean that Jerusalem is eternally safe and secure. It also prevents an exilic reader from imagining that the fall of Jerusalem was some sort of defeat for God, an event beyond God's control. Even if God had once been willing to protect Jerusalem for God's own sake and David's sake (19:34; 20:6), there never had been any absolute guarantees. The fall of Jerusalem was God's will, implied already in Isaiah's oracle given generations earlier.

Hezekiah's response (v. 19) is difficult to interpret. It is tempting to read it as complacent, cavalier, and smug (cf. NEB). Yet this seems out of character for the virtuous Hezekiah described by the narrator (18:3–6; 20:3). Hezekiah as a narrative character may be a fool, but he is not impious. It is better to read his response as one of submission: God's word is good ("appropriate, well-said"; I Sam. 9:10; I Kings 2:38) even if it means future doom. Hezekiah is not complacent but grateful. In the divine economy, Hezekiah is in the same place his great-grandson Josiah will be, living in the temporary hiatus before disaster strikes (22:20). The gift of life in quiet times is not a blessing to be scorned.

246

These two narratives offer two different perspectives on the miraculous deliverance of Jerusalem. The first emphasizes God's love for the Davidic dynasty, but makes it clear that such miracles of deliverance depend on prayer and human faithfulness and obedience. The second warns the reader not to take God's deliverance for granted. Do not try to extend the protection God offered from the Assyrians into the situation of the Babylonians. That was a different story. The successes of Nebuchadnezzar were not defeats for God.

On a surface level these stories offer the reader a simple moralistic choice between prayer and obedience (vv. 1–11) and the results of folly (vv. 12–19). But read together on a deeper level, they sketch out the complex interplay between God's grace (Rom. 4) and human obedience (James 2:14–26), which operates at the heart of Christian theology (cf. Nelson, *Dialog* 22:258–63).

II Kings 21
Manasseh, the Worst King Ever

This report of Manasseh's apostasy has little narrative interest on its own. We read what Manasseh "built" and "did" and of what God "said" in response, but this is no self-contained story with narrative tension or plot. It functions almost exclusively to interpret the Book of Kings as a whole. Manasseh proves to be necessary to make the Book of Kings work. The climactic destruction wreaked on Judah requires as its cause a correspondingly horrendous sin. This is a matter of simple dramatic and theological logic, and Kings is explicit about the connection. Manasseh's sins were the cause of Judah's fall (23:12, 26; 24:3; cf. Jer. 15:4).

In order to counter the positive expectations built up in the reader by God's gracious promises to Judah, Jerusalem, and the dynasty (8:19; I Kings 11:13, 32, 36; 14:21; 15:4), Kings seizes on Manasseh as the arch-villain, portraying him in the most lurid light possible. Manasseh was thus made into Judah's "Jeroboam," the figure on whom was concentrated all the sins of the Davidic kings and the people over whom they ruled. Fairly or not, his reign is described as a fifty-five year orgy of apostasy.

His dramatic position between the pious kings Hezekiah and Josiah makes his evil even worse by contrast, at the same time highlighting their obedience. The contrast to Hezekiah and the reversal of his reform is made explicit in verse 3 (cf.

247

18:4, 22). Manasseh also provides plenty of fodder for the reform of Josiah which follows. Josiah will dismantle Manasseh's structure of apostasy piece by piece (23:4, 5, 10, 12, 24).

This report on Manasseh is unified by a network of inner connections, even though its rough order and syntax (vv. 4, 6) betray a complicated literary history.

> *A* open file (v. 1)
>> *B* outer bracket (v. 2*a*) "he did what was evil"
>>> *C* inner bracket (v. 2*b*) "the nations"
>>>> *D* Manasseh's evil (vv. 3–9*a*)
>>> *C'* inner bracket (v. 9*b*) "the nations"
>>>> *E* God's speech (vv. 10–15)
>> *B'* outer bracket (v. 16) "they did what was evil"
> *A'* close file (vv. 17–18)

Framed by the opening and closing of his file (*A* and *A'*; vv. 1, 17–18), the excoriation of Manasseh unfolds as a building series of variations on the theme of verse 2. This verse, together with verse 16, provides a set of brackets (*B* and *B'*) for the whole dreary catalogue of sin and its effects: "he/they did what was evil in the sight of the Lord."

At the same time, verse 2 connects to verse 9 (*C* and *C'*; "the nations whom the Lord drove out/destroyed before the people of Israel") to set off verses 3–9 as a section focusing on Manasseh's evil (*D*). Verses 10–15 constitute a second section, focusing on the consequences of this evil and held together as a direct speech of God (*E*). This second paragraph also connects back to the thematic verse 2 through the use of the key word "abominations" (v. 11). These two sections (vv. 3–9 and 10–15) are further tied together by the repetition of the language of verse 6 by verse 15. In this way the judgment on Manasseh is widened in scope to apply to the whole people. In addition to serving as an inclusive bracket, verse 16 underlines the idea that Manasseh's sin infected the whole people and adds a social crime to the previous catalogue of religious ones.

The sins attributed to Manasseh are intended to convince the reader that he was the worst king Judah ever had. He explicitly, almost studiously, violated the law of Deuteronomy with his "abominations" (v. 2; Deut. 18:9). He worshiped the "host of heaven" (vv. 3, 5) in direct violation of Deuteronomy

17:3. The text of the law itself is quoted to make his outrageous disobedience obvious (v. 6*b* is verbally dependent on Deut. 18:10–11). Manasseh dragged Judah down to the same level as Israel with his worship of the host of heaven (17:16), Baal and Asherah (I Kings 16:31–33), and idols (v. 11 and I Kings 21:26). These sins were the culmination of Judah's long history of abominations like those of the nations (I Kings 14:24), such as child sacrifice (16:3).

Manasseh, however, went beyond any previous king of Judah to "multiply evil" (v. 6 literally, cf. v. 9). The strange phrase "graven image of Asherah" in verse 7 implies something even worse than an ordinary Asherah pole. Certainly the temerity of putting this object right in the temple of Yahweh itself, along with various illicit altars (vv. 4, 5), must have evoked a horrified reaction from the original readers.

Manasseh's reign was oppressive and violent (v. 16, cf. 24:4). Most interpreters, including Josephus (*Ant.* x 3, 1; cf. Martyrdom of Isaiah 5:1; *Yebamoth* 49*b*) have taken this to indicate that Manasseh murdered the prophets, but Kings itself simply indicates bloodshed of a more general nature. The shedding of "innocent blood" was a juridical concept (Deut. 19:10, 13; 21:8, 9), a crime tempting to royalty (I Sam. 19:5; Jer. 22:17). It takes its place in general catalogues of other social crimes (Prov. 6:17; Isa. 59:7; Jer. 7:6; 22:3) and is used once to describe child sacrifice (Ps. 106:38). That totalitarian destruction of national religious institutions goes hand in hand with a disregard for judicial due process and the security of the average citizen should be no surprise to the modern reader.

Manasseh's sins were not his alone. Sin is rarely an individual matter in the Old Testament. The king's guilt infected the entire people. Manasseh "seduced" them into sin (v. 9). He "made Judah sin" with idols (v. 11). The repetition of part of verse 6 (applied to Manasseh) by verse 15 (applied to the people) makes this same point. Manasseh functions in the larger story as a counterpart to Jeroboam, who caused Israel to sin (17:21–22 etc.). The people had always provoked God to anger, ever since the exodus itself (v. 15). Judah's sin was compounded by a refusal to listen to God's covenant demands (v. 9), the same stubbornness that led to Israel's doom (17:14, 40; cf. Judg. 2:2; 6:10).

249

What is particularly sobering about this chapter is the way in which the gracious promises of God are turned inside out and used to expose the depth of Judah's sin. The exodus is mentioned, but only to pinpoint the beginning of disobedience (v. 15). The "name theology" from I Kings 8:16, God's election of the temple and Jerusalem (cf. I Kings 3:2; 5:5; 8:17–20, 29, 43, 44, 48; 9:3), appears in verses 4 and 7 only to underline the horror of what Manasseh did. God "set" the divine name in the temple, but Manasseh "set" the image of Asherah there (v. 7; the Hebrew uses the same verb). God's promise of the land (v. 8) simply puts Manasseh's act in a worse light. The gift of the law of Moses turns into a threat of impending exile; torah obedience becomes a condition for life in the land of promise. God's gracious words are quoted (vv. 7b–8), but now they sound like threats. This ominous development will reach its climax in 23:27.

Another example of a promise used to communicate threat is the reference to the nation as God's "heritage" (v. 14). The people used this concept to comfort themselves with the certainty of election (Ps. 28:9; 78:70–71; 94:14). In their prayers they called upon God to preserve them for this reason (Deut. 9:26, 29; I Kings 8:51, 53). In contrast, the concept of "heritage" here in verse 14 underlines God's threat instead. Even the last remnant of God's heritage, Judah, will be "cast off" (cf. Jer. 12:7; Amos 5:2).

God's patient prophetic admonitions have had no effect, as was earlier the case with Israel (17:13). They too now point instead to the coming doom (24:2, cf. 17:23). The summary of their message carefully follows the traditional forms of prophetic speech: accusation in verse 11, followed by announcement of judgment in verse 12.

Powerful poetic language emphasizes the fearful nature of this doom. The "evil" done by Manasseh (RSV: "things more wicked") leads to God's corresponding "evil" sent upon Jerusalem and Judah (vv. 11–12; cf. 22:16, 20; I Kings 9:9). Ears will tingle (I Sam. 3:11; Jer. 19:3) at the news of this catastrophe. The metaphorical line of demolition (Isa. 34:11; Lam. 2:8) will measure Jerusalem for a destruction like that of Samaria. The plummet which indicated that Ahab's house was so structurally unsound that it had to be razed (cf. Amos 7:8) will condemn Jerusalem to the same fate. Like a dish, the city will be wiped clean (exile) and turned over (reversal of social institutions).

Amon (vv. 19–26) is simply a replay of his father. A few parallel items of apostasy are reported to impress the reader with this similarity, summarized by the observation that he "forsook" Yahweh. His death reminds the reader, strangely enough, of the fate of the pious Joash (12:20–21). The intervention of the "people of the land" leads to a temporarily brighter future.

Matters for Judah have reached a critical point. Manasseh's apostasy is so outrageous that it can lead only to national destruction (cf. Zeph. 1:4–5). It has infuriated God to the breaking point (vv. 6, 15), as had already happened with the Northern Kingdom (17:11, 17). Even though the reader knows that the story will turn out to be a tragedy, dramatic tension remains at the end of chapter 21. What will God do about this? Is the promised "forever" of verse 7 made inoperative by the "if" of verse 8? In the short term, Manasseh's sins will provide tasks for Josiah's hopeful reform, but in the long term, Kings insists that the die has already been cast. Even Josiah's reform cannot stop the inexorable doom set in motion by Manasseh, the worst king ever (22:17; 23:26).

For the original exilic audience, Manasseh served as the focus for a "doxology of judgment," the people's acknowledgment that God had punished them justly and deservedly. A modern preacher or teacher would have no trouble coming up with contemporary catalogues of "abominations" to revitalize this text as a word of threat and warning. Yet there is always more to the biblical word than the Law that kills (Rom. 7:7–13), even here in chapter 21.

The conditional "if" of verse 8 means that exile is inevitable. If there is any hope at all beyond that exile, it is of the very thinnest, implied perhaps in the homey metaphor of the dish. The dish that is Jerusalem will be wiped clean of its inhabitants and turned over, but it is at least not broken, as is so often the case with these ceramic metaphors (Ps. 2:9; Eccles. 12:6; Jer. 19:11). It stands empty, perhaps waiting for further use, resonating with the promise of verse 7: ". . . in Jerusalem . . . I will put my name for ever."

Later tradition (II Chron. 33:12–13; Prayer of Manasseh) was able to convert Manasseh into a glorious example of repentance. This goes completely beyond the information provided in Kings, but does follow up on the intention of this chapter, to bring readers to repentance.

II Kings 22:1—23:30
Josiah, the Best King Ever

Apparently dialectical theology (the theological paradox of asserting two seemingly opposite truths at the same time) is not the exclusive domain of modern thinkers! This section of Kings simultaneously advances two ideological themes which remain in stark, unrelieved tension with each other. On the one hand, Kings insists that Josiah was the most righteous king Judah ever had. Everything we readers have come to learn about God from the book so far leads us to expect God to forgive Judah on the basis of Josiah's repentence. Therefore we are shocked and surprised by the theological counter theme: God has irreversibly decided to destroy Judah anyway. Nothing in this narrative relaxes this ideological paradox or relieves it in any way. It seems that God's ways are more complex than a simple application of the principle that apostasy leads to punishment and reform to reward.

We shall first point out some things which are often assumed about this story but which are not explicitly stated by it. Next we shall look closely at the narrative itself to see how a pattern of five royal initiatives structure the plot and advance the theme of Josiah's righteousness. Then follows a look at the counter theme of inevitable disaster. Finally we shall examine the implications of this narrative for the theology of the Book of Kings as a whole and for present-day readers.

What the Narrative Does Not Say

These two chapters do not actually report many of the things that tend to be assumed about the reformation of Josiah. For example, the narrative does not explicitly report that the discovery of the law book was the result of temple reconstruction or the emptying of the money chest. The narrative gap between 22:7 and 8 leaves readers the option of drawing this conclusion if they choose. Yet Hilkiah actually says nothing about the circumstances of his find, and Shaphan's report is equally ambiguous (22:9–10).

Moreover, Kings never hints that Josiah's reforms have anything to do with any lapse in his vassal status to Assyria or with any nationalistic revival made possible by Assyrian weakness. All of this is simply a construct of modern historians who have interpreted the evidence in this way. They may well be correct, but it is entirely possible to reconstruct Josiah's history as an uninterrupted alliance with Assyria (Nelson, *"Realpolitik in Judah,"* pp. 183–86). No matter what the actual historical circumstances were, however, as far as the Book of Kings is concerned, Josiah's reforms were motivated by the newly-discovered book of the law, not by any "anti-Assyrian" policy. In a similar way, Kings ignores any possible economic or social motives implicit in Josiah's cult centralization. Only the reforming eighteenth year is of any interest to the narrator. Nothing is reported about any other year except the year of Josiah's death. From the standpoint of international events, these were very exciting years, but for the Book of Kings they do not matter.

Kings does not report that Josiah died in heroic battle against the overwhelming might of Pharaoh Neco. Kings mentions neither a Judahite army nor a battle. It is from the Chronicler that we first hear of a battle in a report constructed for theological purposes out of I Kings 22:29–38. Other plausible historical reconstructions from the vague, non-specific report in Kings are certainly possible (again Nelson, pp. 186–89). Did he die in battle? by treachery? Was he trying to stop Neco or was Neco an ally of Judah? The narrator seems so little interested in political matters that Kings certainly reports Egypt's relationship with Assyria incorrectly. Neco was going up to aid the Assyrians, contrary to the Masoretic text, which suggests that he was going to attack them.

The Basic Structure: Five Royal Initiatives

The reader is convinced in a variety of ways that Josiah was the best king ever, particularly in the central narrative which focuses on Josiah's five commands (22:3—23:24) and in the evaluative statements that frame them (22:2 and 23:25). These framing verses make the claim that, like Hezekiah (18:3, 5), Josiah was another David, a perfect king after the pattern of Deuteronomy 17:18–20 in the tradition of Joshua (Josh. 1:7–8).

253

Josiah is in near total control of events in this central narrative. The story is framed and held together as the actions of his eighteenth year (22:3; 23:23) and by the discovery of the book of the law (22:8–10; 23:24). Five royal initiatives drive the action in five sections:

1. Discovery of the book (22:3–11; "sent," v. 3)
2. Inquiry about the book (22:12–20; "commanded," v. 12)
3. Covenant and the book (23:1–3; "sent," v. 1)
4. Reforms from the book (23:4–20; "commanded," v. 4)
5. Passover from the book (23:21–24; "commanded," v. 21)

The first section centers on the law book itself and provides the narrative exposition (characters, setting, and problem). The narrative problem is that Judah has been disobedient and this law book curses the disobedient with doom. It concludes with Josiah's reaction to this dilemma (22:11), which leads naturally into the second episode. This second section introduces a complication to the resolution of the problem in the form of Huldah's shocking oracle. God appreciates Josiah's repentance but will not revoke the doom implicit in the curses of the law book. The second section concludes with the messengers' report to the king (22:20).

The last three sections move toward a partial resolution of the narrative problem as the apostasy of Judah is effectively reversed. The brief third section centers on the people as a whole and a universal renewal of the covenant. The fourth royal command leads to a long, disorderly catalogue of Josiah's reforms and concludes with his return to Jerusalem (23:20). The fifth royal initiative institutes a centralized Passover. This section concludes with a summary of Josiah's deeds (23:24) and returns us full circle to the dating in the eighteenth year and Hilkiah's discovery.

Josiah, the best king ever, is at the center of every section. The newly-discovered law book is the focus of four of them (22:3–11, four times; 22:12–20, three times; 23:1–3, twice; 23: 21–24, twice), and certainly implicit, but never explicitly mentioned, in the fourth section.

First Episode: Discovery (22:3–11)

The discovery section opens with royal command and closes with royal reaction. Josiah's words repeat the details of his ancestor Joash's temple reform (cf. vv. 4–7, 9 to 12:9–15), although none of these details play any real part in the following story. The discovery of the book is not related to any temple reconstruction, nor is any such reconstruction itself actually reported! This is character background in the sense that it demonstrates Josiah's piety even before the book is found. It was not the threat of doom that frightened Josiah into righteousness. He was already as righteous as good king Joash. A general reform had already at least been started before the law book specified its direction and intensity. These details are something of a mood setter, giving a sense of returning balance after the excesses of Manasseh. Otherwise the story could just as well have begun with verses 8 and 10.

Although the story of discovery is complex, it really fails to tell us how or where the book was found. Retaining an appropriate aura of mystery, it rushes over the details of discovery to get the book into a chain of transmission which ends in the king's hands. This extended chain of transmission (Hilkiah to Shaphan to Josiah) creates dramatic delay (v. 9). It also provides the book with a pedigree, its "provenance" as archaeologists would say, from temple via priest and secretary to the king and eventually to the whole people (23:2).

The identity of the book is no mystery. The narrator and the first readers knew it to be Deuteronomy (cf. Deut. 31:9, 24–26). How or when it became "lost" is of no apparent interest to the narrator. What is important is that Hilkiah found it and passed it on to Josiah. In contrast to Shaphan, who reads the book and still calls it simply "a book," Josiah unerringly recognizes its import, even without knowing its provenance (note that Shaphan fails to tell him).

The king's reaction introduces the narrative problem, to be made more explicit by verses 16, 19. The first readers knew that Deuteronomy ends with a collection of vivid and fearful curses on the disobedient. As it will turn out, nothing can be done about the curses (vv. 12–20), but at least the disobedience can be reversed (23:1–24).

Second Episode: Inquiry (22:12–20)

The second section complicates the narrative problem with the shocking news that no repentance, no reformation will stop the onrush of doom for Judah. The large size of the committee sent to Huldah signals the seriousness of the situation. Huldah's careful identification undergirds the authenticity of the mes-

255

sage she delivers. It emphasizes that she was a real person in real time. The original readers would have known her neighborhood, if not her husband's family. It is to be noted that the narrative makes absolutely nothing of her being a woman. Her status as a prophet of God is not affected by her sex. We get the impression that women prophets were not so uncommon as to require special comment.

The king's question (v. 13) is not about the authenticity of the book, which everyone takes for granted (the reader included under the guidance of the narrator). He wants to know about his fate and the fate of the nation. In fact, his question is really a summary of where the plot of Kings stands at this point. The kings and the people have disobeyed, as the narrator has taken such pains to point out. Now what? Will the promises (8:19; I Kings 11:36; 15:4) and Josiah's righteousness prevail, or will God's anger (21:11–15) swamp them both?

Huldah's oracle falls into two halves (vv. 15–17 and 18–20), each introduced by an address and containing the prophetic messenger formula. The first half points to the grim conclusion of the Book of Kings. The second half points to Josiah's personal exemption from the general catastrophe.

The address of the first half ("the man who sent you") puts emotional distance between God and the king, appropriate to the introduction of the complicating counter theme of irrevocable doom ("it will not be quenched"). The key word "wrath" picks up this theme from Josiah's question, and the words "evil" and "place" carry it forward into verses 19–20. Huldah reports that God (using Deuteronomistic language) agrees with the narrator's own analysis of the situation. Judah has forsaken God (I Kings 9:9) with apostate incense sacrifice (17:11; cf. 23:5), angering God (21:15; cf. 23:26) with the "work of their hands" (that is "idols," Deut. 27:15).

The address of the second half ("the king of Judah") is less distant, appropriate to a limitation of this doom ("the words that you have heard") for Josiah personally. In form, this is recognizable as a weal oracle to an individual. Josiah has reacted to the law book's announcement of judgment as Ahab ("you humbled yourself," cf. I Kings 21:27, 29) and Hezekiah (20:3) had. Thus he has earned a postponement of punishment similar to theirs. God has "heard" Josiah's response, just as Solomon's prayer (I Kings 8:27–30) had foretold, just as God had once "heard" Jehoahaz (13:4) and Hezekiah (20:5). Josiah will

256

die "in peace," without experiencing the coming judgment.

Yet doom really dominates this second half as well. Huldah's unambiguous sealing off of any penitential escape route for the nation as a whole makes it clear that the reforms yet to come will not suffice to avert the wrath of God. Josiah receives a personal exemption, but the irreversible prediction of disaster still stands. The trajectory of the curses of Deuteronomy (Deut. 28:15, 45; the "desolation" of 22:19 is from Deut. 28:37) launched by God's threat in I Kings 9:6–9 (cf. Deut. 29:24–25) will reach its point of impact after Josiah's peaceful burial.

To die "in peace" usually referred to a natural death at a ripe old age (Gen. 15:15) and certainly not by the sword (Jer. 34:4–5). But the holocaust facing Judah will be so terrible that even normal burial following violent death (23:29–30) must be considered to be "in peace" by comparison.

Three Responses: Covenant, Reform, Passover (23:1–24)

The third episode is Josiah's first response, a covenant ceremony (vv. 1–3). Josiah is the instigator, the grammatical subject. Absolutely everyone is present, emphasizing the thoroughness of reform. In this context, the law book acquires a new name as "the book of the covenant" (cf. v. 21), carefully identified with its pedigree once more. The king "stood" by the pillar (the proper procedure for such events, 11:14). Likewise the people "stood" (RSV "joined") in the covenant.

Throughout the Book of Kings, the covenant relationship has been the benchmark of God's grace to the people (Mosaic covenant, I Kings 8:9, 21; Davidic covenant, I Kings 8:24; patriarchal covenant, 13:23; also 11:17 and 17:35). It also was the benchmark for judgment (17:15; I Kings 11:11; 19:10, 14). For a moment at least, Judah is returning to the good old days of covenant renewal (Deut. 31:10–13).

The king's fourth command launches the reform section (vv. 4–20). Basically, this is a disorderly and grammatically rough catalogue of reforming verbs with the king as the subject. Overall, there is a geographical movement from the temple and the area around Jerusalem to Bethel, but the arrangement is really more paratactic (see Introduction) than logical. The cumulative effect is one of ruthlessness ("he broke down"; "he pulled down"), completeness ("all the priests"; "from Geba to Beersheba"), and desecrating zeal ("he defiled"; "bones"). What is first burned is then pounded into dust and once even trans-

257

ported out of Judah (v. 4). Color and credibility are enhanced by specific names, places, and details. The king even violates Deuteronomy 18:6–8 to attain complete decontamination.

This reform reaches back past Manasseh and the other kings of Judah (v. 12; 21:5) to undo apostasy as venerable as Solomon's (v. 13; I Kings 11:5–7) and beyond the borders of Judah to reverse that of Jeroboam (vv. 15–20).

Readers were expected to react with horror at how deeply apostasy had penetrated (vv. 4, 6–7). Later generations of readers participated in the desacralization of these foreign gods by spelling their names with the vowels of the word "shame" (*bosheth;* thus Topheth, Molech, Ashtoreth; cf. the change of the Mount of Olives to "Mount of Corruption" in v. 13).

The catalogue pauses at Bethel (vv. 15–19), and Josiah is abruptly transported there personally to undo the foundational sin of Jeroboam. High place and altar are completely wiped out—pulled down, crushed to dust, even burned (MT)! The modern reader is reminded of the extraordinary efforts required to clean up a waste dump or decontaminate the site of a nuclear accident.

The next section (vv. 16–18) is a flashback which considers the events of verse 15 more closely. In an almost fundamentalistic way, the prophetic word (I Kings 13:2, 32) receives precise fulfillment even over a gap of three centuries. Spotting the cairn or upright stone marking the grave of the man of God "who came from Judah," Josiah posthumously rewards the conviction of the prophet "who came out of" (that is "was from," JB; cf. I Chron. 2:55) the province of Samaria (where Bethel was located, in contrast to Judah). The emphasis on precise prophetic fulfillment supports *both* themes of this section. It exemplifies Josiah's reforming righteousness, but at the same time underscores Huldah's announcement of destruction by insisting on the inevitable fulfillment of prophetic words. A whirlwind reform in Samaria undoes the rest of Jeroboam's apostasy (v. 19, cf. I Kings 12:31; 13:2,32; 23:20). Josiah's return to Jerusalem (v. 20) closes off this episode.

The king's fifth initiative begins the Passover episode (vv. 21–24). Josiah's reform now reaches back all the way to the days of Joshua (Josh. 5:10–12) to reestablish a passover of the sort commanded in the law book (Deut. 16:5–7), a passover held not in homes or in local villages but centralized in Jerusalem. The summary of verse 24 nails down specifically the undoing of Manasseh's crimes (21:6*b*) and reminds the reader one last time of the source of Josiah's inspiration (cf. 23:24*b* with 22:8*a*).

The Counter Theme of Doom (23:26–30)

Following the five royal initiatives, the counter theme of inevitable disaster, introduced already by Huldah's oracle, takes over and dominates the presentation (vv. 26–27). Josiah's righteous reform will not derail the coming judgment. The horrible sentence of 21:10–15 is reiterated.

The reader might have hoped for something better. Of course the sentence is perfectly just. The narration of generations of apostasy over the course of the Book of Kings has made that abundantly clear. Yet at the same time, a glimmer of hope might still seem possible, given the gracious relationship between God and the Davidic kings (8:19; I Kings 11:36; 15:4). Obedience is supposed to result in success (I Kings 2:3). Solomon's temple prayer rested on the principle that repentance leads to forgiveness (I Kings 8:30, 33–34, 35–36). Certainly King Hezekiah is an example of a pious king who was healed and saw the Assyrians turned back at the very walls of Jerusalem. The reader might have hoped for something better, but all such hope is quashed by the narrator's comments and Josiah's tragic death.

The details of this death did not matter (see above). Only the sheer fact that the king died and was buried in comparative "peace" counted. This report recalls the comparable death of Ahab (I Kings 22:37). The contrast of their characters simply increases the poignancy of Josiah's youthful demise. The everfaithful people of the land (11:14, 18–20; 21:24) carry on, bypassing Jehoiakim and anointing Josiah's second son Jehoahaz.

Theological Implications

In a way similar to the church, Josiah is portrayed as living under both the paradox of grace and punishment and the challenge of canonical Scripture.

The ideological paradox is almost unbearable. The irresolvable tension between God's gracious promise and Judah's richly deserved punishment, a tension which underlies the entire Book of Kings, here reaches its sharpest point. The idea that Josiah was the best king Judah ever had stands in stark, unrelieved tension with God's determination to destroy Judah. Reading these two assertions side by side produces a frustrating theological stress, made all the more acute in that the text works so hard to underscore both sides of the dialectic.

The tension between the grace of God and the wrath of God and the relationship of human behavior to them both runs throughout the Bible, from the expulsion from Eden to Paul's formulation of justification by grace through faith. Kings' own special expression of this tension finds its focus in the figure of Josiah. The neat theological formula which insists that righteousness leads inevitably to success (I Kings 2:3) and repentance to forgiveness is fatally undercut. God's gracious promises to David and Jerusalem (23:27) are in abeyance. Josiah's token reward of a peaceful death simply serves to underscore the coming judgment (22:20). God's good gift of covenant law (Deuteronomy) becomes transformed into a word of frightful judgment when it is addressed to an irredeemable situation (22:16; cf. Rom. 3:19–20).

Kings provides no theoretical answer to the theological paradox it creates, but Josiah's own behavior exemplifies the only practical solution. He faithfully obeys God anyway, without regard to any hope of reward. Huldah's oracle has cut off any future for his people. Josiah can do nothing about the wrath of God. Yet Josiah's righteousness and faith were such that he responded to the law book with reforming zeal nonetheless.

Genuine faith transcends any desire for gain. The covenant relationship with the God of the Bible is no commercial arrangement, no religious transaction entered into with the hope of personal benefit. It is a matter of fidelity and trust, irrespective of any desire for reward or fear of punishment. In this, Josiah is the Old Testament's best example of Deuteronomy's call, not just to fear God or obey God, but to love God with heart and soul and might (Deut. 6:5; cf. 23:25). For the original exilic readers of Kings, who had little or no hope of return to their homeland, the call was clear. Obey God's law and keep the faith, even if you can see no hope of reward.

There is a second point of contact for today's reader. The Christian, like Josiah, lives under the challenge of canonical Scripture. Josiah is presented as one who is confronted by a canon of Scripture addressed not to a dead past but to the immediate present. He speaks of "all that is written concerning

260

us" (22:13). For both king and narrator, the newly-discovered book is authoritative, normative Scripture. This book of the law of Moses, Deuteronomy, was last mentioned by the narrator in 14:6 and implied by 17:37. It is the book according to which the narrator, the prophets, and God have advanced judgments in Deuteronomistic language on every king since Solomon. It has played its role of norm and canon since the day Joshua succeeded Moses (Josh. 1:8; 8:31, 34; 23:6; 24:26). Kings who ruled righteously ruled by it (Deut. 17:18).

Josiah was challenged by a word of Scripture that cut deeply to his core (22:11) and yet shaped his faith and behavior (23:25). For us, this is a difficult, paradoxical narrative. Perhaps those who read it as canonical Scripture must first stand in Josiah's shoes. In what way does this text confront and challenge us as Deuteronomy did Josiah? Will we react to the paradox of God's wrath and grace with ethical paralysis or with love and reforming faith?

II Kings 23:31—25:26
The Promise Dismantled

These last chapters of Kings chronicle the violent dismantling of the nation of Judah. The institutions launched so gloriously by Solomon at the beginning of the book have gradually decayed, chapter by chapter. Now the pace of dissolution snowballs. Judah collapses under the punitive brutality of two Babylonian invasions.

Kings pulls no punches in describing this final catastrophe. By the time the reader reaches the last sentence of this section (25:26), the absolute worst has happened. The kings after David's line are in prison (24:12; 25:7). The skilled and useful classes of Judah's society have been exiled (24:14–16; 25:11) or killed (25:18–21), leaving only the peasantry (25:12). The city and temple have been burned, the wall demolished (25:9–10), the last remnants of Solomonic greatness broken up, melted down, and taken away (24:13; 25:13–17). We shall first trace the brutal way the narrative hammers home the totality of Judah's end, then examine its theological claim that God was the motivating force behind these catastrophes.

261

The End of King and Nation

The narrator takes every opportunity to undercut any last vestige of hope, to explore and expose the nation's pain. Starting with the monarchy, the institutions of nationhood are dismantled.

Josiah's sons and grandson come to the throne one by one. They are condemned by curt, nearly identical formulas and meet their well-deserved fate. The ever-faithful "people of the land," perhaps something like a rural gentry, first bypass Jehoiakim to anoint Jehoahaz. Neco soon removes Jehoahaz, and he dies in Egypt as a sort of down payment on the coming "unexodus" of the whole people (25:26; see below). Clearly nothing but a lackey of Pharaoh (what a contrast to I Kings 3:1!), Jehoiakim extracts tribute for his master from these same "people of the land" with a tax ominously reminiscent of Menahem's (15:20).

Then the Babylonian threat, dormant since 20:16–18, suddenly reappears. Solomon's former sphere of influence (I Kings 8:65) is now dominated by Babylon. In chapter 24 Egyptian resistance ceases (v. 7). Jehoiakim dies prematurely, and his son Jehoiachin faces the tragic consequences of his father's rebellion. He surrenders and is exiled. Note how the phrase "to Babylon" is hammered home three times in verses 15–16.

Zedekiah is under the thumb of Nebuchadnezzar, just as his brother Jehoiakim had been under Pharaoh's (cf. v. 17 and 23:34). As the narrator's evaluation in verse 19 indicates, Zedekiah also followed his brother's disastrous foreign policy, resulting in another round of rebellion, defeat, and deportation. This second time, the result is incalculably worse. Zedekiah brings on the devastating holocaust of punishment that was first threatened by God in I Kings 9:9 and has overshadowed the history of Judah ever since. The last sight Zedekiah sees is the murder of his sons. Then he too is carried off to Babylon.

With the monarchy shattered, in chapter 25 the destruction of all other vital national institutions happens quickly. Jerusalem is gutted by fire. In losing its walls it effectively loses its status as a city. Exile sweeps up both loyalist and collaborator (v. 11). Those who are left, the poorest, serve as agricultural laborers in Babylonian state service (v. 12). The valuable parts of the ruined temple are carted off as bullion and scrap bronze. The narrator lingers over this humiliating tragedy with obvious verbal references to the past glory of Solomon (cf. vv. 13–17 with I Kings 7:15–45). The elite of the priesthood and of the faithful people of the land are executed, along with representatives of the military and administrative leadership (vv. 18–21).

Verse 21*b* wraps up the whole catastrophe in a simple summary that coordinates it with the fate of the Northern Kingdom, earlier summarized by 17:23*b*. The two phrases are identical in Hebrew: Israel was exiled from its land/Judah was exiled from its land.

A change in chronology underscores the totality of this destruction of national life. The royal chronology of Judah continues through these last four kings. With Jehoiachin's surrender, however, an alien chronology intrudes itself (24:12). The solemn repetition of foreign chronological formulas periodizes the last crisis (vv. 1, 2–3, 8). In the end the chronology of Judah is overwhelmed by that of Babylon (v. 8).

The incident of Gedaliah's murder is the final act played out on Judah's soil. It nails the lid on the coffin, effectively quashing any residual hope or optimism. The author has abridged Jeremiah 40:7—41:18 to recount this story, omitting any narrative details which would not directly contribute to its function at the end of Kings. Any hopes the reader may harbor for Jerusalem are undercut by the transfer of the provincial administration to Mizpah. Hopes for a revival of the royal family in Palestine are undercut by Ishmael's futile act of political violence. The reduced scale of the action, with ten men wiping out an entire administration, lends a comic opera tone to the incident. We have descended from the grand scale of an independent nation to that of petty local government.

God Did It

Following the Gedaliah episode, "all the people, both small and great" flee to Egypt (25:26; cf. 23:34). Theologically, the sky has fallen as far as salvation history is concerned. The worst possible thing has happened. The exodus from Egypt has been undone! The election of God's chosen people has been called into question. Kings had pointed to the exodus over and over as God's central act of election (17:7, 36; 21:15; I Kings 6:1; 8:9, 16, 21, 51, 53; 9:9). But now this saving event has been reversed in a thudding anti-climax. The worst possible outcome of the open-ended choice given Israel (Deut. 30:15–20) has occurred. They have chosen death instead of life. The horrible curses of

263

Deuteronomy 28:30–37, 47–57, 63–67 have fallen on nation and king. The return to Egypt, the "un-exodus" presaged by Deuteronomy 17:16 and 28:68, has taken place.

The narrator wishes to leave no doubt as to the real cause of Judah's defeat and exile. God did it. The surprising grammatical subject change of 24:2 makes this clear. It was really God and not Nebuchadnezzar who sent this international assortment of raiders to soften up Judah. Because this divine punishment happened in line with the prophetic word (24:2–4 corresponds to 21:10–15 and 24:13 more loosely to 20:17), there can be no doubt. God did it.

Judah was thus removed from God's sight (23:27; 24:3; cf. 17:18, 23). This was God's punishment for Manasseh's sin (21:16; 23:26). Even though a willingness to "pardon" (24:4) had been characteristic of God earlier in the Book of Kings, for example in Solomon's prayer (I Kings 8:20, 34, 36, 39, 50), Manasseh's sins have changed things irreversibly. Under the pressure of obstinate disobedience, God's will has been modified (contrast 8:19 and 13:23 with 24:4).

This theological point is underscored by the basic organization of this section. These grim events are structured not so much by the chronology of either Judah or Babylon as by the repeated formula that leads up to each of the two sieges of Jerusalem (cf. also 13:23; 17:20):

> Surely because of the anger [LXX; cf. JB] of the Lord it came to pass in Judah that he removed them out of his presence (24:3).

* * * *

> For because of the anger of the Lord it came to pass in Judah that he cast them out of his presence (24:20).

The flight of "all the people" back into Egypt, reversing the divine act that had made them God's people, is the final blow. All hope is destroyed. The promise of God has been dismantled.

The original exilic audience had to hear this word of death and come to terms with it before any life could be possible for them in exile. Denial and false hope had to be destroyed so that they could face the future. Beyond this, the best the narrator can do is to offer the exilic audience a bit of common-sense advice through Gedaliah: "serve the king of Babylon, and it shall be well with you" (25:24; cf. I Kings 8:46–50).

So the next-to-the-last word of Kings is utterly hopeless and negative: " . . . the Lord would not pardon" (24:4). God ". . . cast them out from his presence" (24:20). The Bible has other texts like this, where hope has run out, where God has called a halt to the charade, where the inflated currency of cheap grace will no longer buy a future. Just a few of these are the parable of the vineyard (Luke 20:9–16), the judgment of the Son of Man (Matt. 25:31–46), the fall of Babylon the great (Rev. 18).

At points there is an insistent urgency to the biblical message, reflected most clearly in the kingdom preaching of Jesus (Mark 1:14–15), based on the conviction that there are indeed such "too late" times with the God of the Bible. The parables of Jesus call for immediate decision in the face of the onrushing kingdom (for example, Matt. 13:44–49; 25:1–12). A handwritten slogan once spotted in an inner city store-front captures this concern perfectly: "Repent and be forgiven. This offer good for a limited time only."

The smoking ruins of Jerusalem are not hard for us to recreate in our imaginations. The devastated city could well be the symbol of our age: Warsaw and Berlin, Dresden and Stalingrad, Hiroshima and Nagasaki. We can trace the contribution to such horrors made by the sin and folly of our contemporary Jehoiakims and Zedekiahs. Whether we also have the theological vision to see in them the hand of God is another matter.

"Come, behold the works of the Lord, how he has wrought desolations in the earth" (Ps. 46:8). Modern warfare and modern international politics have within them the potential for a planet-wide holocaust. The challenge for us is to believe that God is as active and real in our world as God was to the author and readers of the Book of Kings and to grasp the urgency of the modern crisis before it is too late.

II Kings 25:27–30
Can the Promise Live?

The story of the nation has come to an end. The narrative has done everything it could to put to rest false hopes on the part of its exilic readers. "Our hope is lost; we are clean cut off" (Ezek. 37:11) seems to be the proper reaction. Then comes this odd little notice about King Jehoiachin's rehabilitation. Is this

265

last paragraph vital to the theology of Kings or simply a post-script? Does it advocate hope or merely underscore despair?

This problem has long been a bone of contention for scholars. Some think that this last paragraph must be highly important because of its concluding position. Others point out that paratactic structures (see Introduction) simply end when the subject matter runs out and insist that heavy stress on this final episode is unwarranted. Many read the description of Jehoiachin's status in the Babylonian court, a puppet king with a meaningless throne, as a completely negative ending, cutting off all future hope for the Davidic monarchy. Others see in Evil-Merodach's gracious words and actions a sign of better times to come, a quasi-messianic expectation that David's line would someday reign again.

The Last Nail in the Coffin

The details of the episode are clear enough. After thirty-seven years as a prisoner, Jehoiachin was "graciously freed" as part of Evil-Merodach's accession-year amnesty. Literally, the Babylonian king "lifted up his head from prison." He was granted covenant status as a vassal, indicated by standard treaty language: "he spoke kindly to him." As a mark of honor, Jehoiachin was set on a throne above the other captive kings (cf. Ps. 18:43). His new status was indicated by a change from prison garments and a permanent invitation to the royal table.

Was this supposed to be good news or bad news for the exilic readers? Given the context of cumulative disaster in which it is set (chaps. 24–25), the reader is predisposed to see this episode as one more blow to any hope for a restored Judah. In contrast to Solomon's glorious throne (I Kings 10: 18–20), his exalted status above other kings (I Kings 10:23–25), the extravagant supplies required for his table (I Kings 4:22–23), this "favor" shown Jehoiachin sounds hollow, ironic. Jehoiachin is only a king in a gilded cage. His position is a joke. The trappings of royalty are only the costume of a clown. Jehoiachin's fate is the final proof of the Deuteronomistic thesis of Kings.

On the surface, the theology of Kings seems to be uniformly negative throughout the book. God has punished first Israel and then Judah because of their repeated violations of the law. The prophets, the narrator, and God too, push this point of view from start to finish with increasing stridency. David

266

started the ball rolling with a classic bit of Deuteronomistic theology:

> Keep the charge of the Lord ... keeping his statutes, his commandments, his ordinances, and his testimonies, as it is written in the law of Moses, that you may prosper in all that you do and wherever you turn" (I Kings 2:3).

Of course the opposite happened. Soon Solomon (I Kings 8:46–50), God (I Kings 9:6–9), the prophets (21:10–15; 22:16–17), the narrator (24:3–4), and even King Josiah (22:13), join in a nagging chorus promoting the Deuteronomistic key to the exiles' situation: If you had obeyed, you would have prospered; but because you did not, you have been cast away.

All that Kings had ever promised in the way of a future for exilic readers was that if they repented their lives in exile would be more bearable (I Kings 8:46–50). In this light, the limited improvement of Jehoiachin's lot is a foretaste of the gray future which the captive nation faces. Nothing more than this can be expected, for Josiah's fruitless reform has demonstrated that the mind of God cannot be changed. Judah has been cast out of the sight of God, and that is that. Even the most exemplary repentance and obedience will make no difference.

The Wild Card

Yet beneath this negative surface message, something else is going on as well. There are cracks in the Deuteronomistic theology of Kings through which other points of view show. Even when the last nail has been driven into the coffin of Judah's national hopes, not everything has been said. There is a wild card in the theological deck!

Underneath the negative message of sin and well-deserved punishment, a quieter voice has been speaking a more hopeful word. The promise of an unending reign in Jerusalem for David's descendants (8:19; I Kings 11:36; 15:4) has been spoken and not repudiated. The hint that Judah and Israel can look forward to a reunification under Davidic rule (I Kings 11:39) still hangs suspended in mid-air. When the context of the entire Book of Kings is taken into account, Jehoiachin's experience becomes richly ambiguous rather than merely negative. A certain openness to the future is indicated. Jehoiachin did not die a prisoner but as an honored guest of Babylon's king. At least the possibility of a return for David's dynasty remains.

267

Such a possibility, however, rests only on God's promise, not on human obedience or repentance. Repentance in itself will lead to nothing better than a good life in exile (I Kings 8:50). The narrator's only evaluative word on Jehoiachin is that he had done evil like his father (24:9). Thus the imprisoned king's release is not a matter of Deuteronomistic reward. Instead it must be based on covenant promise, the principle advanced by the Nathan oracle of II Samuel 7:14–16: Scions of the Davidic house may be punished with human penalties, but God's covenant love will never desert them; ". . . your throne shall be established for ever" (v. 16; see 8:19; I Kings 11:36; 15:4).

The wild card in the theology of Kings is God, who refuses to be pinned down even by the orthodox formulas of Deuteronomistic ideology. As Kings as a whole tells the story, God seems to have a change of heart over the years. At first God was not willing to destroy Judah, in spite of their imitation of Ahab's sins, even to the point of erecting a Baal temple in Jerusalem (8:18–19; 11:18). But by the reign of Manasseh, God was ready to throw Judah to the wolves (21:11–15), in spite of the promises made to David.

The Deuteronomistic party line was that if the people through their king had repented and returned to full obedience to the law they would have prospered. Yet Josiah, the one king who truly did repent and truly did keep the law "with all his heart and with all his soul and with all his might" (23:25) was cut down in the prime of his life. God rushed to carry out the sentence of destruction, ignoring Josiah's reform entirely. To put it bluntly, God seemed to change the ground rules.

Does this Deuteronomistic narrator really know what is going on in the mind of God after all? In the end, the story that the narrator has told actually undercuts the theology it is explicitly intended to support. The key to the future lies in the mind of God and not in a Deuteronomistic theological formula.

So the Book of Kings concludes on a thoroughly ambiguous note. It remains open-ended to whatever future God may determine to send. God is the wild card in the deck. This surprising God goes so far as to use lies to implement the divine plan (to Ben-hadad, 8:10; to Ahab, I Kings 22:20–23). This amazing God makes sweeping dynastic promises to David which fly in the face of Deuteronomistic orthodoxy. In the case of Josiah, this unpredictable God undercuts Deuteronomistic principles to punish the people in outraged wrath. Such a God may also have other surprises in store for readers.

The first exilic readers were to remain open to whatever future God might send them. Once false hopes had been put behind them, they could wait in obedient and repentant faith, open to the sort of amazing grace discovered by Jehoiachin in the thirty-seventh year of his exile. Their hope could not be fixed on any particular institution, whether land, king, or temple. It was to be centered on the God of surprising grace.

The Davidic kings never reigned in Jerusalem again. The promise of an eternal Davidic dynasty points straight out into the void, unfulfilled in any political sense. Christians, however, see this promise as charged with new meaning by the reign of Jesus Christ. New Testament tradition saw Jesus as a direct descendant of Jehoiachin (at least according to Matt. 1:12, Jechoniah) and insisted he had been born as a king (Matt. 2:2, 6). Jesus, like Jehoiachin, acted out a royal role (Matt. 21:6–9) with strong elements of mocking farce to it ("Hail, King of the Jews!" Mark 15:17–19). New Testament theology continued to use kingship as a way of communicating Christ's saving rule (John 18:36; Col. 1:13–14; Heb. 7:1–2).

Kings concludes with God's options held wide open. In this, the book is a paradigm of all biblical faith. The key to the future lies with God alone. The experience of both Israel and the church testifies that the God of the Bible is the God of surprise happy endings and amazing grace. This is, after all, the God who raised Jesus from the dead.

BIBLIOGRAPHY

1. For further study

COHN, ROBERT L. "Composition and Creativity in the Book of Kings," *Catholic Biblical Quarterly* 47:603–16 (1984).

———. "Literary Technique in the Jeroboam Narrative," *Zeitschrift für die alttestamentliche Wissenschaft* 97:23–35 (1985).

DEVRIES, SIMON J. *1 Kings*. WORD BIBLE COMMENTARY 12 (Waco, TX: Word Books, 1985).

FRETHEIM, TERENCE E. *Deuteronomistic History* (Nashville: Abingdon Press, 1983).

GRAY, JOHN. *I & II Kings: A Commentary*, 2nd edition. OLD TESTAMENT LIBRARY (Philadelphia: Westminster Press, 1970.

HOBBS, T. R. *2 Kings*. WORD BIBLE COMMENTARY 13 (Waco, TX: Word Books, 1985).

———. "2 Kings 1 and 2: Their Unity and Purpose," *Studies in Religion* 13:327–34 (1984).

JONES, GWILYM H. *1 and 2 Kings*. NEW CENTURY BIBLE COMMENTARY (Grand Rapids, MI: Wm. B. Eerdmans, 1984).

LONG, BURKE O. "A Darkness between Brothers," *Journal for the Study of the Old Testament* 19:79–84 (1981).

———. *1 Kings; with an Introduction to Historical Literature*. THE FORMS OF THE OLD TESTAMENT LITERATURE 9 (Grand Rapids, MI: Wm. B. Eerdmans, 1984).

MAYES, A. D. H. *The Story of Israel between Settlement and Exile: A Redactional Study of the Deuteronomistic History* (London: SCM Press, 1983).

PORTEN, BEZALEL. "The Structure and Theme of the Solomon Narrative (1 Kings 3—11)," *Hebrew Union College Annual* 38: 93–128 (1967).

ROBERTSON, DAVID. "Michaiah ben Imlah: A Literary View," *The Biblical Mosaic*. Edited by Robert M. Polzin and Eugene Rothman (Philadelphia: Fortress Press, 1982), pp. 139–46.

SETERS, JOHN VAN. *In Search of History: Historiography in the Ancient World and the Origins of Biblical History* (New Haven: Yale, 1983).

2. Literature cited

ACKROYD, PETER R. "Historians and Prophets," *Svensk Exegetisk Årsbok* 33:18–54 (1968).

———. "An Interpretation of the Babylonian Exile: A Study of 2 Kings 20," *Scottish Journal of Theology* 27:329–52 (1974).

BEGG, CHRISTOPHER T. "Unifying Factors in 2 Kings 1:2–17a," *Journal for the Study of the Old Testament* 32:75–86 (1985).

BRUEGGEMANN, WALTER. "The Kerygma of the Deuteronomistic Historian," *Interpretation* 22:387–402 (1968).
CHILDS, BREVARD S. "On Reading the Elijah Narratives," *Interpretation* 34:128–37 (1980).
COHN, ROBERT L. "Form and Perspective in 2 Kings 5," *Vetus Testamentum* 33:171–84 (1983).
———. "The Literary Logic of 1 Kings 17—19," *Journal of Biblical Literature* 101:333–50 (1982).
DOZEMAN, THOMAS B. "The 'Troubler' of Israel: 'kr in 1 Kings 18:17–18," *Studies in Bible and Theology* 9:81–93 (1979).
GROSS, WALTER. "Lying Prophet and Disobedient Man of God in 1 Kings 13: Role Analysis," *Semeia* 15:97–135 (1979).
JOBLING, DAVID. *The Sense of Biblical Narrative: Three Structural Analyses in the Old Testament.* JOURNAL FOR THE STUDY OF THE OLD TESTAMENT SUPPLEMENT SERIES 7 (Sheffield: JSOT Press, 1978).
JONES, G. (see Bibliography 1).
KOCH, KLAUS. *The Growth of the Biblical Tradition.* Translated by S. M. Cupitt (New York: Scribner's & Sons, 1969).
LA BARBERA, ROBERT. "The Man of War and the Man of God; Social Satire in 2 Kings 6:8—7:20," *Catholic Biblical Quarterly* 46: 637–51 (1984).
LEVENSON, JON D. "The Paronomasia of Solomon's Seventh Petition," *Hebrew Annual Review* 6:135–38 (1982).
LONG, BURKE O. "Historical Narrative and the Fictionalizing Imagination," *Vetus Testamentum* 35:405–16 (1985).
———. "2 Kings 3 and Genres of Prophetic Narrative," *Vetus Testamentum* 23:337–48 (1973).
———. (See Bibliography 1.)
NAPIER, DAVIE. "The Inheritance and the Problem of Adjacency," *Interpretation* 30:3–11 (1976).
NELSON, RICHARD D. *"Realpolitik* in Judah (687–609 B.C.E.)," *Scripture in Context II.* Edited by W. W. Hallo et al. (Winona Lake, IN: Eisenbrauns, 1983), pp. 177–89.
———. "Was Not Abraham Justified by Works?" *Dialog* 22:258–63 (1983).
NOTH, MARTIN. *The Deuteronomistic History.* JOURNAL FOR THE STUDY OF THE OLD TESTAMENT SUPPLEMENT SERIES 15 (Sheffield: JSOT Press, 1981).
OLYAN, SAUL. "Hasalom: Some Literary Considerations of 2 Kings 9," *Catholic Biblical Quarterly* 46:652–668 (1984).
PRITCHARD, JAMES D. *Ancient Near Eastern Texts Relating to the Old Testament.* 3rd edition with supplement (Princeton: Princeton University, 1969).
RAD, GERHARD VON. "Naaman: A Critical Retelling," *God's Work in Israel.* Translated by H. H. Marks (Nashville: Abingdon Press, 1980), pp. 47–57.
RAST, WALTER E. *Joshua, Judges, Samuel, Kings.* PROCLAMATION COMMENTARIES (Philadelphia: Fortress, 1978).

SIMON, URIEL. "1 Kings 13: A Prophetic Sign—Denial and Persistance," *Hebrew Union College Annual* 47:81–117 (1976).

WOLFF, HANS W. "The Kerygma of the Deuteronomic Historical Work," The *Vitality of Old Testament Traditions*. Edited by W. Brueggemann and H. W. Wolff (Atlanta: John Knox Press, 1975), pp. 83—100.